TEACHER'S EDITION

1a 1b 1

Lecturas para hispanohablantes

CON PREPARACIÓN PARA LOS EXÁMENES

Printed in United States of America

ISBN-13: 978-0-618-75251-5
ISBN-10: 0-618-75251-X 11 12– 0982– 16 15 14
Internet: www.holtmcdougal.com 4500480464

1

Lecturas para hispanohablantes

CON PREPARACIÓN PARA LOS EXÁMENES

What Is *Lecturas para hispanohablantes*?

A book that allows native Spanish speakers to develop stronger reading skills by encouraging the use of a variety of comprehension and critical-thinking strategies.

All levels include

- Reading support throughout the selections
- A consumable format that allows students to mark up the text
- Vocabulary practice and enrichment
- Spelling and pronunciation practice with an emphasis on sound/symbol correspondence
- Comprehension questions and short writing practice and enrichment
- Bilingual glossaries of literary and academic reading terms
- Academic and informational reading with bilingual strategies
- Test preparation models, bilingual strategies, and practice

Lecturas para hispanohablantes
Level 1

Includes
- 3 units of *En voces* readings with a cultural focus
- 9 selections of additional literature for more reading practice and enrichment
- Academic and informational reading
- Test preparation models, strategies, and practice

Lecturas para hispanohablantes
Level 2

Includes
- 2 units of *En voces* readings with a cultural focus
- 10 selections of additional literature for more reading practice and enrichment
- Academic and informational reading
- Test preparation models, strategies, and practice

Lecturas para hispanohablantes
Level 3

Includes
- 1 unit of *En voces* readings with a cultural focus
- 11 selections of additional literature for more reading practice and enrichment
- Academic and informational reading
- Test preparation models, strategies, and practice

Lecturas literarias
Level 4

Includes
- 16 literature selections for reading practice and enrichment
- Academic and informational reading
- Test preparation models, strategies, and practice

The Interactive Reading Process

Lecturas para hispanohablantes

encourages students to write in their books!

Lecturas para hispanohablantes provides students and teachers with a unique resource that fosters reading comprehension. ***Lecturas para hispanohablantes*** encourages students to engage or *interact* with the text. Activities before, during, and after reading a selection prompt students to ask themselves questions, clarify their ideas, and make personal connections—all thinking processes performed by proficient readers.

The following features help students interact with the text:

PARA LEER ***Estrategia de lectura*** and ***Datos para tener en cuenta*** give students concrete ways to approach the selection, as well as the background knowledge and context necessary to understand it.

During Reading ***A pensar...*** This feature appears at the key point of each reading and signals that students need to stop and answer the questions in the margins. These questions allow students to learn and practice a variety of reading skills and strategies, including

- summarizing
- questioning
- predicting
- visualizing
- connecting
- clarifying
- evaluating
- drawing conclusions
- inferring
- locating main ideas
- making judgments
- analyzing
- identifying cause-and-effect relationships

A pensar...

1. ¿Por qué crees que el poeta compara el tomate con el sol? **(Sacar conclusiones)**
2. ¿Qué crees que quiere decir la frase **la cintura del verano? (Analizar)**

MÁRCALO At specific points in each selection, students are directed to underline, circle, or highlight text that features key vocabulary, pronunciation, spelling, or grammar concepts. In the *Literatura adicional* section, students focus on one aspect of literary analysis and mark up the text accordingly. Literary terms are defined in a bilingual glossary.

Palabras clave Vocabulary words that are key to understanding the reading are highlighted in bold and definitions are provided at the bottom of the page.

Consejo para la lectura Useful, specific reading tips appear at points where language is difficult.

ESTRATEGIA DEL BUEN LECTOR

Estrategia del buen lector Specifically for struggling readers, these strategies are helpful for all types of learners. The strategies support those students who encode more easily through visuals, those who retain more easily through repetition, and those who just need a little extra help. In every selection, these notes give useful tips for comprehending vocabulary, context, concepts, and more.

ESTRATEGIA DEL BUEN LECTOR Haz una lista de los datos que has aprendido sobre el coquí al leer este artículo. Por ejemplo: Los **coquíes** viven en los árboles.

Desafío These activities help students develop critical-thinking skills and encourage them to apply concepts beyond the printed page. The exercises actively engage students while highlighting the richness of the selections and literature.

DESAFÍO Escribe un párrafo breve sobre un animal de tu elección. Describe la apariencia del animal, di dónde vive y comenta cómo es el clima en el hábitat del animal. **(Ampliar)**

Vocabulario de la lectura Words boldfaced and defined in the selection are reviewed, requiring students to use the words contextually.

Pronunciación y ortografía These activities reinforce pronunciation concepts, with an emphasis on accentuation and correct spelling. Words introduced to students in the selection are presented both in the context of the selection and in other contexts. The ***MÁRCALO Pronunciación*** and ***MÁRCALO Ortografía*** exercises included with the selection complement these activities.

¿Comprendiste? Comprehension activities require students to use their understanding of the selection to extend their reading skills.

Conexión personal These brief writing activities help students connect the reading to their own lives.

Ongoing Assessment

In addition to increasing students' involvement in the reading process, ***Lecturas para hispanohablantes*** offers you, the teacher, a window on students' progress and problems. Students' notes, responses, and other markings could be looked at regularly as part of the ongoing informal assessment process.

Inclusion in the Foreign Language Classroom

Making Reading More Accessible

En voces* and *Literatura adicional Spanish educators encounter a wide variety of native speakers in their classes. Looking at an individual student's profile, there are those who are fully bilingual with good reading skills in both languages, those who are literate in Spanish but not English; those who are not literate but can listen and speak in English and/or Spanish; and those who can listen and speak in Spanish but have an irregular educational history.

Lecturas para hispanohablantes includes more students before, during, and after they read through the enormous range of support and options. Students are reading with the kind of accommodations that they need. Every student learns the same information, just not in the same way.

Before students read, they are given the critical background information they need. These connections and critical background help students with the different cultural backgrounds and make no assumptions about what a student is supposed to already know.

While students read, they interact with what they are reading through point-of-use notes in the margins. Good readers apply certain strategies instinctively when reading. By making these strategies overt, more students can learn to use these strategies and, in turn, learn better reading habits.

Here are some of the features from ***Lecturas para hispanohablantes*** that help students while they are reading.

- *Consejo para la lectura*
- *Estrategia del buen lector*
- *Márcalo*
- Readings on Audio
- *En voces* Reading Summaries on Audio
- Bilingual Glossary of Literary Terms
- *Literatura* on Audio
- *Palabras clave*
- *Desafío* Activities

Lecturas para hispanohablantes teaches students how to self-monitor, take notes, and apply new reading strategies when they encounter readings in classes, on tests, and in everyday life.

After the selection, the activities concentrate on vocabulary, sound/symbol correspondence, comprehension, and personal connections. All three types of activities cement students' retention by developing their skills from controlled one-right-answer exercises to personalized open-ended critical thinking activities. This range addresses the broader range of students. Some students are more comfortable beginning with the bigger picture and then citing evidence; others are better at finding the details and then connecting those details to create the bigger picture. Ultimately, students could become comfortable going both from detail to world and from world to detail.

The more vocabulary students build through the rich assortment of readings, the better students are able to think critically and creatively. The use of graphic organizers helps students encode the information in two different ways: linguistically and visually. This helps with retention. Providing students with the opportunity to personalize their thoughts about the selection makes the selection stick. It has been encoded into their brain three ways: through words, through visuals, and through personalization. Therefore, they are much more likely to remember the selection. It has become meaningful to them even if they did not like it. The *Conexión personal* section of the reading gives the student the opportunity to say why.

Making Strategies More Effective

Academic and Informational Reading

This section of ***Lecturas para hispanohablantes*** shares with students the unique strategies they need with each of these types of reading. The strategies are in both English and Spanish, and there is a bilingual glossary of terms. Often students are asked to research, yet students do not know how to access different types of readings. This section is a sampling of the different types of tasks that students are asked to perform in school and on standardized tests:

- Analyzing Text Features
- Understanding Visuals
- Recognizing Text Structures
- Reading in the Content Areas
- Reading Beyond the Classroom

This array will develop students' strategies as well as serve as a resource so that when they come across a certain type of reading that they are unfamiliar with, they can see how to get the most out of the reading in the shortest amount of time.

Making Test Taking More Strategic

Test Preparation

The final section of ***Lecturas para hispanohablantes*** features test preparation for reading, revising, editing, and writing. The section opens with general test-taking strategies in both English and Spanish.

Each type of test begins with an annotated model that shows students how to analyze the readings, the writing prompts, the direction lines, the questions, and the distractors, as well as work through standardized tests efficiently and effectively. Annotations are in both English and Spanish. The second step is for the students to practice with the same type of test. The final step is a self-check where students can verify their answers and self-evaluate areas where they may need more practice. This three-step process makes test-taking more transparent for students–demonstrating that it's not just a matter of a lucky guess, but that there are ways to make educated guesses.

This section shows students that once they learn and practice the strategies and avoid the pitfalls, they will be more confident when the *real* test takes place.

Making Students More Successful

At the end of the year, educators want students to walk out of the classroom knowing more than they did in September. Regardless of the level, students can progress. Below are general strategies for all levels of students. When a student can see his or her individual progress, that is when the student will be motivated to continue studying Spanish.

Strategies by Student Group	
Strategies for Advanced Group Advanced students will be placed in accelerated classes in 9th grade and in Sophomore Honors, take the AP Language test (SAT-2) at the end of Junior year, and take the AP Literature test (SAT-2) at the end of Senior year. They will progress rapidly through the basics of the oral language and begin studying literature.	**1.** Involve students in a Pen Pal project to develop cummunication skills with peers in foreign countries. **2.** Schedule meetings between Foreign Language and English teachers to develop common rubrics for literary analysis. **3.** If taught in a heterogeneous class, substitute more challenging assignments for easier ones. **4.** Make sure instruction is sufficiently complex and in-depth.
Strategies for Grade Level Group Grade level students are usually college-oriented, have an adequate foreign language reading level, but need lots of visuals for instruction.	**1.** Assess what these students already know and adjust the rate of introduction of new material based on frequent assessments during instruction. **2.** Provide cumulative review of sound/symbol relationships, vocabulary and grammatical forms taught; use flash cards for class and partner review. **3.** Progress through the Spanish program at the recommended pace and sequence.
Strategies for Students with Learning Difficulties Group Learners have the lowest functional vocabulary level, are very visual learners, and need more cumulative review.	**1.** Assess what these students already know and adjust the rate of introduction of new material based on frequent assessments during instruction. **2.** Focus primarily on oral language. **3.** Explicitly teach sound/symbol relationships, separating difficult discrimination in introduction. **4.** Introduce vocabulary through drawings and personalize vocabulary. **5.** Provide daily oral practice through group responding, partner practice, and short presentations.
Strategies for Students Needing Intensive Help (Special Education) Intensive needs students are those whose performance is two or more standard deviations below the mean on standardized measures. These students will probably be eligible for special education services. This is a very small percentage of the general population.	**1.** Determine reading level in English to guide the introduction of oral language content. **2.** Follow the guidelines given for Students with Learning Difficulties. **3.** Use a very visual approach and concentrate on oral language. **4.** Directly teach sound-symbol relationships and vocabulary by clustering vocabulary words using sound-symbol relationships. **5.** Place these students in lower grade level material if at all possible.

Chart written by Linda Carnine and Doug Carnine

Reaching All Readers

Spanish teachers may find it challenging to accommodate the wide range of reading abilities and interests among their native speaker students. For those students who are hooked on reading, the challenge is to provide a steady diet of rich materials. But for many students, reading is a chore that requires enormous effort and yields little success.

Students who are not able to read at grade level often do not succeed in school. While much of the focus of the early grades is on learning to read, the focus shifts in the middle grades to reading to learn. Students who do not have a strong foundation in basic decoding and comprehension skills become struggling readers. Their poor reading ability denies them access to the content of the textbooks; as a result, they fall behind in almost every subject area. Below-level reading ability most often is the result of inadequate decoding skills, poor comprehension, or a combination of both.

Decoding skills provide readers with strategies for determining the pronunciation of the written word. Basic decoding skills involve matching letters and letter combinations with spoken sounds and blending those sounds into words. As students encounter longer–multisyllabic–words, they need to divide these words into manageable chunks or syllables.

Decoding is an enabling skill for comprehension. Comprehension is a process of constructing meaning from text. Readers integrate the information in the text with their prior knowledge to make sense of what they read. Specific comprehension skills and strategies, such as main idea, sequence, and visualizing, can help students recognize the relationships among ideas, figure out text structures, and create pictures of what they read.

Developing Fluency in All Readers

Reading fluency is the ability to automatically recognize words so that attention can be focused on the meaning of the written material. Fluency involves both decoding and comprehension skills; fluent readers decode text with little or no effort as they construct meaning from that text. Teachers can usually spot readers who struggle with decoding the text. Other readers, however, may be able to say the words and sound as though they are reading, but they have little or no understanding of what they read. These readers often go unnoticed, especially in the content areas.

Fluency is a developmental skill that improves with practice. The more students read, the better readers they become. The reading level at which a student is fluent is called his or her *independent reading level.* However, a student's independent reading level may vary with the type of material he or she is reading. For example, reading a short story is often easier than reading a textbook.

A key part in developing reading fluency is determining a student's independent reading level and then providing a range of materials at that level. Developing Fluent Readers on pages T12–T13 offers diagnostic tools for determining reading levels and tips for improving fluency.

Helping All Readers Break the Code

There are many reasons that some students struggle with reading. Often poor readers spend most of their mental energy trying to figure out, or decode, the words. With their brains focused on the letters and corresponding sounds, there is little attention left to think about what the words mean. Until readers achieve a basic level of automaticity in word recognition, they are not reading for meaning.

Although most students do have a knowledge of basic phonics, some students fail to develop strategies for using the letter-sound correspondences. They often have difficulty decoding new words, and multisyllabic words are especially problematic. As students encounter longer words, they need to be able to break these words into parts.

Establishing a Reading Process

Good readers are strategic in how they approach reading. They consciously or unconsciously do certain things before, during, and after reading. Poor readers, however, often possess few or none of the strategies required for proficient reading. To help struggling readers, establish a routine for reading that involves strategies before, during, and after reading.

- **Before Reading** New ideas presented in reading materials need to be integrated with the reader's **prior knowledge** for understanding to occur. Have students preview the material to see what it is about. Discuss what they already know about the topic and have them **predict** new information they might learn about it. Talk about a **purpose** for reading and have students think about reading strategies they might use with the material.
- **During Reading** Good readers keep track of their understanding as they read. They recognize important or interesting information, know when they don't understand something, and figure out what to do to adjust their understanding. Poor readers are often unaware of these **self-monitoring strategies**. To help these readers become more involved in their reading, suggest that they read with a pencil in hand to jot down notes and questions as they read. If students own the reading materials, they can mark the text as they read. ***Lecturas para hispanohablantes*** is ideal for this type of work.
- **After Reading** Provide opportunities for readers to reflect on what they have read. These can involve group or class discussion and writing in journals and logs.

Creating Independent Readers

As you work to give students the skills they need to read for themselves, you can also incorporate some basic routines into your classroom that will help your students extend their understanding.

- **Read aloud.** People of all ages love a good story. Read aloud to your students and hook them on some authors and genres they might not have tackled themselves. For most material, students' listening comprehension is more advanced than their comprehension of written material. Listening helps them develop the thinking skills needed to understand complex text.
- **Write daily.** Writing is a powerful tool for understanding. Encourage students to use writing to work through problems, explore new ideas, or respond to the literature they read. Encourage students to keep journals and learning logs.
- **Read daily**. Allow time for sustained silent reading. Set aside classroom time for students to read self-selected materials. Students who read become better readers, and students are more likely to choose to read if they can pursue ideas they find interesting.
- **Build a classroom library**. If possible, provide a wide range of reading materials so that students are exposed to diverse topics and genres. Respect students' reading choices. Struggling readers need first to view themselves as readers.
- **Promote discussion**. Set ground rules for discussion so that all opinions are heard. Model good discussion behaviors by asking follow-up questions, expanding on ideas presented, and offering alternate ways of viewing topics.

Developing Fluent Readers

Good readers are fluent readers. They recognize words automatically, group individual words into meaningful phrases, and apply phonic, morphemic, and contextual clues when confronted with a new word. Fluency is a combination of accuracy (number of words identified correctly) and rate (number of words per minute) of reading. Fluency can be taught directly, and it improves as a consequence of students' reading a lot of materials that are within their instructional range.

Understanding Reading Levels

Every student reads at a specific level regardless of the grade in which he or she is placed. Reading level in this context is concerned with the relationship between a specific selection or book and a student's ability to read that selection. The following are common terms used to describe these levels:

- **independent level**–The student reads material in which no more than 1 in 20 words is difficult. The material can be read without teacher involvement and is likely to be material students would choose to read on their own.
- **instructional level**–The student reads material in which no more than 2 in 20 words are difficult. The material is most likely found in school and read with teacher involvement.
- **frustration level**–The student reads material in which significantly more than 2 in 20 of the words are difficult. Students will probably get little out of reading the material.

If students read only material that's too easy, growth in skill, vocabulary, and understanding is too slow. If students read only difficult material, they may give up in frustration much too early.

Providing Reading Materials in the Student's Instructional Range

Most states have testing programs that provide information about each student's reading ability. Once you determine a student's general reading level, you can work with the library media teacher to identify reading materials that will be within the student's instructional level. To develop fluency, students should read materials that contain a high proportion of words that they know already or can easily decode. Work with each student to develop a list of books to read, and have students record their progress on a Reading Log.

Repeated Oral Readings

Repeated oral readings of passages is a strategy that improves fluency. Oral reading also improves prosody, which is the art of sounding natural when you read, or reading with appropriate intonation, expression, and rhythm.

Beginning readers sound awkward when they read aloud. They pause and halt at the wrong places; they emphasize the wrong syllables; they may read in a monotone. Repeated oral readings can increase fluency and prosody as students 1) identify words faster and faster each time they read; 2) correctly identify a larger percentage of words; 3) segment text into appropriate phrases; 4) change pitch and emphasis to fit the meaning of the text.

To improve fluency and prosody, select passages that are brief, thought provoking, and at the student's current independent level of reading. You may choose narrative or expository text, or have the student choose something he or she enjoys. Performing a play, practicing to give a speech, reading to younger students, and rereading a passage to find evidence in support of an argument are all activities that provide opportunities to reread. For the following exercise, you may choose to pair students together and have them read to each other, or use this as a one-on-one teacher-student or tutor-student activity.

1. Select an excerpt within the student's reading level.
2. Have the student read the passage aloud to a partner. The partner records the number of seconds it takes to read the whole passage, and notes the number of errors. Reverse roles so that each student has a chance to read to the other.
3. Read the passage aloud to the students so that students can hear it read correctly.
4. As homework, or as an in-class assignment, have students practice reading the passage out loud on their own.
5. After practice, have each student read aloud again to his or her partner, who records the time and the number of errors.
6. After repeated practice and readings the student will read the passage fluently, that is, with a moderate rate and near 100% accuracy.

Repeated Silent Readings

Having students silently read and reread passages that are at their instructional level also improves fluency. As they practice, students will recognize words more quickly each time, will group words into meaningful phrases more quickly, and will increase their reading rate. One nice thing about repeated silent reading is that a student can do it individually. Many students enjoy timing themselves when they read and seeing improvement over time. Have them keep a record on a piece of graph paper.

Modeling

Students benefit from repeated opportunities to hear Spanish spoken fluently. By listening to live models or CDs, listeners can understand the rhythm of the language and the pitch and pronunciation of particular words and phrases. They can hear when to pause, when to speed up, and what words to emphasize. In addition, you can model or ask an experienced reader to read passages aloud. At most advanced levels, this technique is particularly useful to introduce students to various forms of dialect. As you play the CDs aloud, have students read along silently or chorally, or pause the CDs after each paragraph and have the students try reading the same passage aloud.

Phrase-Cued Text

Less proficient readers may not know when to pause in text. They may pause in the middle of a phrase, or run through a comma or period. They may not recognize verb phrases, prepositional phases, or even phrases marked by parentheses or brackets as words that "go together." This makes their reading disjointed and choppy, or gives it a monotone quality. Some poems have essentially one phrase per line and can be used to demonstrate to students how to phrase text. Or, you may take a passage and have students rewrite it with one phrase per line, so that they pause at the end of each line. Alternatively, you can show them how a passage should be read by inserting slash marks or blank spaces at appropriate places to pause. Choose passages appropriate to the students' reading level. Have students read and then reread the passage, stopping to pause at each slash mark.

Reciprocal Teaching

Reciprocal teaching refers to an instructional activity that teaches students concrete, specific, "comprehension-fostering" strategies they will need whenever they approach the reading of a new text. The activity consists of a dialogue between students and teacher, with each taking a turn in the role of the teacher or leader. Classroom use of this activity has been found to improve the reading comprehension of both good and struggling readers.

Step 1: Have everyone silently read a short passage (one or several paragraphs) of a new text. Model the following four thinking strategies using only the part of the reading that has been read.

- **Questioning** – Ask the class to think of a question that everyone can answer because everyone has read the same text. Model by generating a question for the class. Call on a student to answer your question. Ask that student to then generate a question for the class and to call on another student to answer her question. Repeat this procedure until you think all students are thoroughly familiar with the facts and details of the passage. (If students do not ask a question beginning with *why*, model one for them to move their thinking from literal to inferential comprehension.)
- **Clarifying** – Model for the class a confusion you need to clarify; for example, a word or a phrase that caused you to pause as you initially read the passage. Think aloud as you discuss your mental engagement with this section, explaining to the class how you figured it out. Ask students if they found any confusing parts when they read the passage. Have a dialogue about the problem-solving methods used by students to make sense of confusing parts.
- **Summarizing** – After students have comprehended the passage as a result of the reciprocal questioning and clarifying strategies, ask them to think of a one-sentence summary for the passage. Ask a volunteer to share his summary statement. Encourage others to revise, if needed, the shared summary by elaborating and embellishing its content. Identify the best summary through a dialogue with class members.
- **Predicting** – Now that students know what the first passage in the reading means, ask them to predict what the author will discuss next.

Step 2: Ask everyone to silently read another portion of text. Have a student volunteer repeat step 1, serving as the teacher/leader, over this new portion.

Step 3: In groups of four, have students silently read the next portion of text, taking turns role-playing the leader and following the four-step procedure.

Teacher's Role: Guide students' practice by monitoring the student dialogue in each group during steps 2 and 3. Remind students of the procedure and give additional modeling of the steps.

Reciprocal Teaching training provides students with explicit ways to interact with new text.

An ongoing review of all of the strategies provides a helpful reminder to students and encourages their pursuit of independent reading.

Strategies for Reading
Copymaster

These comprehension and critical-thinking strategies can help you gain a better understanding of what you read. Whenever you find yourself having difficulty making sense of what you're reading, choose and use the strategy that seems most likely to help.

Visualize
Visualize characters, events, and setting to help you understand what's happening. When you read nonfiction, pay attention to the images that form in your mind as you read.

Cause/Effect
Try to figure out what will happen next and how the selection might end. Interpret the facts and infer the effects. Then read on to see how accurate your guesses are.

Compare/Contrast
Connect personally with what you're reading. Think of similarities and differences between the descriptions in the reading and what you have personally experienced, heard about, or read about.

Analyze
Question what happens while you read. Searching for reasons behind events and characters' feelings can help you feel closer to what you are reading. Look for patterns, hidden meanings, and details.

Synthesize
Review your understanding of what you read. You can do this by **summarizing** what you have read, identifying the **main idea**, and **making inferences**–drawing conclusions from the information you are given. Reread passages you don't understand.

Evaluate
Form opinions about what you read, both as you read and after you've finished. Develop your own ideas about characters and events.

Estrategias de lectura
Hoja de duplicación

Estas estrategias de comprensión y razonamiento crítico pueden ayudarte a entender mejor lo que lees. Siempre que tengas problemas para captar el sentido de lo que lees, elige y usa la estrategia que te parezca más adecuada para ayudarte.

Visualizar
Visualiza los personajes, los sucesos y el ambiente para ayudarte a entender lo que está sucediendo. Cuando leas obras de no ficción, presta atención a las imágenes que se forman en tu mente a medida que lees.

Causa/Efecto
Trata de averiguar lo que ocurrirá después y cómo puede terminar el fragmento. Interpreta los hechos e infiere los efectos. Luego sigue leyendo para comprobar lo acertadas que son tus suposiciones.

Comparar/Contrastar
Relaciona lo que lees con tu experiencia personal. Piensa en las semejanzas y las diferencias entre las descripciones de la lectura y lo que tú has vivido, oído o leído.

Analizar
Pregúntate qué pasa a medida que lees. Buscar razones detrás de los sucesos y de los sentimientos de los personajes puede ayudarte a sentir más de cerca lo que lees. Busca patrones, significados ocultos y detalles.

Sintetizar
Repasa lo que has comprendido de la lectura. Puedes hacer esto **resumiendo** lo que has leído, identificando la **idea principal** y **haciendo inferencias,** sacando conclusiones de la información de que dispones. Vuelve a leer los pasajes que no entiendas.

Evaluar
Forma opiniones acerca de lo que lees, tanto al leer como después de haber terminado. Desarrolla tus propias ideas acerca de los personajes y sucesos.

1a, 1b, 1

Lecturas para hispanohablantes

CON PREPARACIÓN PARA LOS EXÁMENES

McDougal Littell
A DIVISION OF HOUGHTON MIFFLIN COMPANY
Evanston, Illinois • Boston • Dallas

Cover photo *top right* David Ryan/Lonely Planet Images; *all others* Martha Granger/EDGE Productions

Acknowledgments

"Cumpleaños," from *Family Pictures/Cuadros de familia* by Carmen Lomas Garza. Copyright © 1990 by Carmen Lomas Garza. All rights reserved. Reprinted with the permission of the publisher, Children's Book Press, San Francisco, CA.

"La exclamación," and "En Uxmal" by Octavio Paz. © Octavio Paz, 1970. Reprinted by permission.

"Palma sola" by Nicolás Guillén. © Herederos de Nicolás Guillén. Reprinted by permission of Herederos de Nicolás Guillén c/o Agencia Literaria Latinoamericana.

From *Como agua para chocolate* by Laura Esquivel. Copyright © 1989 by Laura Esquivel. Used by permission of Doubleday, a division of Random House, Inc.

"Oda al tomate," from *Odas elementales* by Pablo Neruda. Fundación Pablo Neruda, 1954. Reprinted with the permission of Agencia Literaria Carmen Balcells, S.A., Barcelona, Spain.

From *El cuento del cafecito* by Julia Alvarez. Copyright © 2001, 2002. Translated by Daisy Cocco de Filippis. Published by Chelsea Green Publishing Company, 2001. Reprinted by permission of Susan Bergholz Literary Services, New York. All rights reserved.

"Economía doméstica," from *Meditation on the Threshold* by Rosario Castellanos. Copyright © Rosario Castellanos. Copyright © 1988 by Bilingual Press/Editorial Bilingüe. Reprinted by permission of Bilingual Press/Editorial Bilingüe, Arizona State University, Tempe, AZ.

From *Cajas de cartón* by Francisco Jiménez. Copyright © Francisco Jiménez. Reprinted with permission from the author.

Illustration and **Photography Credits** appear on page 224.

ISBN-13: 978-0-618-76606-2
ISBN-10: 0-618-76606-5 2 3 4 5 6 7 8 9 10 – VEI – 12 11 10 09 08 07
Internet: www.mcdougallittell.com

Table of Contents

Literatura adicional

Each authentic literature selection is self-contained, so that the *Literatura adicional* may be presented in any order, according to students' needs and interests.

Test Preparation Strategies 170

Introducing *Lecturas para hispanohablantes*

Lecturas para hispanohablantes is a new kind of reading text. As you will see, this book helps you become an active reader. It is a book to mark up, to write in, and to make your own. You can use it in class and take it home.

Reading Skills Improvement– in Spanish *and* English

You will read selections from your textbook, as well as great literature. In addition, you will learn how to understand the types of texts you read in classes, on tests, and in the real world. You will also study and practice specific strategies for taking standardized tests.

Help for Reading

Many readings in Spanish are challenging the first time you encounter them. ***Lecturas para hispanohablantes*** helps you understand these readings. Here's how.

Para leer The page before each reading gives you background information about the reading and a key to understanding the selection.

Reading Strategy Reading strategies help you decide how to approach the material.

What You Need to Know A preview of every selection tells you what to expect before you begin reading.

Reading Tips Useful, specific reading tips appear at points where language is difficult.

A pensar... Point-of-use, critical-thinking questions help you analyze content as you read.

Márcalo This feature invites you to mark up the text by underlining and circling words and phrases right on the page.

Gramática As you read, this feature highlights key grammar concepts.

Vocabulario This feature helps you with the new vocabulary as you read the selection.

Pronunciación and ***Ortografía*** These features help you improve your pronunciation and your spelling skills.

Análisis This feature appears in the *Literatura adicional* section and encourages you to focus on one aspect of literary analysis as you read.

Reader's Success Strategy These notes give useful and fun tips and strategies for comprehending the selection.

Challenge These activities keep you challenged, even after you have grasped the basic concepts of the reading.

Vocabulary Support

Palabras clave Important new words appear in bold. Their definitions appear in a *Palabras clave* section at the bottom of any page where they occur in the selection. You will practice these words after the selection.

Vocabulario de la lectura A vocabulary activity follows each selection and gives you the opportunity to practice the *Palabras clave.*

Comprehension and Connections

¿Comprendiste? Questions after each selection check your understanding of what you have just read.

Conexión personal These short writing activities ask you to relate the selection to your life and experiences to make what you have read more meaningful.

Complements your Spanish Program!

When using McDougal Littell's Spanish Program, you will find ***Lecturas para hispanohablantes*** to be a perfect companion. ***Lecturas para hispanohablantes*** lets you mark up the selections as you read, helping you understand and remember more.

Read on to learn more!

Academic and Informational Reading

Here is a special collection of real-world examples–in English with bilingual reading strategies–to help you read every kind of informational material, from textbooks to technical directions. Why are these sections in English with bilingual reading strategies? Because the strategies you learn will help you on tests, in other classes, and in the world outside of school. You will find strategies for the following:

Analyzing Text Features This section will help you read many different types of magazine articles and textbooks. You will learn how titles, subtitles, lists, graphics, many different kinds of visuals, and other special features work in magazines and textbooks. After studying this section you will be ready to read even the most complex material.

Understanding Visuals Tables, charts, graphs, maps, and diagrams all require special reading skills. As you learn the common elements of various visual texts, you will learn to read these materials with accuracy and skill.

Recognizing Text Structures Informational texts can be organized in many different ways. In this section you will study the following structures and learn about special key words that will help you identify the organizational patterns:

- Main Idea and Supporting Details
- Problem and Solution
- Sequence
- Cause and Effect
- Comparison and Contrast
- Persuasion

Reading in the Content Areas You will learn special strategies for reading social studies, science, and mathematics texts.

Reading Beyond the Classroom In this section you will encounter applications, schedules, technical directions, product information, Web pages, and other readings. Learning to analyze these texts will help you in your everyday life and on some standardized tests.

Test Preparation Strategies

In this section, you will find bilingual reading strategies and practice to help you succeed on many different kinds of standardized tests. After closely studying a variety of test formats through annotated examples, you will have an opportunity to practice each format on your own. Additional support will help you think through your answers. You will find strategies for the following:

Successful Test Taking This section provides many suggestions for preparing for and taking tests. The information ranges from analyzing test questions to tips for answering multiple-choice and open-ended test questions.

Reading Tests: Long Selections You will learn how to analyze the structure of a lengthy reading and prepare to answer the comprehension questions that follow it.

Reading Tests: Short Selections These selections may be a few paragraphs of text, a poem, a chart or graph, or some other item. You will practice the special range of comprehension skills required for these pieces.

Functional Reading Tests These real-world texts present special challenges. You will learn about the various test formats that use applications, product labels, technical directions, Web pages, and more.

Revising-and-Editing Tests These materials test your understanding of English grammar and usage. You may encounter capitalization and punctuation questions. Sometimes the focus is on usage questions such as verb tenses or pronoun agreement issues. You will become familiar with these formats through the guided practice in this section.

Writing Tests Writing prompts and sample student essays will help you understand how to analyze a prompt and what elements make a successful written response. Scoring rubrics and a prompt for practice will prepare you for the writing tests you will take.

En voces

Point-of-use comprehension support helps you read selections and develop critical-thinking skills.

Estrategia de lectura
This feature provides reading tips and strategies that help you effectively approach the material.

Datos para tener en cuenta
This section provides a key to help you unlock the selection so that you can understand and enjoy it.

Para leer *Una encuesta escolar*

Estrategia de lectura

USAR PISTAS DEL CONTEXTO Puedes usar el contexto para adivinar el significado de las palabras desconocidas. El contexto es lo que viene antes y después de la palabra. Los dibujos a menudo son parte del contexto también. ¿Qué piensas que significan las palabras resaltadas? Escribe las respuestas en el cuadro siguiente.

- Una encuesta **escolar** entre estudiantes y maestros
- Los **resultados** de la encuesta dicen qué clase es la más popular.

Palabra	Definición
escolar	
resultados	

Datos para tener en cuenta

En México, los niños tienen que asistir a la escuela pública o privada hasta el grado nueve. Hay seis grados de educación primaria y tres grados de educación secundaria. El horario para los primeros grados normalmente es de 9 a.m. a 12:30 p.m. Y para los grados de secundaria es de 7:30 a.m. a 2:30 p.m. La mayoría de los estudiantes mexicanos asisten a escuelas públicas, aunque en las ciudades muchos asisten a escuelas privadas. Los estudiantes que quieren seguir su educación después de la secundaria toman clases de preparatoria para la universidad durante otros tres años o asisten a una escuela profesional, después de la cual pueden solicitar el ingreso en una universidad. En México, tanto las universidades públicas como las privadas tienen exámenes de admisión altamente competitivos que los solicitantes tienen que pasar para ser admitidos.

24 Lecturas para hispanohablantes Nivel 1

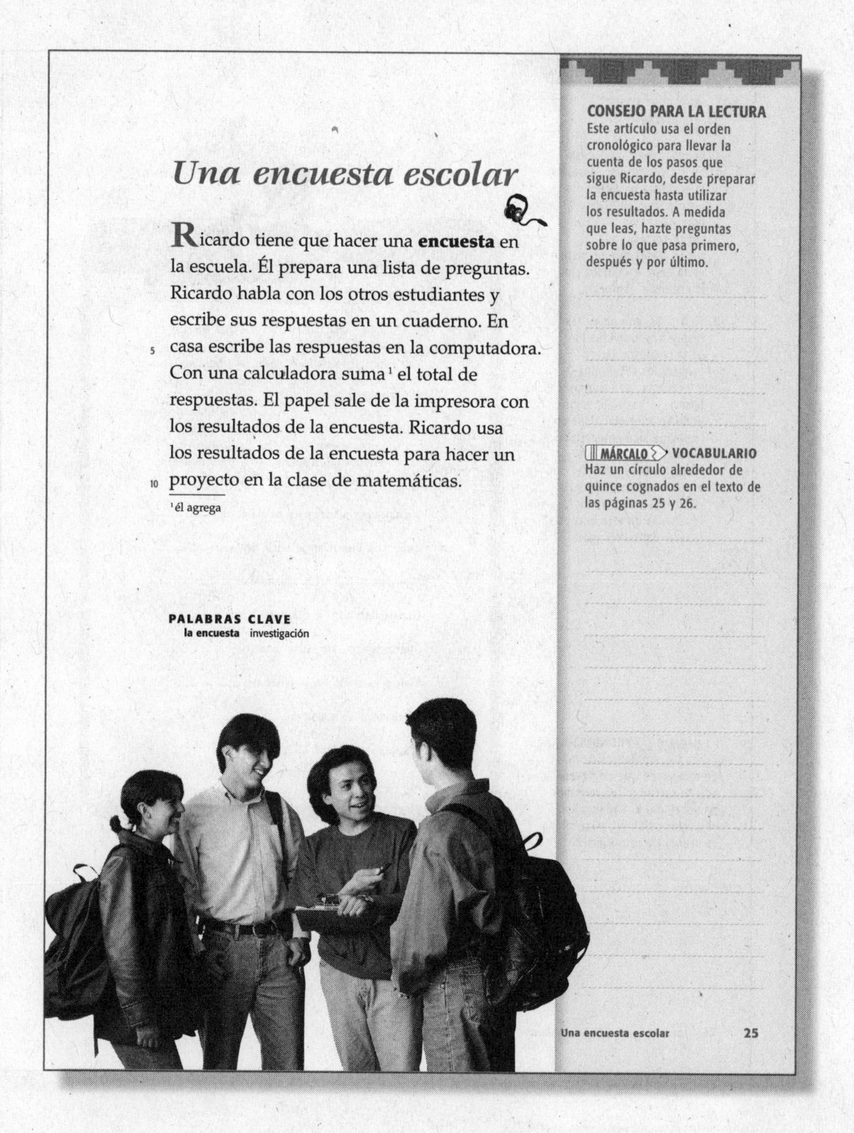

CONSEJO PARA LA LECTURA
Este artículo usa el orden cronológico para llevar la cuenta de los pasos que sigue Ricardo, desde preparar la encuesta hasta utilizar los resultados. A medida que leas, hazte preguntas sobre lo que pasa primero, después y por último.

Una encuesta escolar

Ricardo tiene que hacer una **encuesta** en la escuela. Él prepara una lista de preguntas. Ricardo habla con los otros estudiantes y escribe sus respuestas en un cuaderno. En
5 casa escribe las respuestas en la computadora. Con una calculadora suma[1] el total de respuestas. El papel sale de la impresora con los resultados de la encuesta. Ricardo usa los resultados de la encuesta para hacer un
10 proyecto en la clase de matemáticas.

[1] él agrega

MÁRCALO VOCABULARIO
Haz un círculo alrededor de quince cognados en el texto de las páginas 25 y 26.

PALABRAS CLAVE
la encuesta investigación

Una encuesta escolar 25

MÁRCALO

VOCABULARIO
This feature helps you with the new vocabulary as you read the selection. Underlining or circling the example makes it easier for you to find and remember.

PALABRAS CLAVE
Important vocabulary words appear in bold within the reading. Definitions are given at the bottom of the page.

A pensar...

Point-of-use questions check your understanding and ask you to think critically about the passage.

MÁRCALO

PRONUNCIACIÓN

This feature helps you improve your pronunciation skills. There are also **Márcalo Ortografía** activities to practice spelling.

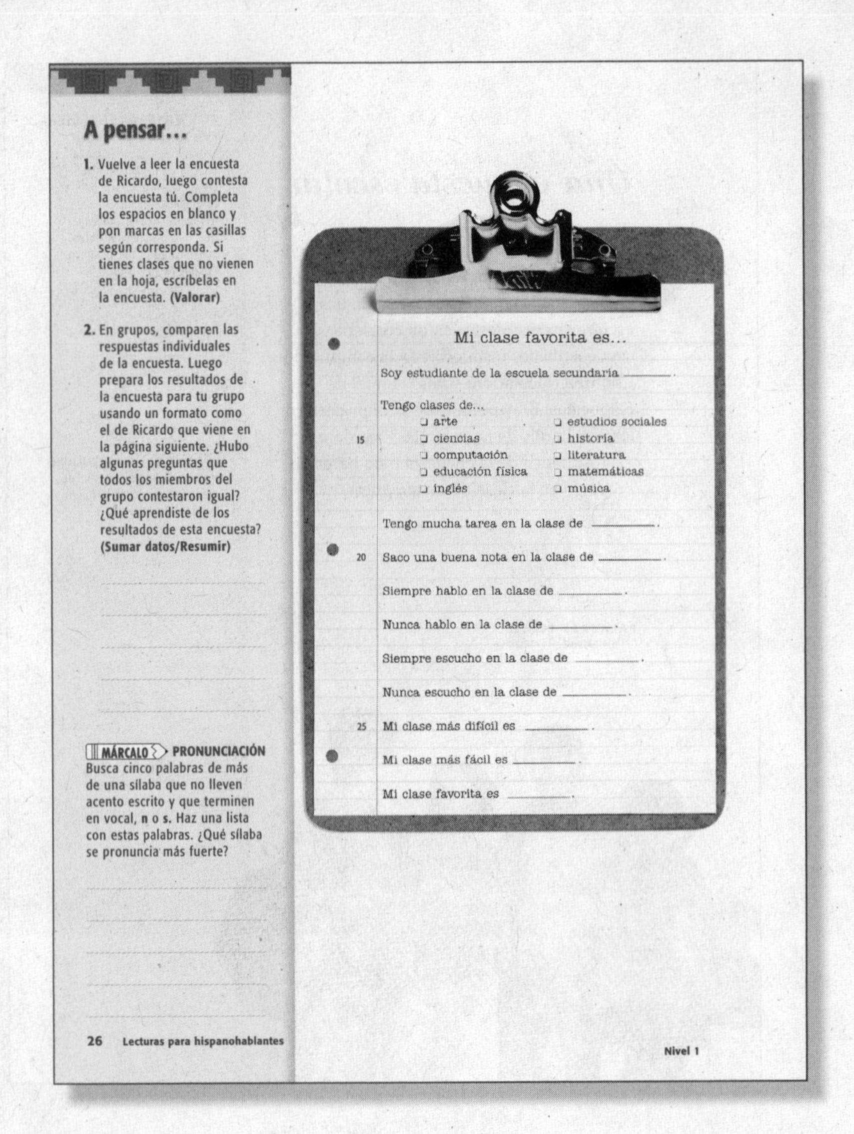

A pensar...

1. Vuelve a leer la encuesta de Ricardo, luego contesta la encuesta tú. Completa los espacios en blanco y pon marcas en las casillas según corresponda. Si tienes clases que no vienen en la hoja, escríbelas en la encuesta. **(Valorar)**

2. En grupos, comparen las respuestas individuales de la encuesta. Luego prepara los resultados de la encuesta para tu grupo usando un formato como el de Ricardo que viene en la página siguiente. ¿Hubo algunas preguntas que todos los miembros del grupo contestaron igual? ¿Qué aprendiste de los resultados de esta encuesta? **(Sumar datos/Resumir)**

MÁRCALO **PRONUNCIACIÓN**
Busca cinco palabras de más de una sílaba que no lleven acento escrito y que terminen en vocal, **n** o **s**. Haz una lista con estas palabras. ¿Qué sílaba se pronuncia más fuerte?

Mi clase favorita es...

Soy estudiante de la escuela secundaria ______.

Tengo clases de...
- ❑ arte
- ❑ ciencias
- ❑ computación
- ❑ educación física
- ❑ inglés
- ❑ estudios sociales
- ❑ historia
- ❑ literatura
- ❑ matemáticas
- ❑ música

Tengo mucha tarea en la clase de ______.

Saco una buena nota en la clase de ______.

Siempre hablo en la clase de ______.

Nunca hablo en la clase de ______.

Siempre escucho en la clase de ______.

Nunca escucho en la clase de ______.

Mi clase más difícil es ______.

Mi clase más fácil es ______.

Mi clase favorita es ______.

26 Lecturas para hispanohablantes

Nivel 1

Los resultados

Una encuesta a 50 estudiantes

30 Clase con más tarea: matemáticas
(25 estudiantes)

Los estudiantes sacan más buenas notas en la clase de: música
(35 estudiantes)

Los estudiantes hablan más en la clase de: literatura
35 *(30 estudiantes)*

Los estudiantes nunca hablan en la clase de: inglés
(25 estudiantes)

Los estudiantes escuchan más en la clase de: ciencias
(40 estudiantes)

40 Los estudiantes nunca escuchan en la clase de: historia
(20 estudiantes)

La clase más difícil es: ciencias
(35 estudiantes)

La clase más fácil es: arte
45 *(45 estudiantes)*

La clase favorita es: literatura
(30 estudiantes)

ESTRATEGIA DEL BUEN LECTOR Usa una tabla como la siguiente para comparar y contrastar los cursos que se ofrecen en la escuela de Ricardo con los que se ofrecen en tu escuela.

La escuela de Ricardo
Mi escuela

DESAFÍO Fíjate en los resultados de la encuesta de Ricardo. Fíjate en el título para saber a cuántos estudiantes él encuestó en total. Luego convierte el número de estudiantes de cada subcategoría al porcentaje de estudiantes encuestados. **(Calcular)**

Modelo: Clase con más tarea: matemáticas (25 estudiantes: 50%)

Una encuesta escolar 27

ESTRATEGIA DEL BUEN LECTOR

Notes like this one provide ideas to help you read the selection successfully. For example, some notes suggest that you fill in a chart while you read. Others suggest that you mark key words or ideas in the text.

DESAFÍO

This feature asks you to expand upon what you have learned for enrichment.

Vocabulario de la lectura

Vocabulary practice follows each reading, reinforcing the *Palabras clave* that appear throughout the selection.

Pronunciación y ortografía

This part of the vocabulary support presents an explanation of basic pronunciation or spelling rules, then offers activities to practice the information just learned.

Vocabulario de la lectura

Palabras clave

la calculadora máquina que hace cálculos como la suma y la resta
la computadora máquina para el tratamiento de la informacion
la encuesta investigacion
la impresora máquina que permite la salida de resultados escritos sobre papel

Escribe la **palabra clave** que mejor complete cada oración.

Ricardo prepara una lista de preguntas para su ______ (1) escolar.
Primero, escribe las respuestas de los otros estudiantes en un cuaderno.
Cuando llega a casa, escribe las respuestas en la ______ (2).
Usa una ______ (3) para sumar el total de respuestas.
El papel sale de la ______ (4) con los resultados.

Pronunciación y ortografía

Cada palabra en español tiene una sílaba que se pronuncia más fuerte. Este acento o *golpe* está determinada por las dos siguientes reglas:

1) Una palabra que termina en vocal, **n** o **s** se pronuncia más fuerte en la penúltima sílaba (cuando no hay un acento escrito).
a-**cen**-to **di**-ce pre-**pa**-ran pre-**gun**-tas

2) Una palabra que termina en consonante, excepto **n** o **s**, se pronuncia más fuerte en la última sílaba (cuando no hay un acento escrito).
to-**tal** con-tes-**tar** ciu-**dad** re-**loj**

A. Pronuncia las siguientes palabras y subraya la sílaba que pronuncias más fuerte.
1. escuchan **2.** notas **3.** papel **4.** hacer **5.** proyecto

B. Repite cada palabra y determina cuál de las dos reglas de acentuación determina la sílaba fuerte, **1** o **2**.
1. escuchan ____ **2.** notas ____ **3.** papel ____
4. hacer ____ **5.** proyecto ____

28 Lecturas para hispanohablantes Nivel 1

¿Comprendiste?

1. ¿Qué tiene que hacer Ricardo?

2. ¿Qué usa Ricardo para escribir la encuesta?

3. ¿Los estudiantes hablan mucho o poco en la clase de inglés?

4. ¿Es difícil la clase de música o arte en la escuela de Ricardo?

5. ¿Qué clase es la clase favorita de los estudiantes?

Conexión personal

¿Cuál es tu clase favorita? ¿Por qué te gusta? Escribe las respuestas en la red siguiente.

Me gusta leer.

mi clase favorita: inglés

Una encuesta escolar 29

¿Comprendiste?

Comprehension questions check your understanding and provide the opportunity to practice new vocabulary words.

Conexión personal

These short writing activities help you see connections between what happens in the selection and in your own life.

Literatura adicional

Notes in the margins make literature from the Spanish-speaking world accessible and help you read works by famous authors such as Neruda and Paz.

Estrategia de lectura
This feature provides reading tips and strategies that help you effectively approach the material.

Datos para tener en cuenta
This section provides a key to help you unlock the selection so that you can understand and enjoy it.

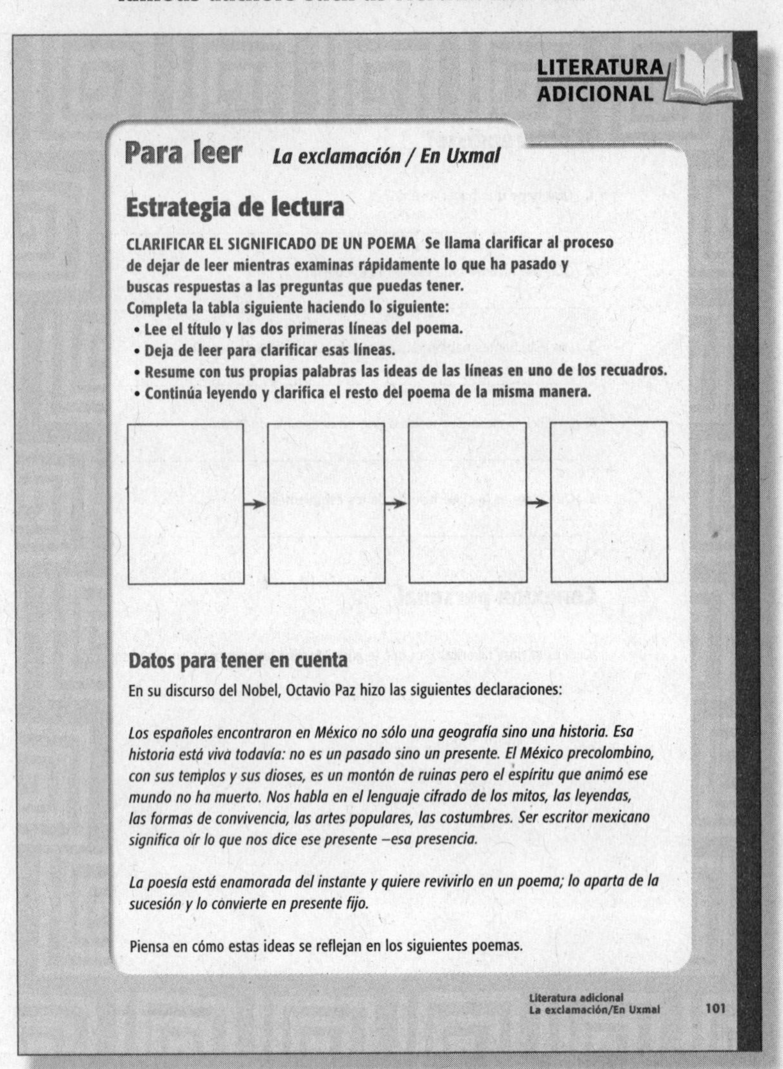
LITERATURA ADICIONAL

Para leer *La exclamación / En Uxmal*

Estrategia de lectura

CLARIFICAR EL SIGNIFICADO DE UN POEMA Se llama clarificar al proceso de dejar de leer mientras examinas rápidamente lo que ha pasado y buscas respuestas a las preguntas que puedas tener.
Completa la tabla siguiente haciendo lo siguiente:
- **Lee el título y las dos primeras líneas del poema.**
- **Deja de leer para clarificar esas líneas.**
- **Resume con tus propias palabras las ideas de las líneas en uno de los recuadros.**
- **Continúa leyendo y clarifica el resto del poema de la misma manera.**

Datos para tener en cuenta

En su discurso del Nobel, Octavio Paz hizo las siguientes declaraciones:

Los españoles encontraron en México no sólo una geografía sino una historia. Esa historia está viva todavía: no es un pasado sino un presente. El México precolombino, con sus templos y sus dioses, es un montón de ruinas pero el espíritu que animó ese mundo no ha muerto. Nos habla en el lenguaje cifrado de los mitos, las leyendas, las formas de convivencia, las artes populares, las costumbres. Ser escritor mexicano significa oír lo que nos dice ese presente —esa presencia.

La poesía está enamorada del instante y quiere revivirlo en un poema; lo aparta de la sucesión y lo convierte en presente fijo.

Piensa en cómo estas ideas se reflejan en los siguientes poemas.

Literatura adicional
La exclamación/En Uxmal 101

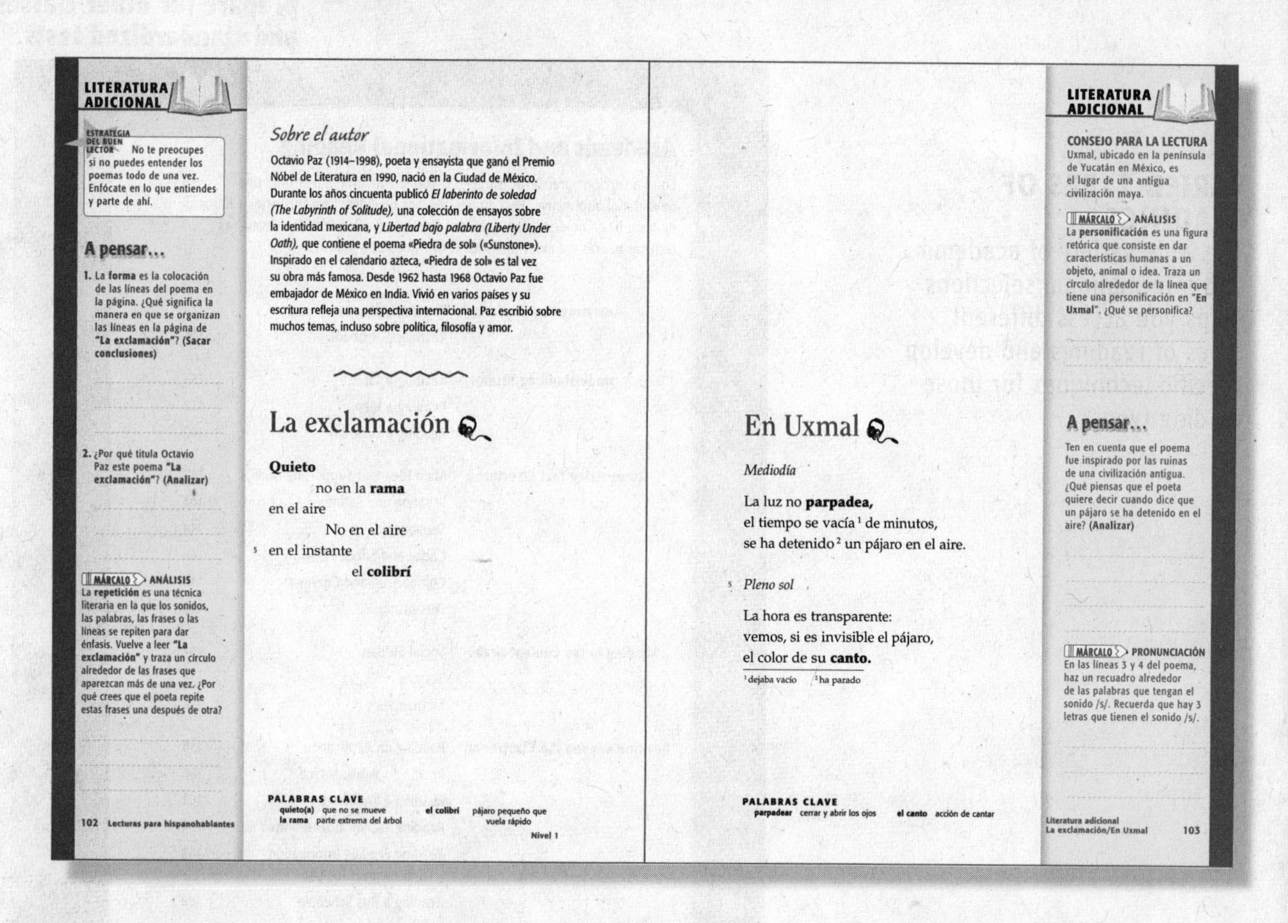

LITERATURA ADICIONAL

ESTRATEGIA DEL BUEN LECTOR No te preocupes si no puedes entender los poemas todo de una vez. Enfócate en lo que entiendes y parte de ahí.

A pensar...

1. La **forma** es la colocación de las líneas del poema en la página. ¿Qué significa la manera en que se organizan las líneas en la página de **"La exclamación"**? **(Sacar conclusiones)**

2. ¿Por qué titula Octavio Paz este poema **"La exclamación"**? **(Analizar)**

MÁRCALO ANÁLISIS
La **repetición** es una técnica literaria en la que los sonidos, las palabras, las frases o las líneas se repiten para dar énfasis. Vuelve a leer **"La exclamación"** y traza un círculo alrededor de las frases que aparezcan más de una vez. ¿Por qué crees que el poeta repite estas frases una después de otra?

Sobre el autor

Octavio Paz (1914–1998), poeta y ensayista que ganó el Premio Nóbel de Literatura en 1990, nació en la Ciudad de México. Durante los años cincuenta publicó *El laberinto de soledad (The Labyrinth of Solitude),* una colección de ensayos sobre la identidad mexicana, y *Libertad bajo palabra (Liberty Under Oath),* que contiene el poema «Piedra de sol» («Sunstone»). Inspirado en el calendario azteca, «Piedra de sol» es tal vez su obra más famosa. Desde 1962 hasta 1968 Octavio Paz fue embajador de México en India. Vivió en varios países y su escritura refleja una perspectiva internacional. Paz escribió sobre muchos temas, incluso sobre política, filosofía y amor.

La exclamación

Quieto
no en la **rama**
en el aire
No en el aire
5 en el instante
el **colibrí**

PALABRAS CLAVE
quieto(a) que no se mueve
la rama parte extrema del árbol
el colibrí pájaro pequeño que vuela rápido

102 Lecturas para hispanohablantes Nivel 1

En Uxmal

Mediodía

La luz no **parpadea,**
el tiempo se vacía[1] de minutos,
se ha detenido[2] un pájaro en el aire.

5 *Pleno sol*

La hora es transparente:
vemos, si es invisible el pájaro,
el color de su **canto.**

[1] dejaba vacío [2] ha parado

PALABRAS CLAVE
parpadear cerrar y abrir los ojos
el canto acción de cantar

LITERATURA ADICIONAL

CONSEJO PARA LA LECTURA
Uxmal, ubicado en la península de Yucatán en México, es el lugar de una antigua civilización maya.

MÁRCALO ANÁLISIS
La **personificación** es una figura retórica que consiste en dar características humanas a un objeto, animal o idea. Traza un círculo alrededor de la línea que tiene una personificación en **"En Uxmal"**. ¿Qué se personifica?

A pensar...

Ten en cuenta que el poema fue inspirado por las ruinas de una civilización antigua. ¿Qué piensas que el poeta quiere decir cuando dice que un pájaro se ha detenido en el aire? **(Analizar)**

MÁRCALO PRONUNCIACIÓN
En las líneas 3 y 4 del poema, haz un recuadro alrededor de las palabras que tengan el sonido /s/. Recuerda que hay 3 letras que tienen el sonido /s/.

Literatura adicional
La exclamación/En Uxmal 103

Sobre el autor

Each literary selection begins with a short author biography that provides cultural context.

This icon indicates that there is audio for this selection.

MÁRCALO ANÁLISIS

This feature encourages you to focus on one aspect of literary analysis as you read.

ESTRATEGIA DEL BUEN LECTOR

Notes like this one provide ideas to help you read the selection successfully. For example, some notes suggest that you fill in a chart while you read. Others suggest that you mark key words or ideas in the text.

Academic and Informational Reading

This section helps you read informational material and prepare for other classes and standardized tests.

VARIED TYPES OF READINGS

The wide variety of academic and informational selections helps you access different types of readings and develop specific techniques for those reading types.

Academic and Informational Reading

En esta sección aprenderás estrategias que te ayudarán a leer todo tipo de material informativo. Encontrarás muchos ejemplos, desde revistas y libros de texto hasta horarios de autobuses. Al emplear estas sencillas y efectivas técnicas podrás entender todos los textos que ves a diario.

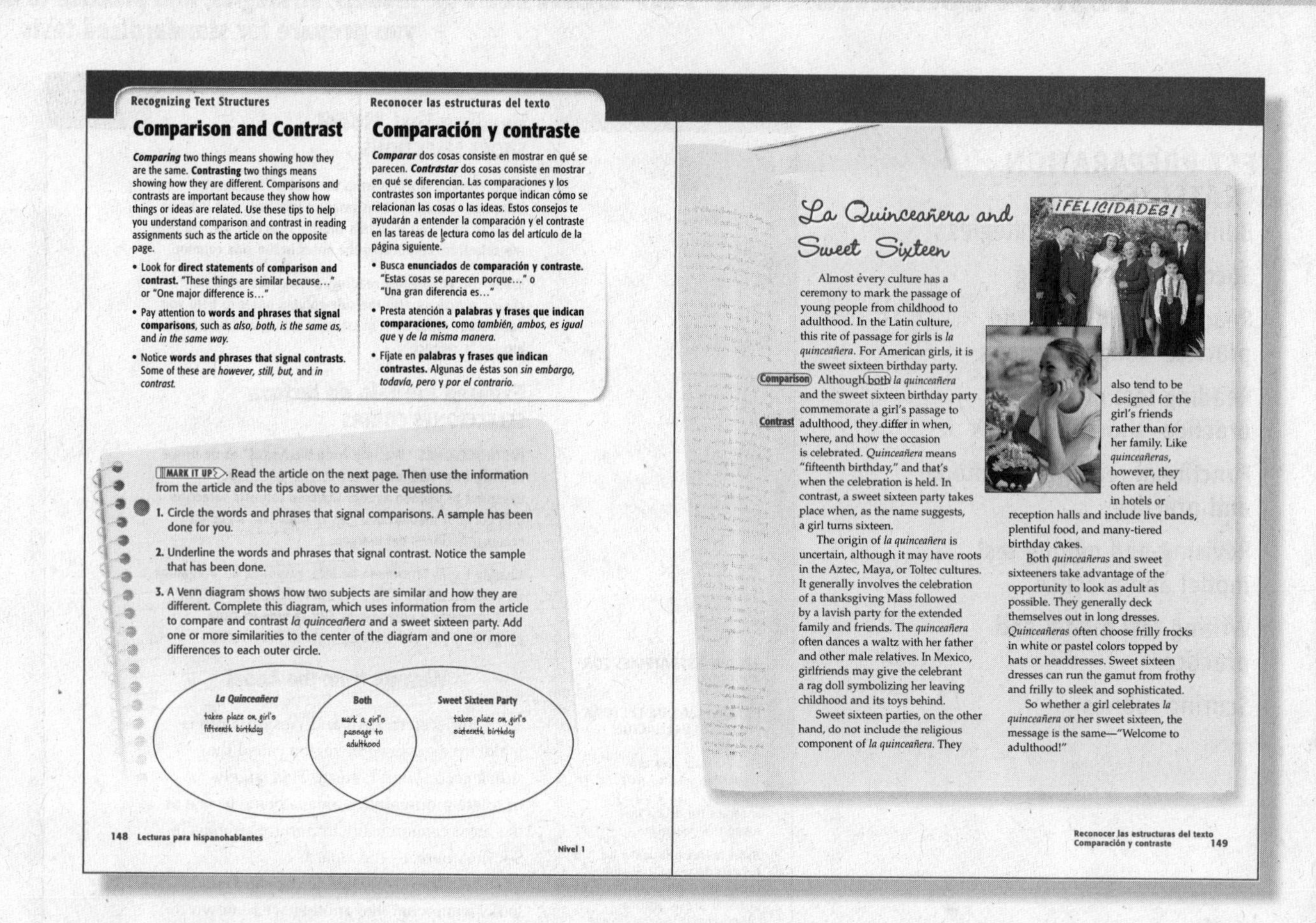

Recognizing Text Structures

Comparison and Contrast

Comparing two things means showing how they are the same. **Contrasting** two things means showing how they are different. Comparisons and contrasts are important because they show how things or ideas are related. Use these tips to help you understand comparison and contrast in reading assignments such as the article on the opposite page.

- Look for **direct statements** of **comparison and contrast.** "These things are similar because..." or "One major difference is..."
- Pay attention to **words and phrases that signal comparisons**, such as *also, both, is the same as,* and *in the same way.*
- Notice **words and phrases that signal contrasts**. Some of these are *however, still, but,* and *in contrast.*

Reconocer las estructuras del texto

Comparación y contraste

Comparar dos cosas consiste en mostrar en qué se parecen. ***Contrastar*** dos cosas consiste en mostrar en qué se diferencian. Las comparaciones y los contrastes son importantes porque indican cómo se relacionan las cosas o las ideas. Estos consejos te ayudarán a entender la comparación y el contraste en las tareas de lectura como las del artículo de la página siguiente.

- Busca **enunciados** de **comparación y contraste.** "Estas cosas se parecen porque..." o "Una gran diferencia es..."
- Presta atención a **palabras y frases que indican comparaciones,** como *también, ambos, es igual que* y *de la misma manera.*
- Fíjate en **palabras y frases que indican contrastes.** Algunas de éstas son *sin embargo, todavía, pero* y *por el contrario.*

MARK IT UP Read the article on the next page. Then use the information from the article and the tips above to answer the questions.

1. Circle the words and phrases that signal comparisons. A sample has been done for you.
2. Underline the words and phrases that signal contrast. Notice the sample that has been done.
3. A Venn diagram shows how two subjects are similar and how they are different. Complete this diagram, which uses information from the article to compare and contrast *la quinceañera* and a sweet sixteen party. Add one or more similarities to the center of the diagram and one or more differences to each outer circle.

148 Lecturas para hispanohablantes

Nivel 1

La Quinceañera and Sweet Sixteen

Almost every culture has a ceremony to mark the passage of young people from childhood to adulthood. In the Latin culture, this rite of passage for girls is *la quinceañera*. For American girls, it is the sweet sixteen birthday party.

Comparison Although both *la quinceañera* and the sweet sixteen birthday party commemorate a girl's passage to Contrast adulthood, they differ in when, where, and how the occasion is celebrated. *Quinceañera* means "fifteenth birthday," and that's when the celebration is held. In contrast, a sweet sixteen party takes place when, as the name suggests, a girl turns sixteen.

The origin of *la quinceañera* is uncertain, although it may have roots in the Aztec, Maya, or Toltec cultures. It generally involves the celebration of a thanksgiving Mass followed by a lavish party for the extended family and friends. The *quinceañera* often dances a waltz with her father and other male relatives. In Mexico, girlfriends may give the celebrant a rag doll symbolizing her leaving childhood and its toys behind.

Sweet sixteen parties, on the other hand, do not include the religious component of *la quinceañera*. They also tend to be designed for the girl's friends rather than for her family. Like *quinceañeras*, however, they often are held in hotels or reception halls and include live bands, plentiful food, and many-tiered birthday cakes.

Both *quinceañeras* and sweet sixteeners take advantage of the opportunity to look as adult as possible. They generally deck themselves out in long dresses. *Quinceañeras* often choose frilly frocks in white or pastel colors topped by hats or headdresses. Sweet sixteen dresses can run the gamut from frothy and frilly to sleek and sophisticated.

So whether a girl celebrates *la quinceañera* or her sweet sixteen, the message is the same—"Welcome to adulthood!"

Reconocer las estructuras del texto
Comparación y contraste 149

SKILL DEVELOPMENT

These activities offer bilingual instructions, graphic organizers, Mark It Up features, and other reading support to help you comprehend and think critically about the selection.

Test Preparation for All Learners

***Lecturas para hispanohablantes* offers models, strategies, and practice to help you prepare for standardized tests.**

TEST PREPARATION STRATEGIES

- Bilingual reading strategies
- Successful test taking
- Reading test model and practice–long selections
- Reading test model and practice–short selections
- Functional reading test model and practice
- Revising-and-editing test model and practice
- Writing test model and practice
- Scoring rubrics

APUNTES

Reading Test Model
SHORT SELECTIONS

DIRECTIONS "Warmth from the Andes" is a short informative article. The strategies you have just learned can also help you with this shorter selection. As you read the selection, respond to the notes in the side column.

When you've finished reading, answer the multiple-choice questions. Use the side-column notes to help you understand what each question is asking and why each answer is correct.

Examen modelo de lectura
SELECCIONES CORTAS

INSTRUCCIONES "Warmth from the Andes" es un breve artículo informativo. Las estrategias que acabas de aprender te pueden ayudar también con esta selección más corta. A medida que leas la selección, sigue las recomendaciones del margen.

Cuando hayas terminado de leer, responde las preguntas de elección múltiple. Usa las anotaciones del margen para ayudarte a entender lo que se pide en cada pregunta y por qué esa respuesta es la correcta.

READING STRATEGIES FOR ASSESSMENT

ESTRATEGIAS DE LECTURA PARA LA EVALUACIÓN

Find the main idea and supporting details. Circle the main idea of this article. Then underline the details that support the main idea.

Busca la idea principal y los detalles de apoyo. Traza un círculo alrededor de la idea principal de este artículo. Luego subraya los detalles que apoyan la idea principal.

Warmth from the Andes

Southeastern Peru and Western Bolivia make up a geographic region called the *Altiplano*, or High Plateau. This largely desolate mountainous area is home to one of the most economically important animals in South America—the alpaca.

The alpaca is related to the camel and looks somewhat like another well-known South American grazing animal, the llama. Alpacas live at elevations as high as 16,000 feet. At such altitudes, oxygen is scarce. Alpacas are able to survive because their

196 Lecturas para hispanohablantes

Nivel 1

Writing Test Model

DIRECTIONS Many tests ask you to write an essay in response to a writing prompt. A writing prompt is a brief statement that describes a writing situation. Some writing prompts ask you to explain *what, why,* or *how.* Others ask you to convince someone of something.

As you analyze the following writing prompts, read and respond to the notes in the side columns. Then look at the response to each prompt. The notes in the side columns will help you understand why each response is considered strong.

Examen modelo de escritura

INSTRUCCIONES En muchos exámenes se te pide escribir un ensayo en respuesta a una sugerencia. Una sugerencia es una explicación breve que describe una situación sobre la que se te pide escribir. Algunas sugerencias te piden explicar *qué, por qué o cómo.* En otras se te pide convencer a alguien de algo.

A medida que analizas las sugerencias siguientes, lee y sigue las recomendaciones de las anotaciones de los márgenes. Luego mira la respuesta para cada sugerencia. Las anotaciones de los márgenes te ayudarán a comprender por qué se considera buena cada respuesta.

Prompt A

Some child-rearing experts believe that young people should be kept busy after school and on the weekends with a variety of structured activities, such as music lessons, sports, dance classes, and so on. Others say that young people today have been "overscheduled" and need more time to themselves—to read, think about the future, and even just to daydream.

ANALYZING THE PROMPT

ANALIZAR LA SUGERENCIA PARA ESCRIBIR

Identify the focus. What issue will you be writing about? Circle the focus of your essay in the first sentence of the prompt.

Identifica el tema central. ¿De qué vas a escribir? Traza un círculo alrededor del tema central del ensayo en la primera oración de la sugerencia.

Understand what's expected of you. First, circle what the prompt asks you to do. Then identify your audience. What kinds of details will appeal to this audience?

Entiende lo que se te pide. Primero, traza un círculo alrededor de lo que se te pide hacer en la sugerencia. Luego identifica a quién va dirigido el ensayo. ¿Qué tipo de detalles atraerán a estos lectores?

Revising-and-Editing Test Model

DIRECTIONS Read the following paragraph carefully. Then answer the multiple-choice questions that follow. After answering the questions, read the material in the side columns to check your answer strategies.

Examen modelo para revisar y corregir

INSTRUCCIONES Lee con atención el párrafo siguiente. Luego responde las preguntas de elección múltiple que se dan a continuación. Después de responder las preguntas, consulta la información de los márgenes para comprobar tus estrategias para responder las preguntas.

[1]Madrid, the capital of Spain. [2]It is home to one of that nations cultural treasures—the Prado museum. [3]The building was constructed in the late eighteenth century as a museum of natural science. [4]Then they decided to change it to an art museum in 1819 and it has more than 9,000 works of art. [5]The museum is located on a street called the Paseo del Prado. [6]Their are many famous paintings they're, including works by El Greco, Velázquez, and Goya.

1. Which sentence in the paragraph is actually a fragment, or incomplete thought?

   A. sentence 5

   B. sentence 3

   C. sentence 1

   D. sentence 4

READING STRATEGIES FOR ASSESSMENT

ESTRATEGIAS DE LECTURA PARA LA EVALUACIÓN

Watch for common errors. Highlight or underline errors such as incorrect spelling or punctuation; fragments or run-on sentences; and missing or misplaced information.

Ten cuidado con errores comunes. Marca o subraya errores ortográficos o de puntuación; oraciones incompletas o seguidas; información que falta o está fuera de lugar.

ANSWER STRATEGIES

ESTRATEGIAS PARA CONTESTAR LAS PREGUNTAS

Incomplete Sentences. A sentence is a group of words with a subject and a verb that expresses a complete thought. If either the subject or the verb is missing, the group of words is an incomplete sentence.

Oraciones incompletas. Una oración es un grupo de palabras con un sujeto y un verbo que expresa una idea completa. Si falta el sujeto o el verbo, el grupo de palabras es una oración incompleta.

Answers: 1. C

Para leer *Los latinos de Estados Unidos*

Estrategia de lectura

MIRAR ANTES LOS GRÁFICOS Piensa en cómo lees un artículo. ¿Te fijas en las fotos u otros gráficos antes de leer? Mira los gráficos que vienen en esta lectura, luego predice de lo que trata la lectura. Después de leer, determina si tu predicción fue acertada o tienes que cambiarla un poco.

Predicción: ______________________________

____

____

____

¿Acertaste con tu predicción? ______________________________

____

____

____

____

Datos para tener en cuenta

Cada diez años, los años que terminan en cero, el gobierno de Estados Unidos cuenta a toda la población de Estados Unidos. A esto se le llama el censo de los EE.UU. La Constitución de los EE.UU. pide que se cuente a todas las personas que viven en los Estados Unidos. No importa la edad, el lugar de nacimiento, ni el idioma de las personas. Además para contar a toda la población, el censo también recoge información como el idioma que se habla en casa, el lugar de nacimiento y el origen nacional. En los últimos años, las personas nacidas o procedentes de un país hispanohablante se han convertido en el grupo minoritario más grande de los Estados Unidos.

The audio is on CD 1 of ***Lecturas para hispanohablantes,*** Track 1.

Los latinos de Estados Unidos

En **Estados Unidos** hay personas de muchos países de Latinoamérica.

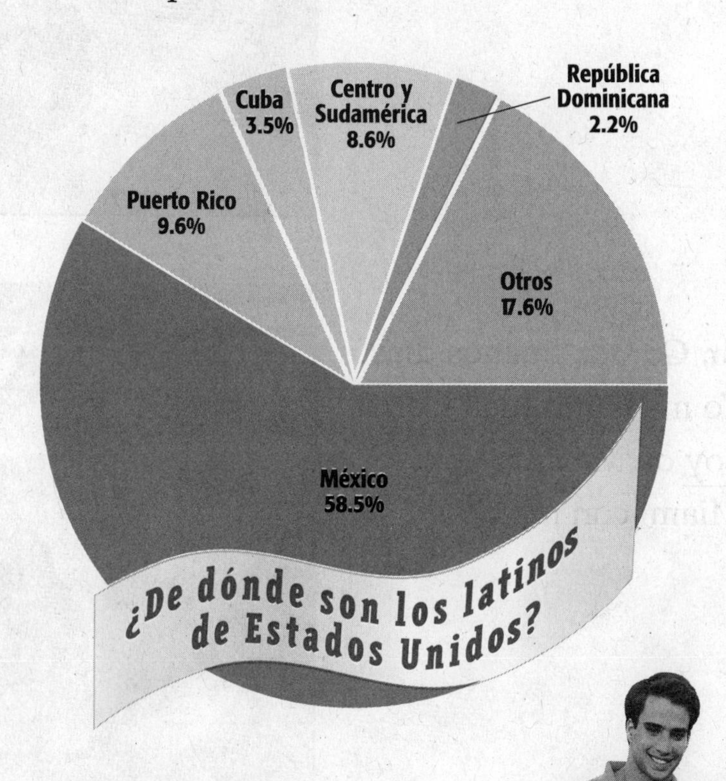

Francisco: ¿Qué tal? Me llamo Francisco García Flores. Soy de Puerto Rico, pero vivo en Miami. El hombre de México es mi papá. La mujer es mi mamá.

PALABRAS CLAVE

Estados Unidos país de Norteamérica
Centroamérica tierra entre Norteamérica y Sudamérica
República Dominicana país caribeño
México país de Norteamérica
Sudamérica parte del continente americano

CONSEJO PARA LA LECTURA Escucha el disco mientras sigues atentamente el libro. Fíjate en los diferentes acentos de los hablantes. ¿Sabes de qué país es cada uno? Ahora lee otra vez el artículo por tu cuenta.

A pensar...

Una gráfica de pastel es una gráfica circular cortada en partes como pedazos de pastel. Divide la información y muestra partes de un todo. Mira la gráfica de pastel de la izquierda. ¿De dónde indica la gráfica que son los latinos? ¿De qué dos países son la mayoría de los residentes de Estados Unidos descendientes de latinos? Escribe la respuesta a continuación. **(Analizar)**

La gráfica indica que los latinos de los Estados Unidos son de todas partes del mundo hispanohablante. México y Puerto Rico son los países de origen de la mayoría de los latinos de Estados Unidos.

APUNTES

APUNTES

MÁRCALO GRAMÁTICA
Subraya todos los verbos de esta página y escribe los infinitivos abajo.

llamar, ser, trabajar, vivir

APUNTES

Sra. García: Me llamo
10 Anita García. También
soy de Puerto Rico pero
trabajo como doctora en
Miami.

Sr. García: Buenos días.
15 Yo me llamo Juan García.
Soy de México. Vivo en
Miami con mi familia.

Sr. Estrada: Hola. Me
llamo Felipe Estrada.
20 Yo soy de Cuba, pero
vivo en Miami.

Arturo: Hola. Me llamo Arturo. Soy estudiante en Miami, pero soy
25 de la República Dominicana.

Alma: Mi nombre es Alma. Soy de Colombia, pero también vivo
30 en Miami.

ESTRATEGIA DEL BUEN LECTOR Identifica la parte de la gráfica de la página 3 que corresponde a cada persona de la lectura. Para Alma, primero fíjate en un mapa para ver dónde está Colombia.

Francisco:	Puerto Rico
Sra. García:	Puerto Rico
Sr. García:	México
Sr. Estrada:	Cuba
Alma:	Centro y Sudamérica
Arturo:	República Dominicana

APUNTES

DESAFÍO ¿Por qué piensas que una persona elegiría irse a vivir a otro país? Escribe algunas ideas a continuación. **(Sacar conclusiones)**

Respuestas modelo:
por oportunidades profesionales o de empleo; por oportunidades educativas; para estar con miembros de la familia

Vocabulario de la lectura

Palabras clave

Centroamérica tierra entre Norteamérica y Sudamérica
Estados Unidos país de Norteamérica
México país de Norteamérica
República Dominicana país caribeño
Sudamérica parte del continente americano

Escribe la **palabra clave** correcta en cada uno de los espacios en blanco.

Los latinos de ___Estados Unidos___ (1) son de muchos países diferentes. Francisco y su papá son de ___México___ (2). Arturo es de la ___República Dominicana___ (3). Alma es de Colombia, un país de ___Sudamérica___ (4). Muchas otras personas son de Costa Rica, El Salvador, Guatemala, Honduras, Nicaragua o Panamá; ellas son de ___Centroamérica___ (5).

Pronunciación y ortografía

La letra **a** tiene el sonido de la *a* en la palabra *father* en inglés.

A. Di los nombres de las personas de la lectura y completa cada nombre con la vocal **a**.

1. Fr_a_ncisco **2.** _A_rturo **3.** _A_nit_a_

4. Felipe Estr_a_d_a_ **5.** _A_lm_a_

B. Identifica a cada persona. Di su nombre y escríbelo mientras lo pronuncias. Si no recuerdas, búscalo en la lectura.

1. Soy de la República Dominicana. ___Arturo___

2. Trabajo como doctora en Miami. ___Anita García___

3. Soy de México. ___Juan García___

4. Soy de Cuba. ___Felipe Estrada___

5. Soy de Colombia. ___Alma___

¿Comprendiste?

1. ¿De dónde es la doctora? ¿Cómo se llama?

   La doctora es de Puerto Rico. Se llama Anita García.

2. ¿De dónde es el señor García?

   El señor García es de México.

3. ¿Cómo se llama el señor de Cuba?

   El señor de Cuba se llama Felipe Estrada.

4. ¿De dónde es la chica?

   La chica es de Colombia.

5. ¿Cómo se llama el estudiante? ¿De dónde es?

   El estudiante se llama Arturo. Es de la República Dominicana.

Conexión personal

Elige a una persona de la lectura que te gustaría conocer. ¿Qué preguntas te gustaría hacerle? Escribe varias preguntas en español.

Persona: Sra. García

Preguntas:

¿Le gusta ser doctora?

¿Dónde vive ahora?

¿Habla inglés y español?

Para leer *Las celebraciones del año*

Estrategia de lectura

BUSCAR COGNADOS Los cognados son palabras parecidas que tienen un significado semejante tanto en inglés como en español, como europeo y artificiales. ¿Qué otros cognados puedes encontrar en Las celebraciones del año? Escríbelas a continuación.

Los cognados pueden ser: celebraciones, importantes, formas, tradiciones, diferentes, octubre, europeo, cultura, latinoamericana, noviembre, personas, familias, decoran, famosas, tradicional.

Datos para tener en cuenta

Hay muchas fiestas importantes en los países hispanohablantes. Algunas, como la Navidad o el Día de la Madre, se celebran en muchas partes de Latinoamérica y también en los Estados Unidos. Muchas fechas de importancia histórica, como el Día de la Independencia de México, se celebran principalmente en un país. Las comunidades hispanohablantes de los Estados Unidos celebran muchas fiestas tradicionales. Los méxicoamericanos celebran anualmente **el Día de los Muertos**.

The audio is on CD 1 of ***Lecturas para hispanohablantes,*** Track 3.

Las celebraciones del año

Hay muchas fechas importantes durante el año. Los países hispanohablantes celebran estas fechas de varias formas. Algunas celebraciones son iguales que las de Estados 5 Unidos, pero también hay tradiciones diferentes.

CONSEJO PARA LA LECTURA Recuerda que, en español, las fechas se escriben con el número del día primero, luego el número del mes. Por ejemplo, 4/1 quiere decir 4 de enero.

APUNTES

El Día de la Raza

octubre

12/10 El Día de la Raza En este día no hay trabajo. Hay muchos **desfiles.** El día celebra 10 el encuentro del **indígena** con el europeo y el africano. Hoy esta mezcla de razas y tradiciones forma la cultura latinoamericana.

MÁRCALO ORTOGRAFÍA En las líneas 1 y 2 de esta lectura, haz un círculo alrededor de las palabras que tengan el sonido /e/. Pronuncia cada palabra al leerla.

PALABRAS CLAVE
el desfile procesión
el (la) indígena persona nativa

DESAFÍO ¿Por qué crees que los mexicanos tienen fiestas especiales para recordar a los antepasados y familiares que han muerto y para honrar a la familia? Escribe algunas ideas y luego coméntalas en grupos pequeños. **(Discutir)**

Las respuestas van a variar. Respuesta modelo: El concepto de familia es una parte importante de la cultura mexicana.

A pensar...

1. ¿Qué fiestas de las descritas son iguales tanto en países hispanohablantes como en los EE.UU.? ¿Qué fiestas celebran principalmente las personas de los países hispanohablantes? **(Comparar y contrastar)**

   La Nochevieja y **el Año Nuevo** se celebran tanto en Latinoamérica como en los EE.UU. **El Día de la Raza, el Día de Todos los Santos, el Día de los Muertos,** y **el Día de los Reyes** las celebran principalmente las personas de los países hispanohablantes.

2. Nombra dos maneras diferentes de celebrar **la Nochevieja** en España y Latinoamérica. Luego habla de alguna costumbre que se celebre en Nochevieja típica de los Estados Unidos o de tu comunidad. **(Asociar)**

   Las respuestas van a variar. Respuesta modelo: Los ecuatorianos celebran la Nochevieja quemando símbolos del pasado a medianoche. En España es tradicional comer doce uvas. En Estados Unidos...

noviembre

1/11 El Día de Todos los Santos y
15 **2/11 el Día de los Muertos** En estos días todos honran a las personas de su familia. En México las familias decoran las tumbas de sus **antepasados** con flores bonitas.

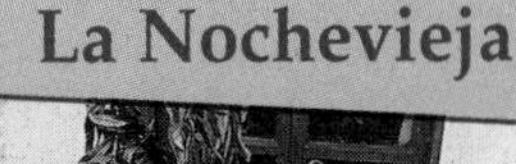

diciembre y enero

20 **31/12 La Nochevieja y**
1/1 el Año Nuevo Hay fuegos artificiales, desfiles o celebraciones en todos los países. En Ecuador los años viejos se representan con figuras grandes de personas
25 famosas de ese año. A medianoche los años viejos se queman. En España es tradicional comer doce uvas a la medianoche.

PALABRAS CLAVE
el (la) antepasado(a) ascendiente de una persona, ancestro
la Nochevieja la última noche del año

enero

6/1 El Día de los Reyes Es el día tradicional
30 para dar regalos de Navidad en los países latinos.

ESTRATEGIA DEL BUEN LECTOR A medida que leas, fíjate en las fotografías que acompañan al texto. Pueden ayudarte a entender cómo se celebran las fiestas.

MÁRCALO › GRAMÁTICA
Traza un círculo alrededor de todas las fechas que aparecen en el artículo. Luego escribe cada una de ellas a continuación, en número y letras.

Modelo: 13/4, el trece de abril

12/10, el doce de octubre
1/11, el primero de noviembre
2/11, el dos de noviembre
31/12, el treinta y uno de diciembre
1/1, el primero de enero
6/1, el seis de enero

Vocabulario de la lectura

Palabras clave

el (la) antepasado(a) ascendiente de una persona, ancestro
el desfile procesión
el (la) indígena persona nativa
la Nochevieja la última noche del año

Completa cada una de las oraciones siguientes con la **palabra clave** apropiada.

1. Hay muchos desfiles en el Día de la Raza.
2. El Día de la Raza celebra el encuentro del indígena, el europeo y el africano.
3. Mis antepasados son de España.
4. El treinta y uno de diciembre es la Nochevieja.

Pronunciación y ortografía

La letra **e** tiene el sonido de la *e* en la palabra *eight* y de la *a* en *ate* en inglés.

A. Completa las siguientes palabras de la lectura con **e** y pronuncia cada palabra al escribirla.

1. c_e_l_e_bracion_e_s
2. d_e_sfil_e_s
3. indíg_e_na
4. m_e_dianoch_e_
5. _e_n_e_ro

B. Escribe la palabra de la lectura escondida en cada grupo de letras.

1. chesfa fechas
2. patnadaseso antepasados
3. yeser reyes
4. eosrlga regalos
5. buerotc octubre

¿Comprendiste?

1. ¿Cómo celebran los latinoamericanos el Día de la Raza?

No hay trabajo. Hay muchos desfiles.

2. ¿Cuáles son las fechas en que los mexicanos honran a su familia?

Son el primero y el dos de noviembre.

3. Describe dos tradiciones del Año Nuevo.

(Two of the following): Hay fuegos artificiales; hay desfiles; los años se representan con figuras grandes y los años se queman; comer doce uvas.

4. ¿En qué fecha dan regalos de Navidad las personas de los países latinos? ¿Cómo se llama ese día?

Dan regalos de Navidad el seis de enero. Se llama el Día de los Reyes.

Conexión personal

Elige una de tus fiestas preferidas. ¿Qué palabras o frases se te ocurren cuando piensas en este día? Escríbelas en la red de palabras.

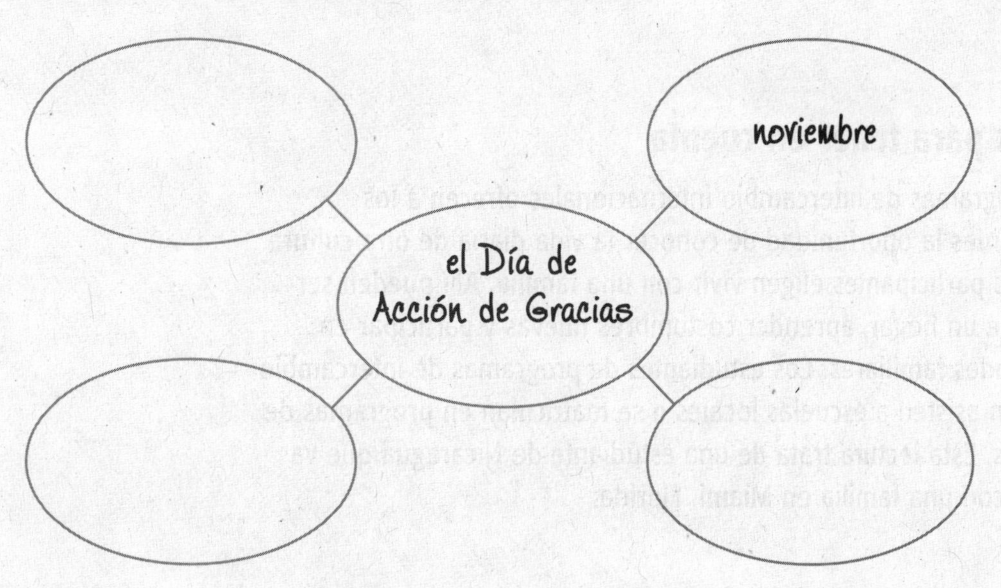

Para leer *Una estudiante de Nicaragua*

Estrategia de lectura

BUSCAR COGNADOS Las palabras que se parecen en español y en inglés se llaman cognados. Los cognados te ayudarán a entender las lecturas. Echa un vistazo rápido a la lectura y escribe todos los cognados que encuentres.

Los cognados pueden ser: estudiante, programa, académico, internacional, practicar, inglés, tímida, aeropuerto, contenta, oficiales, bilingües, familia, norteamericana, emoción.

Datos para tener en cuenta

Los programas de intercambio internacionales ofrecen a los estudiantes la oportunidad de conocer la vida diaria de otra cultura. Muchos participantes eligen vivir con una familia. Allí pueden ser parte de un hogar, aprender costumbres nuevas y participar en actividades familiares. Los estudiantes de programas de intercambio también asisten a escuelas locales o se matriculan en programas de idiomas. Esta lectura trata de una estudiante de Nicaragua que va a vivir con una familia en Miami, Florida.

The audio is on CD 1 of ***Lecturas para hispanohablantes,*** Track 5.

Una estudiante de Nicaragua

Una chica viaja sola en avión a Miami. Se llama Eva. Eva es de Nicaragua, pero este año estudia en Estados Unidos. Eva es estudiante del programa del Intercambio Académico Internacional. A Eva le gusta viajar y le gusta practicar el inglés. Pero ahora Eva está un poco tímida.

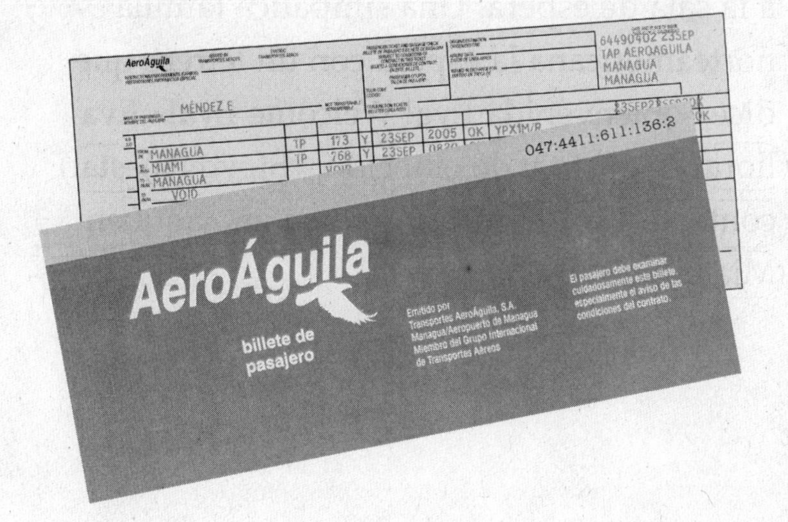

CONSEJO PARA LA LECTURA La muchacha del cuento es de Nicaragua. Fíjate en un mapa o en un atlas para ver dónde está Nicaragua.

ESTRATEGIA DEL BUEN LECTOR A menudo puedes entender mejor un cuento si te pones en la situación de los personajes. Imagina que vas a pasar el próximo año viviendo en otro país como estudiante de intercambio. ¿Cómo te sentirías al llegar al aeropuerto y estar a punto de conocer a la familia con quien vas a vivir?

APUNTES

MÁRCALO GRAMÁTICA Subraya la parte de la lectura que dice lo que a Eva le gusta hacer. Luego escribe una oración a continuación diciendo lo que te gusta hacer a ti.

A mí...

A pensar...

1. ¿Por qué se siente Eva tímida al llegar al aeropuerto de Miami? **(Inferir)**

   Respuesta modelo: Eva se siente tímida porque viaja sola de Nicaragua a los Estados Unidos. Su primera lengua es español y como estudiante de intercambio, va a vivir con una familia que no conoce.

2. ¿Cómo se siente después de ver a la familia con quien va a vivir y por qué? **(Inferir)**

   Respuesta modelo: Al ver a la familia con quien va a vivir, Eva se siente contenta y aliviada, porque sonríen y tienen un cartel de bienvenida con su nombre.

DESAFÍO Escribe un diálogo entre Eva y su nueva familia. Luego represéntenlo en grupos pequeños. **(Ampliar)**

Las respuestas van a variar.

MÁRCALO › ORTOGRAFÍA
En las líneas 18 a 20 de esta lectura, haz un círculo alrededor de las palabras que tengan el sonido /a/. Pronuncia cada palabra al leerla.

10 En el aeropuerto internacional de Miami los **letreros** están en inglés ¡y español! Eva se siente más contenta. Los oficiales de la **aduana** también son **bilingües** y muy simpáticos. Eva ya tiene confianza y va
15 a la sala de espera. Una simpática familia norteamericana la espera con un letrero que dice, «¡Bienvenida Eva! Welcome Eva!» Eva llora de gusto y de emoción. «Sí, voy a estar contenta. ¡Voy a pasar un buen año aquí en
20 Miami!»

PALABRAS CLAVE
el letrero cartel, rótulo, aviso
bilingüe bilingüe
la aduana oficina que controla mercancías en la frontera

Vocabulario de la lectura

Palabras clave

la aduana oficina que controla mercancías en la frontera
bilingüe que habla dos idiomas
el letrero cartel, rótulo, aviso

Escribe una oración con cada una de las **palabras clave**.

____

____

____

Pronunciación y ortografía

La letra **a** tiene el sonido de la *a* en la palabra *father* en inglés.

A. Completa las siguientes palabras de la lectura con la vocal **a** y entonces pronuncia cada palabra.

1. Ev__a__

2. chic__a__

3. __a__hor__a__

4. progr__a__m__a__

5. intern__a__cion__a__l

B. Escribe la palabra correspondiente a cada definición mientras la pronuncias. Si no recuerdas, búscala en la lectura.

1. un medio de transporte que viaja por el aire __avión__

2. el lugar donde revisan las maletas __aduana__

3. amables __simpáticos__

4. mamá, papá, hijos, etc. __fa lia__

5. seguridad que alguien tiene en sí mismo __confianza__

¿Comprendiste?

1. ¿Quién es Eva?

Eva es estudiante.

2. ¿De dónde es ella?

Es de Nicaragua.

3. ¿Adónde viaja?

Viaja a Miami.

4. ¿Qué le gusta?

Le gusta viajar y practicar el inglés.

Conexión personal

Vas a participar en un programa de intercambio internacional. Escribe una carta a la familia con quien vas a vivir para presentarte. Di de qué pueblo o ciudad eres, cómo es tu familia y qué te gusta hacer.

¡Hola! Me llamo...

Para leer *Los Ángeles: Una carta del pasado*

Estrategia de lectura

DESCUBRIR PISTAS EN LOS DIBUJOS Fijarse en los dibujos que tiene una lectura puede ayudarte a entenderla mejor. Fíjate en las ilustraciones de estas páginas. ¿De qué crees que se tratará la lectura? Escribe tus ideas en el espacio siguiente.

___

___

___

___

___

___

Datos para tener en cuenta

En 1769 Gaspar de Portolá, un soldado del ejército español, y Juan Crespi, un sacerdote católico, fueron los líderes de una expedición en la costa de California en una región que ahora es parte de Los Ángeles. Acamparon junto a un río, que llamaron **El Río de Nuestra Señora la Reina de los Ángeles de Porciúncula. Porciúncula** era una capilla de Italia. En 1781 el gobierno español reunió a un grupo de once familias del norte de México para llevarlas a esta región y fundar un **pueblo**, o una aldea. Los habitantes, conocidos como **los pobladores**, eran 11 hombres, 11 mujeres y 22 niños. Ellos llamaron a su nuevo lugar de residencia **El pueblo de Nuestra Señora la Reina de los Ángeles de Porciúncula** por el río cercano. La carta que vas a leer es de un muchacho que vivía en el poblado de Los Ángeles exactamente tres años antes de que llegaran allí las familias fundadoras.

ESTRATEGIA DEL BUEN LECTOR En un mapa mundial, localiza México, Málaga, España y Los Ángeles, California. Imagina qué ruta posiblemente hayan seguido las personas que vinieron de México o de España para llegar a Los Ángeles en el siglo dieciocho.

Los Ángeles: Una carta del pasado

Aquí tienes un fragmento de una carta de Miguel José Guerra, un chico español, que vivía en Los Ángeles en ¡1784!

MÁRCALO > GRAMÁTICA
Subraya la oración en la cual Miguel escribe las edades de él y su hermana. Luego escribe tu edad y la de los hermanos que tengas. Si no tienes hermanos, escoge a un(a) amigo(a).

(Yo) tengo . . . años.
Mi hermano(a) tiene . . . años.

MÁRCALO > GRAMÁTICA
En las líneas 9 y 10 de esta lectura, haz un círculo alrededor de las palabras que tengan el sonido /e/. Pronuncia cada palabra al leerla.

Circle the following words in lines 9 and 10: Pueblo, de, Nuestra, Señora, de, Ángeles, estamos, contentos.

2 de agosto de 1784

Querido primo:

¿Cómo estás? ¿Cómo está toda la familia allá en Málaga? Aquí en el Pueblo de Nuestra Señora de Los Ángeles estamos contentos. ¡Hoy mi familia y yo no trabajamos!

Generalmente, mi hermana y yo trabajamos en el campo con mamá y papá. (Mi hermana ya tiene 15 años y yo tengo 13, pero mi papá es muy viejo —¡él tiene 36 años!) Papá es fuerte y

PALABRAS CLAVE
la carta comunicación escrita
querido(a) expresión de cortesía para empezar una carta

muy moreno por el sol del campo.
Mamá es muy fuerte también y siempre
muy bonita.

20 Hoy es el día de Nuestra Señora de Los
Ángeles, la patrona de mi pueblo.
Hay celebración y fiesta. Llevo mi ropa
elegante y mi hermana también.
Vamos a la capilla con mamá y papá
25 y con los tíos y los primos de aquí.
Hay música y danzas tradicionales y
¡mucha buena comida!

Un **abrazo** de tu primo,
Miguel José

CONSEJO PARA LA LECTURA
Algunas palabras, como **ropa** en la línea 22, son cognados falsos. Los cognados falsos son palabras que se parecen en inglés y en español, pero tienen significados diferentes. ¿Qué quiere decir **ropa**? ¿Cuál es la palabra del inglés que se le parece?

A pensar…

1. ¿Por qué Miguel tiene un primo y otros familiares en España? **(Inferir)**

Las respuestas van a variar. Respuesta modelo: Miguel es descendiente de españoles. Es probable que su familia viviera en España antes de irse a vivir al poblado de Los Ángeles.

2. ¿Por qué piensas que hasta los niños de la familia de Miguel tenían que trabajar? **(Sacar conclusiones)**

Las respuestas van a variar. Respuesta modelo: En 1784, la ciudad de Los Ángeles estaba todavía en formación y mucha de la tierra que la rodeaba estaba sin habitar. Las familias pioneras que vivían allí tuvieron que construir sus propias casas, establecer sus propios negocios y cultivar su propia comida.

DESAFÍO ¿Por qué crees que una familia tomaría la decisión de dejar su propio país e irse a vivir lejos a un nuevo lugar sin poblar? **(Hacer juicios)**

Las respuestas van a variar.

PALABRAS CLAVE
el abrazo acto de saludar a una persona rodeándola con los brazos, o expresión de saludo al final de una carta

Vocabulario de la lectura

Palabras clave

el abrazo acto de saludar a una persona rodeándola con los brazos, o expresión de saludo al final de una carta

la carta comunicación escrita

querido(a) expresión de cortesía para empezar una carta

Completa la carta con las **palabras clave** correctas.

16 de agosto

___Querido___ primo:

¿Cómo estás? Aquí en Málaga estoy muy contenta. Me gusta esta ciudad. Picasso, el artista, es de aquí. Hoy mis padres y yo vamos a visitar el Museo Picasso. Esta noche, vamos a un restaurante que sirve comida típica de España. ¡Qué chévere! Te escribo otra ___carta___ pronto. Un ___abrazo___ de tu prima,

Manuela

Pronunciación y ortografía

La letra **e** tiene el sonido de la *e* en la palabra *eight* y de la *a* en *ate* en inglés.

A. Completa las siguientes palabras de la lectura con **e** y pronuncia cada palabra al escribirla.

1. __e__spañol

2. h__e__rmana

3. cont__e__ntos

4. __e__l__e__gant__e__

5. g__e__n__e__ralm__e__nt__e__

B. Escribe la palabra de la lectura escondida en cada grupo de letras.

1. stoames ___estamos___

2. jiveo ___viejo___

3. pesimre ___siempre___

4. tisefa ___fiesta___

5. nielcbócear ___celebración___

¿Comprendiste?

1. ¿Quién escribe la carta?

Miguel José Guerra, un chico español, escribe la carta.

2. ¿A quién le escribe? ¿Dónde vive esa persona?

Le escribe a su primo. El primo vive en Málaga, España.

3. ¿Por qué está contento?

Hay celebración y fiesta. No hay trabajo hoy.

4. ¿Cuántos miembros de la familia hay? ¿Quiénes son?

Hay cuatro (pero también hay tíos y primos). Son el padre, la madre, la hermana y Miguel José.

5. ¿Cómo celebran el día?

Hay música y danzas tradicionales y buena comida.

Conexión personal

Escribe una carta a un(a) amigo(a) por correspondencia real o imaginario(a), describiéndote tú y describiendo a tu familia.

Querido(a)...

Para leer *Una encuesta escolar*

Estrategia de lectura

USAR PISTAS DEL CONTEXTO Puedes usar el contexto para adivinar el significado de las palabras desconocidas. El contexto es lo que viene antes y después de la palabra. Los dibujos a menudo son parte del contexto también. ¿Qué piensas que significan las palabras resaltadas? Escribe las respuestas en el cuadro siguiente.

- Una encuesta **escolar** entre estudiantes y maestros
- Los **resultados** de la encuesta dicen qué clase es la más popular.

Palabra	Definición
escolar	
resultados	

Datos para tener en cuenta

En México, los niños tienen que asistir a la escuela pública o privada hasta el grado nueve. Hay seis grados de educación primaria y tres grados de educación secundaria. El horario para los primeros grados normalmente es de 9 a.m. a 12:30 p.m. Y para los grados de secundaria es de 7:30 a.m. a 2:30 p.m. La mayoría de los estudiantes mexicanos asisten a escuelas públicas, aunque en las ciudades muchos asisten a escuelas privadas. Los estudiantes que quieren seguir su educación después de la secundaria toman clases de preparatoria para la universidad durante otros tres años o asisten a una escuela profesional, después de la cual pueden solicitar el ingreso en una universidad. En México, tanto las universidades públicas como las privadas tienen exámenes de admisión altamente competitivos que los solicitantes tienen que pasar para ser admitidos.

The audio is on CD 1 of ***Lecturas para hispanohablantes,*** Track 9.

Una encuesta escolar

Ricardo tiene que hacer una **encuesta** en la escuela. Él prepara una lista de preguntas. Ricardo habla con los otros estudiantes y escribe sus respuestas en un cuaderno. En
5 casa escribe las respuestas en la computadora. Con una calculadora suma[1] el total de respuestas. El papel sale de la impresora con los resultados de la encuesta. Ricardo usa los resultados de la encuesta para hacer un
10 proyecto en la clase de matemáticas.

[1] él agrega

PALABRAS CLAVE

la encuesta investigación

CONSEJO PARA LA LECTURA

Este artículo usa el orden cronológico para llevar la cuenta de los pasos que sigue Ricardo, desde preparar la encuesta hasta utilizar los resultados. A medida que leas, hazte preguntas sobre lo que pasa primero, después y por último.

MÁRCALO > VOCABULARIO

Haz un círculo alrededor de quince cognados en el texto de las páginas 25 y 26.

Students should circle any 15 of the following words: prepara, lista, estudiantes, computadora, calculadora, total, papel, resultados, proyecto, clase, matemáticas, secundaria, arte, ciencias, educación física, estudios sociales, historia, literatura, música, favorita.

A pensar...

1. Vuelve a leer la encuesta de Ricardo, luego contesta la encuesta tú. Completa los espacios en blanco y pon marcas en las casillas según corresponda. Si tienes clases que no vienen en la hoja, escríbelas en la encuesta. **(Valorar)**

2. En grupos, comparen las respuestas individuales de la encuesta. Luego prepara los resultados de la encuesta para tu grupo usando un formato como el de Ricardo que viene en la página siguiente. ¿Hubo algunas preguntas que todos los miembros del grupo contestaron igual? ¿Qué aprendiste de los resultados de esta encuesta? **(Sumar datos/Resumir)**

MÁRCALO > PRONUNCIACIÓN
Busca cinco palabras de más de una sílaba que no lleven acento escrito y que terminen en vocal, **n** o **s**. Haz una lista con estas palabras. ¿Qué sílaba se pronuncia más fuerte?

clase, favorita, estudiante, escuela, secundaria, Tengo, clases, arte, estudios, sociales, ciencias, historia, literatura, mucha, tarea, Saco, una, buena, nota, Siempre, hablo, Nunca, escucho

Estas palabras se pronuncian más fuerte en la penúltima sílaba.

Mi clase favorita es...

Soy estudiante de la escuela secundaria ______.

Tengo clases de...

- ❑ arte
- ❑ ciencias (15)
- ❑ computación
- ❑ educación física
- ❑ inglés
- ❑ estudios sociales
- ❑ historia
- ❑ literatura
- ❑ matemáticas
- ❑ música

Tengo mucha tarea en la clase de ______.

20 Saco una buena nota en la clase de ______.

Siempre hablo en la clase de ______.

Nunca hablo en la clase de ______.

Siempre escucho en la clase de ______.

Nunca escucho en la clase de ______.

25 Mi clase más difícil es ______.

Mi clase más fácil es ______.

Mi clase favorita es ______.

Los resultados

Una encuesta a 50 estudiantes

30 Clase con más tarea: matemáticas
(25 estudiantes)

Los estudiantes sacan más buenas notas en la clase de: música
(35 estudiantes)

Los estudiantes hablan más en la clase de: literatura
35 *(30 estudiantes)*

Los estudiantes nunca hablan en la clase de: inglés
(25 estudiantes)

Los estudiantes escuchan más en la clase de: ciencias
(40 estudiantes)

40 Los estudiantes nunca escuchan en la clase de: historia
(20 estudiantes)

La clase más difícil es: ciencias
(35 estudiantes)

La clase más fácil es: arte
45 *(45 estudiantes)*

La clase favorita es: literatura
(30 estudiantes)

ESTRATEGIA DEL BUEN LECTOR Usa una tabla como la siguiente para comparar y contrastar los cursos que se ofrecen en la escuela de Ricardo con los que se ofrecen en tu escuela.

La escuela de Ricardo
Mi escuela

DESAFÍO Fíjate en los resultados de la encuesta de Ricardo. Fíjate en el título para saber a cuántos estudiantes él encuestó en total. Luego convierte el número de estudiantes de cada subcategoría al porcentaje de estudiantes encuestados. **(Calcular)**

Modelo: Clase con más tarea: matemáticas (25 estudiantes: 50%)

(35 estudiantes: 70%)

(30 estudiantes: 60%)

(25 estudiantes: 50%)

(40 estudiantes: 80%)

(20 estudiantes: 40%)

(35 estudiantes: 70%)

(45 estudiantes: 90%)

(30 estudiantes: 60%)

Vocabulario de la lectura

Palabras clave

la calculadora máquina que hace cálculos como la suma y la resta
la computadora máquina para el tratamiento de la informacíon
la encuesta investigacíon
la impresora máquina que permite la salida de resultados escritos sobre papel

Escribe la **palabra clave** que mejor complete cada oración.

Ricardo prepara una lista de preguntas para su encuesta (1) escolar.
Primero, escribe las respuestas de los otros estudiantes en un cuaderno.
Cuando llega a casa, escribe las respuestas en la computadora (2).
Usa una calculadora (3) para sumar el total de respuestas.
El papel sale de la impresora (4) con los resultados.

Pronunciación y ortografía

Cada palabra en español tiene una sílaba que se pronuncia más fuerte.
Este acento o *golpe* está determinada por las dos siguientes reglas:

1) Una palabra que termina en vocal, **n** o **s** se pronuncia más fuerte en la penúltima sílaba (cuando no hay un acento escrito).

a-**cen**-to **di**-ce pre-**pa**-ran pre-**gun**-tas

2) Una palabra que termina en consonante, excepto **n** o **s,** se pronuncia más fuerte en la última sílaba (cuando no hay un acento escrito).

to-**tal** con-tes-**tar** ciu-**dad** re-**loj**

A. Pronuncia las siguientes palabras y subraya la sílaba que pronuncias más fuerte.

1. escuchan **2.** notas **3.** papel **4.** hacer **5.** proyecto

B. Repite cada palabra y determina cuál de las dos reglas de acentuación determina la sílaba fuerte, **1** o **2.**

1. escuchan 1 **2.** notas 1 **3.** papel 2

4. hacer 2 **5.** proyecto 1

¿Comprendiste?

1. ¿Qué tiene que hacer Ricardo?

   Tiene que hacer una encuesta escolar.

2. ¿Qué usa Ricardo para escribir la encuesta?

   Usa una computadora.

3. ¿Los estudiantes hablan mucho o poco en la clase de inglés?

   Hablan poco.

4. ¿Es difícil la clase de música o arte en la escuela de Ricardo?

   No, son fáciles.

5. ¿Qué clase es la clase favorita de los estudiantes?

   La clase favorita de los estudiantes es la literatura.

Conexión personal

¿Cuál es tu clase favorita? ¿Por qué te gusta? Escribe las respuestas en la red siguiente.

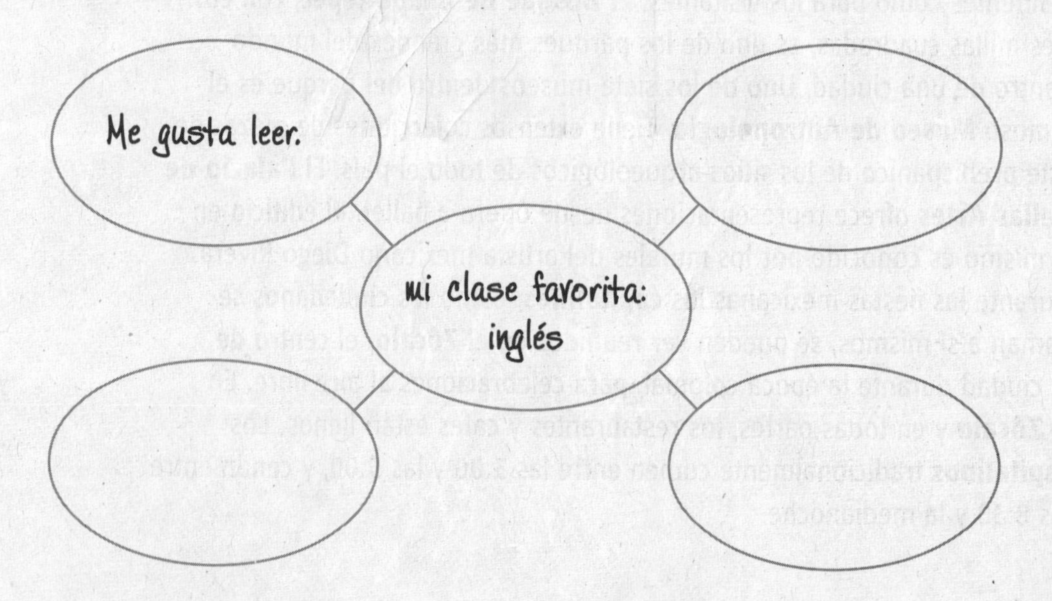

Para leer *México y sus jóvenes*

Estrategia de lectura

LEER POR ENCIMA Antes de leer un pasaje largo, conviene leer rápidamente para tener una idea general de lo que se trata. Lee los párrafos por encima, y anota las pistas que indiquen el tema o el asunto central. Cuando se lee por encima, se puede saber rápidamente de qué trata la lectura. Luego será más fácil hacer una lectura más detallada. Después de leer por encima México y sus jóvenes, escribe a continuación algunas palabras o frases que indiquen de lo que se trata.

Las respuestas van a variar: jóvenes, escuela, tarea, teatros, museos, tiendas, parques, fines de semana, viernes, sábados, domingos, libres, descansar.

Datos para tener en cuenta

La ciudad de México ofrece una variedad de atracciones tanto para los residentes como para los visitantes. **El Bosque de Chapultepec**, con casi tres millas cuadradas, es uno de los parques más grandes del mundo dentro de una ciudad. Uno de los siete museos dentro del parque es el famoso **Museo de Antropología**. Tiene extensas colecciones de piezas de arte prehispánico de los sitios arqueológicos de todo el país. El **Palacio de Bellas Artes** ofrece representaciones desde ópera a ballet. El edificio en sí mismo es conocido por los murales del artista mexicano Diego Rivera. Durante las fiestas mexicanas los **capitalinos**, como los ciudadanos se llaman a sí mismos, se pueden ver reunidos en el **Zócalo**, el centro de la ciudad durante la época colonial, para celebraciones al aire libre. En el **Zócalo** y en todas partes, los restaurantes y cafés están llenos. Los **capitalinos** tradicionalmente comen entre las 3:00 y las 5:00, y cenan entre las 8:30 y la medianoche.

The audio is on CD 1 of ***Lecturas para hispanohablantes,*** Track 11.

México y sus jóvenes

¿Qué hacen los mexicanos jóvenes? De lunes a viernes los muchachos que tienen menos de 18 años van a la escuela. Tienen muchas materias— a veces tienen hasta ocho clases en un día. Y también tienen mucha tarea. Por eso, después de clases muchos de los estudiantes van a sus casas para hacer la tarea y después descansar.

En la Ciudad de México hay muchos **teatros, museos, tiendas y parques.** En cada lugar es posible ver a muchos jóvenes, especialmente los fines de semana.

PALABRAS CLAVE

teatro sitio donde se pueden ver obras dramáticas o musicales
museo lugar de colecciones culturales
tienda lugar donde se vende cosas al público
parque jardín público

CONSEJO PARA LA LECTURA
Muchas veces puedes adivinar lo que significan las palabras que no reconoces al buscar pistas en el contexto. Intenta adivinar el significado de una palabra antes de buscarla en el diccionario.

MÁRCALO **PRONUNCIACIÓN**
En las tres primeras oraciones, haz un círculo alrededor de las palabras que contengan un diptongo, es decir un sonido combinado de una vocal débil y una fuerte.

Circle the following words in the first three sentences of the selection: viernes, tienen, escuela, Tienen, materias, tienen.

DESAFÍO Imagina que entrevistas a un estudiante de intercambio de la Ciudad de México. ¿Qué te gustaría saber de cómo es la vida en la capital de México? Tal vez quieras preguntarle sobre un típico día de clase, qué hacen los adolescentes para divertirse con sus amigos, qué actividades comparten con la familia o algo más que te interese. A continuación escribe en español tres preguntas de la entrevista. **(Asociar)**

ESTRATEGIA DEL BUEN LECTOR Marca las palabras del artículo que mencionan lugares que visitan los jóvenes de México durante los fines de semana.

MÁRCALO VOCABULARIO
Acabas de aprender palabras y frases para describir actividades del tiempo libre. Usando este vocabulario, pon una leyenda para cada una de las fotografías de estas páginas.

Se dan respuestas modelo debajo de las fotografías.

Las chicas comen una merienda mexicana.

El hombre toca la guitarra.

La gente pasea en el parque.

Los viernes por la tarde, los sábados y los
20 domingos son los días principales en que los jóvenes mexicanos están **libres.** Los domingos hay mucha gente en los parques. Andan en bicicleta, practican deportes o tocan un instrumento. De vez en cuando, para
25 el almuerzo, van a un restaurante con sus familias. El domingo es el día principal para pasear y descansar.

Los jóvenes pasan un rato con los amigos.

Para el almuerzo, esta familia va a un restaurante.

El muchacho camina con los perros.

A pensar...

Piensa en lo que has aprendido sobre cómo pasan el tiempo los adolescentes de la Ciudad de México durante los fines de semana. ¿Les gustan a ti y a tus amigos los mismos tipos de actividades en su tiempo libre? Di algunas actividades que tengas en común con los adolescentes mexicanos y algunas actividades que sean diferentes a las de ellos. **(Comparar y contrastar)**

Las respuestas van a variar.

PALABRA CLAVE
libre sin responsabilidades

Vocabulario de la lectura

Palabras clave

libre sin responsabilidades
el museo lugar de colecciones culturales
el parque jardín público
el teatro sitio donde se pueden ver obras dramáticas o musicales
la tienda lugar donde se venden cosas al público

Para cada **palabra clave** en la columna izquierda, busca la oración en la columna derecha que mejor describa la palabra. Escribe la letra correspondiente en el espacio en blanco.

B **1.** tienda
A **2.** parque
E **3.** teatro
D **4.** museo
C **5.** libre

A. Es donde la gente pasea y descansa.
B. Venden cosas aquí.
C. Alguien que no está ocupado.
D. Tiene cosas muy viejas.
E. Es donde va la gente para ver ballet y escuchar música.

Pronunciación y ortografía

Cuando una vocal débil (**i, u**) se combina con una vocal fuerte (**a, e, o**) o con otra vocal débil, forman un sonido combinado que se llama *diptongo*. Un diptongo es parte de una sola sílaba. Cuando un diptongo se divide en dos sílabas, hay que escribir un acento sobre la primera vocal para indicar la pronunciación correcta. Por ejemplo, el diptongo **ia** en **farmacia** no se divide pero en **día** se divide en dos. La combinación de dos vocales fuertes se divide en dos sílabas como en la palabra **creo**.

A. Pronuncia las siguientes palabras de la lectura y decide si las vocales subrayadas forman un diptongo.

1. v<u>ie</u>rnes si **2.** rest<u>au</u>rante si **3.** tar<u>ea</u> no

4. alm<u>ue</u>rzo si **5.** pas<u>ea</u>r no

B. Pronuncia las siguientes palabras y escribe cuántas sílabas tiene cada una. Si necesitas añadir un acento, escribe la palabra con su acento y entonces el número de sílabas.

1. materias 3 **2.** dia diá, 2 **3.** museos 3

4. ciudad 2 **5.** teatros 3

¿Comprendiste?

1. ¿Qué hacen los jóvenes de lunes a viernes?

Van a la escuela. Hacen mucha tarea.

2. ¿Adónde van muchos jóvenes los fines de semana en la Ciudad de México?

Van a los teatros, a los museos, a las tiendas y a los parques.

3. ¿Qué actividades hacen los domingos?

Andan en bicicleta, practican deportes o tocan un instrumento.

4. ¿Qué hace a veces una familia los domingos?

Va a un restaurante para el almuerzo.

Conexión personal

¿Cómo describirías un sábado ideal? Escribe algunas de tus actividades favoritas de los fines de semana en el espacio de la derecha.

Los sábados, me gusta...

1. andar en bicicleta
2.
3.
4.

Para leer *Una leyenda azteca: El origen de la Ciudad de México*

Estrategia de lectura

BUSCAR PISTAS EN EL CONTEXTO A primera vista, puede parecer que no puedes entender muchas palabras de la lectura. Para mejorar tu comprensión, usa esta estrategia: Lee las oraciones completas en vez de traducir palabra por palabra.

Datos para tener en cuenta

Se cree que las personas que fundaron la capital azteca Tenochtitlán llegaron al sur desde un lugar llamado Aztlán. Aztlán está en la región actual del norte de México o del sur de Arizona. El nombre azteca se deriva de la palabra *Aztlán*. Tenochtitlán, la ciudad más grande del imperio azteca, se construyó en un lago. Se conectaba con la tierra por medio de tres grandes pasos elevados. A principios del siglo quince, los aztecas tenían una de las más avanzadas civilizaciones del mundo. Aunque se encontraron con una fuerte resistencia, los españoles finalmente destruyeron Tenochtitlán en 1521. Construyeron la ciudad de México en el lugar de la capital azteca. La bandera mexicana tiene un águila sobre un cacto de nopal con una serpiente cascabel en la boca. Se inspiró en la leyenda azteca acerca de Tenochtitlán. Esta leyenda es el tema de esta lectura.

ESTRATEGIA DEL BUEN LECTOR Usa las ilustraciones de estas páginas para ayudarte a reconstruir la leyenda.

Una leyenda azteca

El origen de la Ciudad de México

MÁRCALO > PRONUNCIACIÓN Todas las palabras de más de una sílaba tienen una sílaba que se pronuncia más fuerte. Por ejemplo, en "palabra", se pronuncia "la" más fuerte–es el acento o *golpe*. En la primera oración de la lectura, subraya las sílabas acentuadas en las palabras.

MÁRCALO > GRAMÁTICA Acabas de aprender las formas del singular y del plural de los adjetivos posesivos. Busca y traza un círculo alrededor de todos los adjetivos posesivos que encuentres en la lectura.

Los estudiantes deben trazar un círculo alrededor de **su, su, nuestro, nuestra, su** y **sus.**

Los aztecas, una tribu de **guerreros,** deciden dejar su casa en el norte por necesidades económicas. Caminan todos los días por mucho tiempo buscando un lugar nuevo. Pasan por muchos lugares pero no encuentran el lugar perfecto. Esperan ansiosos la señal[1] de su dios, Huitzilopochtli.

Pasa mucho tiempo y están los aztecas muy cansados. Llegan a un lago donde miran la señal en medio del lago. Está un **águila** sobre un **cacto,** ¡con una **serpiente** en la boca! Todos miran y hablan.

[1] mensaje

PALABRAS CLAVE

el guerrero soldado, que hace la guerra
el águila (f.) ave grande cazadora
el cacto planta de tierras secas
la serpiente culebra

—¡Ésta es la señal que esperamos! ¡Ésta es la señal de nuestro dios!

20 —¡Aquí es donde preparamos nuestra ciudad!

Y así, en el lago de Texcoco, los aztecas empiezan a construir su ciudad. Usan tierra y raíces[2] para crear pequeñas **islas.** Construyen sus casas en las islas.

25 Y así fue la creación, en el año 1325, de la gran Tenochtitlán, que ahora es la maravillosa Ciudad de México.

[2] parte de las plantas que está abajo tierra

CONSEJO PARA LA LECTURA
Esta lectura contiene algunas palabras en Náhuatl, la lengua azteca. Escucha el disco para ver cómo se pronuncian.

A pensar...

1. ¿Qué empiezan a hacer los aztecas después de ver al águila en un cacto con una serpiente en la boca y por qué? **(Clarificar)**

   Respuesta modelo: Empiezan a construir Tenochtitlán. El dios Huitzilopochtli les dijo a los aztecas que construyeran su ciudad en el lugar donde encontraron un águila en un cacto comiendo una serpiente.

2. Mira el dibujo de la bandera mexicana. ¿Cuál es el símbolo de la bandera? ¿Qué significa? **(Clarificar)**

   Respuesta modelo: La bandera mexicana tiene un águila en un cacto comiéndose una serpiente. Esa era la señal que Huitzilopochtli les dijo a los aztecas que buscaran.

DESAFÍO ¿Qué puedes inferir del papel de la religión en la vida de los aztecas al leer esta leyenda? Marca todas las partes que apoyen tus ideas. **(Inferir)**

Las respuestas van a variar. Respuesta modelo: La religión fue importante en la vida azteca. Los aztecas de la leyenda buscaron una señal de su dios para que les dijera donde tenían que vivir.

Vocabulario de la lectura

Palabras clave

el águila ave grande cazadora
el cacto planta de tierras secas
el guerrero soldado, que hace la guerra
la serpiente culebra

Completa cada oración con la forma correcta de una de las **palabras clave**.

1. Los aztecas son un tribu de ___guerreros___.

2. En un lago, hay un ___águila___ con una ___serpiente___ en la boca.

3. El águila está sobre un ___cacto___.

Pronunciación y ortografía

Cada palabra en español tiene una sílaba que se pronuncia más fuerte. Este acento o *golpe* está determinada por las dos siguientes reglas:

1. Una palabra que termina en vocal, **n** o **s** se pronuncia más fuerte en la penúltima sílaba (cuando no tiene un acento escrito).

a-**cen**-to **di**-ce pre-**pa**-ran pre-**gun**-tas

2. Una palabra que termina en consonante, excepto **n** o **s**, se pronuncia más fuerte en la última sílaba (cuando no tiene un acento escrito).

to-**tal** con-tes-**tar** ciu-**dad** re-**loj**

A. Pronuncia las siguientes palabras de la lectura y subraya la sílaba que pronuncias más fuerte.

1. origen **2.** tribu **3.** dejar **4.** lago **5.** señal

B. Repite cada palabra y determina cuál de las dos reglas de acentuación determina la sílaba fuerte, 1 ó 2.

1. origen ___1___ **2.** tribu ___1___ **3.** dejar ___2___

4. lago ___1___ **5.** señal ___2___

¿Comprendiste?

1. ¿Quiénes son los aztecas?

Son una tribu de guerreros.

2. ¿Qué buscan?

Buscan un lugar nuevo.

3. ¿Cuál es la señal que reciben?

En medio de un lago hay un águila sobre un cacto con una serpiente en la boca.

4. ¿Qué es Tenochtitlán?

Es la ciudad de los aztecas. Hoy es la Ciudad de México.

Conexión personal

Supón que eres parte de una excavación arqueológica en el sitio de una civilización azteca. ¿Qué es lo que más te gustaría encontrar? Escribe una lista a la derecha.

Busco...

casas

Para leer *Una leyenda mexicana: La Casa de los Azulejos*

Estrategia de lectura

SEGUIR LA TRAMA Usa un cuadro para ayudarte a seguir lo que pasa en esta leyenda. Indica el principio, el medio y el final del cuento. ¿Qué hacen el padre y el hijo en cada momento del cuento?

	Principio	Medio	Final
Padre			
Hijo			

Datos para tener en cuenta

En 1737, el Conde y la Condesa del valle de Orizaba ordenaron una reconstrucción de su casa de la Ciudad de México y la cubrieron de azulejos azules y blancos. Las casas de azulejos fueron una muestra de prosperidad en México durante la época colonial y eran ya populares en la ciudad de Puebla, donde la condesa había vivido antes de mudarse a la Ciudad de México. La Casa de los Azulejos, como la antigua casa del conde y de la condesa se conoce hoy, es uno de los monumentos más antiguos de la Ciudad de México. Su patio de dos pisos es ahora un restaurante y la escalera al segundo piso tiene un mural del famoso artista mexicano Orozco. La siguiente leyenda cuenta la historia de la Casa de los Azulejos.

Una leyenda mexicana

La Casa de los Azulejos

En la Ciudad de México hay una casa muy famosa. Hay muchas leyendas de esta casa. Una de ellas va así...

En la **época colonial,** el señor **conde** de Valle tiene un hijo que no trabaja y no estudia. Sólo va a muchas fiestas de noche y descansa de día. Sólo quiere llevar ropa elegante. Su padre está muy triste. Piensa que su hijo nunca va a hacer nada bueno. Por fin, un día dice: —Veo, hijo mío, que tú nunca vas a trabajar, nunca vas a estudiar y nunca vas a hacer tu casa de azulejos como la gente buena de esta ciudad.

ESTRATEGIA DEL BUEN LECTOR En español, se usan a menudo los guiones para indicar el diálogo, a diferencia de las comillas que se usan en inglés. A medida que leas fíjate quién dice las palabras que siguen al primer guión y quién dice las palabras que siguen al segundo guión.

CONSEJO PARA LA LECTURA
Fíjate que el primer párrafo y el último párrafo de esta lectura tienen una introducción y una conclusión de la leyenda. Describen un edificio que todavía existe hoy en la Ciudad de México.

DESAFÍO ¿Cómo crees que empezó esta leyenda? Intercambien ideas en grupos pequeños. **(Emitir juicios)**

Las respuestas van a variar.

PALABRAS CLAVE
el azulejo ladrillo pequeño
la época colonial el período en el que España gobierna a México
el conde, la condesa títulos de nobleza

MÁRCALO GRAMÁTICA Haz un círculo alrededor de 15 verbos en el texto de esta página y haz una lista de sus infinitivos.

escuchar, contestar, ver, querer, cambiar, ir, abandonar, trabajar, empezar, hacer, enseñar, existir, poder, visitar, ser

MÁRCALO PRONUNCIACIÓN Busca dos palabras que lleven la combinación de la vocal débil **i** con una vocal fuerte **(a, e, o)** y que no lleven acento escrito. Subraya las dos palabras.

A pensar...

1. ¿Por qué está el conde disgustado con su hijo al principio del cuento? **(Aclarar)**

   Respuesta modelo: El hijo del conde pasa la mayoría del tiempo ocioso y yendo a fiestas. Su padre quiere que sea más trabajador.

2. ¿Por qué el hijo del conde decide construir una casa de azulejos? **(Causa y efecto)**

   Las respuestas van a variar. Respuesta modelo: Se siente responsable de la tristeza de su padre y quiere mostrar respeto por los sentimientos de su padre.

El hijo escucha con atención las palabras de
20 su papá por primera vez y contesta: —Lo
veo a usted muy triste por mi culpa[1]. Quiero
cambiar mi vida. Voy a abandonar mi vida de
perezoso y voy a trabajar.

Entonces, el hijo empieza a trabajar mucho.
25 Hace una casa grande y bonita con azulejos
por dentro y ¡por fuera! Es para enseñarle
a su papá que sí escucha sus palabras.

¡Y todavía existe
esta casa! Si vas a la
30 Ciudad de México,
puedes visitarla. Es
un restaurante muy
bonito y famoso.

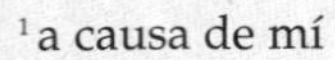

[1] a causa de mí

Vocabulario de la lectura

Palabras clave

el azulejo ladrillo pequeño
el conde, la condesa títulos de la nobleza
la época colonial el período en el que España gobierna a México
la gente conjunto de personas

Escribe la **palabra clave** que mejor complete cada oración.

El señor ___conde___ (1) de Valle vive en la Ciudad de México durante la ___época colonial___ (2). Está triste porque su hijo perezoso no trabaja y no estudia. El hijo ve a su padre muy descontento y por fin decide cambiar su vida. Hace una casa bonita con ___azulejos___ (3) por dentro y por fuera.

Pronunciación y ortografía

Cuando una vocal débil **(i, u)** se combina con una vocal fuerte **(a, e, o)** u otra vocal débil, forman un sonido combinado que se llama *diptongo.* Un diptongo es parte de una sola sílaba. Cuando un diptongo se divide en dos sílabas, hay que escribir un acento sobre la primera vocal para indicar la pronunciación correcta.

El diptongo **ia** en **farmacia** no se divide pero en **día** se divide en dos.
La combinación de dos vocales fuertes se divide en dos sílabas como en la palabra **creo.**

A. Pronuncia las siguientes palabras y decide si las vocales subrayadas forman un diptongo.

1. estud<u>ia</u> ___sí___ **2.** v<u>eo</u> ___no___ **3.** b<u>ue</u>na ___sí___

4. p<u>ie</u>nsa ___sí___ **5.** rest<u>au</u>rante ___sí___

B. Pronuncia las siguientes palabras y escribe cuántas sílabas tiene cada una. Si necesitas dividir dos vocales fuertes, escribe la palabra con su acento y entonces el número de sílabas.

1. ciudad ___2___ **2.** mio ___mío 2___ **3.** colonial ___3___

4. tiene ___2___ **5.** todavia ___todavía 4___

¿Comprendiste?

1. ¿Cómo es el hijo del conde?

Es perezoso.

2. ¿Qué hace todos los días?

No trabaja y no estudia. Sólo va a fiestas y quiere llevar ropa elegante.

3. ¿Qué piensa el padre?

Piensa que su hijo nunca va a hacer nada bueno.

4. Por fin, ¿qué hace el hijo?

Empieza a trabajar mucho y hace una casa con azulejos por dentro y por fuera.

Conexión personal

Si fueras el hijo o la hija de un noble rico, ¿cómo pasarías tu tiempo? Haz una lista de algunas de las cosas que harías en el espacio de la derecha.

ir al teatro

Para leer *Bomba y plena*

Estrategia de lectura

ECHAR UN VISTAZO Se le llama echar un vistazo a leer rápidamente para conseguir un dato determinado. Puede ser el resultado de un partido de fútbol o a la hora de una película. Echa un vistazo al cartel de la página 47 y determina si podrías asistir al festival si tuvieras entrenamiento de béisbol el sábado, 16 de octubre, a las 2:00 p.m. Escribe la respuesta a continuación.

____

____

____

____

Datos para tener en cuenta

Puerto Rico ha desarrollado tradiciones musicales únicas que reflejan la convergencia de culturas indígenas, africanas y europeas. Algunos instrumentos que todavía se usan en la música puertorriqueña se cree que se originaron con los **taínos**. El más notable de ellos es el **güiro**. Este es una calabaza hueca con muescas talladas en su superficie. Se usa para unas formas de música y danza puertorriqueñas llamadas **bomba** y **plena**. Las **maracas**, instrumentos de percusión hechos de **higos**, también datan de los **taínos**. Son una parte importante de la **salsa** del Caribe. Los tambores de **conga**, también usados por los grupos de salsa, tienen sus raíces en instrumentos africanos. Se hacen de troncos huecos y cubiertos con pieles de animales. El **cuatro** de cuatro cuerdas es un instrumento de cuerda adaptado de la guitarra clásica española. Es único en Puerto Rico y tiene mucha importancia en una amplia variedad de la música tradicional y contemporánea puertorriqueña.

The audio is on CD 1 of **Lecturas para hispanohablantes,** Track 17.

CONSEJO PARA LA LECTURA
Mientras lees, mira las fotografías o ilustraciones para ver si puedes identificar los instrumentos que se mencionan en el texto.

APUNTES

MÁRCALO **GRAMÁTICA**
Busca y subraya cada una de las formas del verbo **tener** que aparecen en la lectura. Luego conjuga los verbos **tener** y **venir** abajo.

tener: tengo, tienes, tiene, tenemos, tienen
venir: vengo, vienes, viene, venimos, vienen

MÁRCALO **PRONUNCIACIÓN**
En las líneas 1 a 5 de esta lectura, haz un círculo alrededor de las palabras que tengan el sonido /i/. Pronuncia cada palabra al leerla.

A pensar...

El artículo se refiere a tradiciones musicales de tres culturales mundiales. ¿Cuáles son? ¿Cuál es su relación con el tema de la lectura? **(Analizar)**

Respuesta modelo: El artículo se refiere a la música de Puerto Rico, África y España. La **bomba** y la **plena** y los instrumentos usados para acompañarlas representan una mezcla de estas influencias culturales.

Bomba y plena

La bomba y la plena son danzas típicas de Puerto Rico. Tienen sus orígenes en la música africana. Los instrumentos originales para tocar esta música alegre son los tambores, las **panderetas,** las maracas y el cuatro. El cuatro es un tipo de guitarra española pequeña, originalmente con cuatro **cuerdas.** Las personas que bailan estas danzas llevan ropa de muchos colores. La música tiene mucho ritmo y las personas ¡mueven todo el cuerpo!

PALABRAS CLAVE
la pandereta instrumento de percusión con sonajas y una membrana del piel
la cuerda hilo

PALABRAS CLAVE

la actuación representación
el (la) bailarín/bailarina danzante, que baila

ESTRATEGIA DEL BUEN LECTOR Al leer el cartel para el concierto, hazte las preguntas ¿Quién? ¿Qué? ¿Cuándo? ¿Dónde? Busca las respuestas en el cartel y escríbelas a continuación.

¿Quién? músicos, bailarines

¿Qué? concierto de bomba y plena

¿Cuándo? sábado 16 de octubre a las 5 de la tarde

¿Dónde? el Instituto de Cultura

DESAFÍO ¿Qué clase de música o baile te gusta? Usando el diagrama de Venn, compara esta música o baile con la bomba y la plena. Escribe las diferencias en las partes donde no coinciden los círculos. Escribe las semejanzas en la parte donde coinciden.

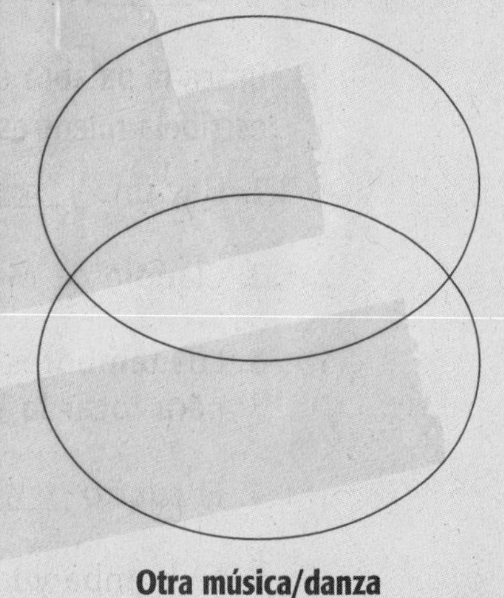

Vocabulario de la lectura

Palabras clave

la actuación representación
el (la) bailarín/bailarina danzante, que baila
la cuerda hilo
la pandereta instrumento de percusión con sonajas y una membrana de piel

Para cada **palabra clave** en la columna izquierda, busca la oración en la columna derecha que mejor describa la palabra. Escribe la letra correspondiente en el espacio en blanco.

C	**1.** cuerdas	A. interpretación o representatación
A	**2.** actuación	B. persona que se dedica al baile
B	**3.** bailarín	C. parte de una guitarra
D	**4.** pandereta	D. un tambor con sonajas

Pronunciación y ortografía

La vocal **i** se pronuncia como la combinación *ee* de la palabra *seek* en inglés.

A. Completa las siguientes palabras de la lectura con i. Luego, escribe la palabra completa y pronúnciala al escribirla.

1. t__í__p__i__cas **2.** r__i__tmo **3.** conc__i__erto

4. or__í__genes **5.** __i__nst__i__tuto

B. Busca la palabra apropiada de la lectura para completar cada oración. Luego, escríbela mientras la pronuncias. Enfoca en los sonidos de **a, e, i**.

1. Hay una __actuación__ especial de baile durante el concierto.

2. Claudio de Mata, Rubén López y Lucio Escobar son músicos __sensacionales__.

3. Los tambores y las panderetas son dos de los __instrumentos__ originales para tocar la bomba y la plena.

4. El cuatro __originalmente__ tenía cuatro cuerdas.

5. La bomba y la plena tienen sus orígenes en la música __africana__.

¿Comprendiste?

1. ¿Cuándo es el concierto?

El concierto es el sábado dieciséis de octubre, a las cinco de la tarde.

2. ¿En qué tienen sus orígenes la bomba y la plena?

Tienen sus orígenes en la música africana.

3. ¿Es una música triste o alegre?

Es una música alegre.

4. ¿Qué es el cuatro?

Es un tipo de guitarra española pequeña, originalmente con cuatro cuerdas.

5. ¿Qué otros instrumentos hay?

Hay tambores, panderetas y maracas.

6. ¿Qué ropa llevan las personas que bailan?

Llevan ropa de muchos colores.

Conexión personal

Diseña tu propio cartel en español para anunciar un evento escolar o un acto cultural local, real o imaginario. Tu objetivo es intentar atraer a la gente para que asista al evento. Asegúrate de poner el nombre del evento, los nombres de todos los actores y la fecha, la hora y el lugar.

Para leer *El coquí*

Estrategia de lectura

DISTINGUIR LOS DETALLES Averigua qué son los coquíes. ¿Qué características tienen? Usa la red de palabras para describir un coquí y nombrar las características que lo identifican.

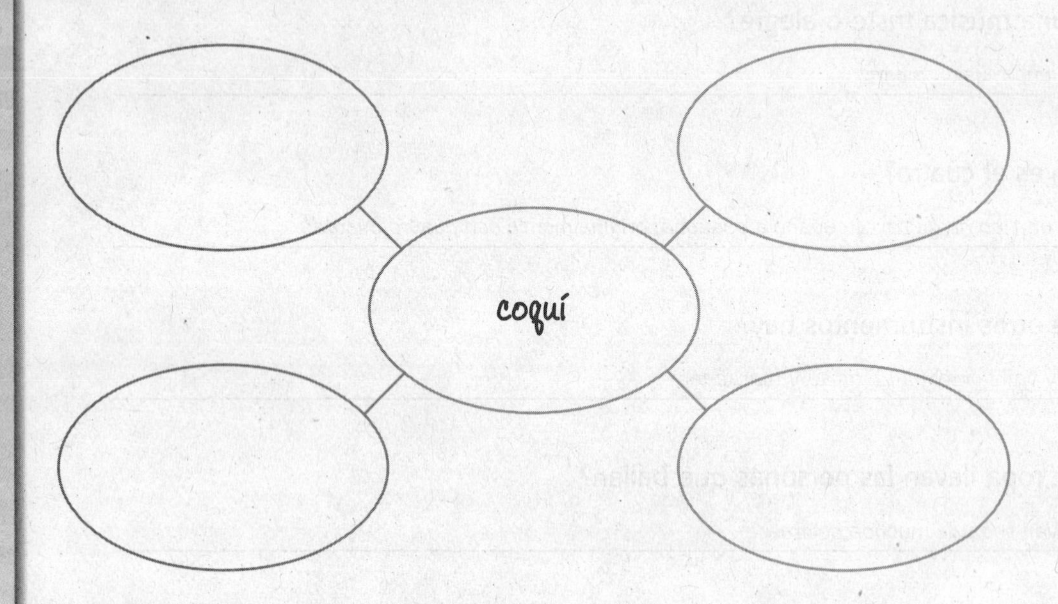

Datos para tener en cuenta

La única selva tropical del Servicio Forestal Nacional de Estados Unidos se encuentra en la isla de Puerto Rico. Está en la **Sierra de Luquillo**, a 25 millas de San Juan. Con 28,000 acres, en **El Bosque Nacional del Caribe**, comúnmente llamado **El Yunque**, viven 240 especies de árboles y plantas. Algunas no se encuentran en ninguna otra parte del mundo. La alta diversidad de la fauna de **El Yunque** tiene 16 tipos de **coquíes**; 11 tipos de murciélagos; y la boa puertorriqueña, una serpiente que puede llegar a tener más de ocho pies de larga. La caza no está permitida en El Yunque, que es refugio y hábitat de ocho especies en peligro de extinción. Una de estas especies es la del extremadamente raro **loro puertorriqueño** o *Puerto Rican Parrot.*

El coquí

No muy lejos de[1] San Juan está el **Bosque** Nacional del Caribe. En este bosque tropical, El Yunque, hay animales y plantas que no ves en ninguna otra parte del mundo. El coquí,
5 el animal más conocido de todo Puerto Rico, vive **protegido** en El Yunque.

[1] cerca de

El Yunque, el Bosque Nacional del Caribe

PALABRAS CLAVE
protegido(a) bajo protección legal
bosque sitio poblado de árboles

CONSEJO PARA LA LECTURA
Mientras lees **El coquí**, usa un marcador para marcar las palabras que te ayudan a visualizar el bosque. Busca palabras que despierten tus sentidos, especialmente la vista y el oído.

APUNTES

MÁRCALO **VOCABULARIO**
Imagina que estás planeando un viaje a El Yunque. Sabes que la temperatura durante el día va aproximadamente de 65°F a 78°F, llueve a menudo y en las elevaciones más altas se puede nadar en las piscinas naturales. Haz una lista de la ropa y accesorios que debes llevar.

Las respuestas van a variar. Respuesta modelo: gorro, impermeable, shorts, traje de baño, bronceador, gafas de sol, paraguas

APUNTES

MÁRCALO **PRONUNCIACIÓN**
En el primer párrafo de la lectura, subraya todas las palabras con la combinación **qu** y una vocal. Luego pronúncialas, y recuerda que la vocal después de la **u** es la vocal pronunciada.

ESTRATEGIA DEL BUEN LECTOR Haz una lista de los hechos que has aprendido acerca del coquí al leer este artículo. Por ejemplo: Los **coquíes** viven en los árboles.

A pensar...

¿Por qué crees que ciertas especies del **coquí** están en peligro de extinción? **(Causa y efecto)**

*Las respuestas van a variar. Respuesta modelo: Algunos tipos de **coquíes** están en peligro a causa de la deforestación. Cuando se destruye el hábitat natural del **coquí** sus huevos se pierden y disminuye su suministro alimenticio.*

DESAFÍO Escribe un párrafo breve sobre un animal de tu elección. Describe la apariencia del animal, di dónde vive y comenta cómo es el clima en el hábitat del animal. **(Ampliar)**

Las respuestas van a variar.

El coquí es una rana de tamaño pequeño que vive en los árboles. Los coquíes son de diferentes colores. Hay coquíes grises, marrones, amarillos y verdes. Reciben su nombre por su **canto** característico. Hay 16 **especies** de coquíes en Puerto Rico, pero sólo dos producen el canto típico «coquí». Dos están en peligro de **extinción**. Casi todos los coquíes empiezan a cantar cuando llega la noche.

Si visitas Puerto Rico, vas a ver imágenes del coquí en muchos lugares — en nombres de tiendas, artículos de promoción y libros. La tradición puertorriqueña es que si ves un coquí vas a tener mucha suerte. Y si quieres tener un bonito recuerdo de Puerto Rico es posible comprar un coquí verde de juguete, símbolo de la isla.

PALABRAS CLAVE
el canto acción de cantar
la especie grupo de animales
la extinción desaparición

Vocabulario de la lectura

Palabras clave

el bosque sitio poblado de árboles
el canto acción de cantar
la especie grupo de animales
la extinción desaparición
protegido(a) bajo protección legal

Escribe la **palabra clave** correcta en cada uno de los espacios en blanco. Usa cada palabra una vez.

El Yunque es un __bosque__ tropical de Puerto Rico. El coquí, una rana pequeña, vive __protegido__ en los árboles del parque. Los coquíes reciben su nombre por su __canto__ típico «coquí». Hay 16 __especies__ de coquí en Puerto Rico, pero dos están en peligro de __extinción__.

Pronunciación y ortografía

La vocal **o** se pronuncia como la *o* de la palabra *open* en inglés. La **u** se pronuncia como la *oo* de la palabra *boot* en inglés. La **u** no tiene sonido cuando sigue las consonantes **g** y **q**. La combinación **gu** se pronuncia con una **g** dura como en la palabra **gustar**, y la vocal después de la **u** es la vocal pronunciada. La combinación **qu** se pronuncia como la *k* en inglés y la vocal después de la **u** es la vocal pronunciada.

A. Completa cada palabra de la lectura con la vocal necesaria. Luego, escríbela mientras la pronuncias.

1. lej__o__s **2.** l__u__gares **3.** pr__o__tegid__o__

4. m__u__nd__o__ **5.** pr__o__d__u__cen

B. Escoge una palabra de la lectura para completar cada oración. Pronuncia cada palabra mientras la escribes. Enfoca en todas las vocales y en las combinaciones de **gu** y **qu**.

1. El __Yunque__ es un bosque tropical importante en Puerto Rico.

2. En este bosque hay animales y plantas que no están en __ninguna__ otra parte del mundo.

3. Hay 16 especies de __coquíes__ en Puerto Rico.

4. El imagen del coquí se usa en muchos __artículos__ de promoción.

5. Un coquí de __juguete__ es un bonito recuerdo de la isla.

¿Comprendiste?

1. ¿Dónde vive el coquí?

Vive en El Yunque.

2. ¿Qué es el coquí? ¿Por qué se llama coquí?

El coquí es una rana. Recibe su nombre por su canto característico.

3. ¿Cómo es el coquí?

Es de tamaño pequeño. Hay coquíes grises, marrones, amarillos y verdes.

4. ¿Cuándo canta el coquí?

Canta cuando llega la noche.

5. ¿Por qué es bueno ver un coquí?

Los puertorriqueños piensan que si ves un coquí vas a tener mucha suerte.

Conexión personal

Describe un parque nacional o zona forestal en la que hayas estado o que te gustaría visitar. ¿Cuáles son sus características geográficas? ¿Cómo es el tiempo? ¿Por qué te gustaría ir a este lugar?

Me gustaría ir a Yosemite, un parque nacional de California...

Para leer *El bohique y los niños*

Estrategia de lectura

USAR EL CONTEXTO Puedes usar el contexto para entender el significado de una palabra. El contexto es lo que viene delante y detrás de la palabra. Escribe las palabras que te ayudan a entender lo que estas palabras quieren decir.

Palabra	Contexto
voz	
areito	

Datos para tener en cuenta

Cuando Cristóbal Colón llegó a Puerto Rico en 1493, la isla estaba habitada por los **taínos**. Los habitantes **taínos** vivían en **bohíos**, cabañas redondas de paja colocadas alrededor de una plaza central. Allí el jefe de la aldea, o **cacique**, tenía su dirección general. El jefe gobernaba el pueblo con la ayuda del **bohique**, un respetado miembro de la sociedad **taína** que actuaba como oráculo o profeta. El **bohique** conocía las propiedades curativas de las hierbas y de los árboles. También se consideraba que era un curandero. Incluso antes de la llegada de los españoles, la supervivencia de los **taínos** había sido amenazada por los guerreros caribes, un pueblo indígena de Sudamérica. A mediados del siglo dieciséis, sin embargo, los **taínos** habían sido destruidos por los europeos.

CONSEJO PARA LA LECTURA
Recuerda el concepto de los cognados falsos, palabras que se parecen en español y en inglés, pero tienen significados diferentes. ¿Puedes encontrar un cognado falso en la línea 2 de esta lectura? ¿A qué palabra en inglés se parece?

El cognado falso es ***rato****, el cual se parece a la palabra inglesa rat.*

A pensar...

1. ¿Cuál de las oraciones siguientes acerca del **bohique** no es verdadera? Táchala. **(Clarificar)**

   Es un miembro respetado de la sociedad **taína**.

   ~~Cuenta su conocimiento por escrito.~~

   Canta canciones que cuentan cuentos.

   Explica la historia de los **taínos**.

2. ¿Cómo transmiten los **taínos** el conocimiento histórico y las tradiciones culturales? **(Resumir)**

   Respuesta modelo: La historia y las tradiciones se transmiten oralmente de generación en generación.

The audio is on CD 1 of ***Lecturas para hispanohablantes,*** Track 21.

El bohique[1] y los niños

Hace sol en las islas del Caribe. Unos niños taínos[2] pasan un buen rato en la playa. Enseñan a hablar a los **loros.** El bohique está en su casa. El bohique es una persona muy importante. Es la persona que sabe toda la historia de su **pueblo.** Es la persona que comunica la historia a su pueblo. El bohique empieza a contar un areito. Un areito es una canción, leyenda o historia.

Cuando los niños escuchan la voz del bohique, uno dice: —Vamos a ir a la casa del bohique. ¡Va a contar un areito! ¡Va a contar la historia de nuestra gente!

[1] cuentista [2] habitantes originales de Puerto Rico

PALABRAS CLAVE
el loro papagayo, pájaro con plumaje colorido
el pueblo personas de una misma nacionalidad

—¡Sí! —dicen todos los niños—. ¡Vamos a
15 escucharlo!
—¡Escuchen! Acaba de empezar el bohique.
Escucho los **tambores.**
—Y tocan las maracas también.
—¡Vamos a cantar con el bohique!
20 —A mí me gustan los areitos. Me gusta bailar
cuando canta el bohique.
—¡Escuchen! El bohique empieza a contar el
areito.

El bohique empieza: «Dicen que de las
25 primeras personas, los taínos, el sol crea todo
el mundo...»

Gracias al bohique que cuenta las historias,
los niños aprenden de la vida de su pueblo.

PALABRAS CLAVE
el tambor instrumento de percusión con una membrana de piel

CONSEJO PARA LA LECTURA
Como has aprendido, los guiones se usan frecuentemente en español para indicar el diálogo o las conversaciones. Además de guiones, este fragmento tiene comillas (fíjate en las líneas 24 y 26), las cuales se usan para separar las citas.

MÁRCALO GRAMÁTICA
Sabes cómo se usa el verbo **gustar** con un infinitivo para hablar de lo que a una persona le gusta hacer. En esta lectura, uno de los niños usa una forma de **gustar** con el infinitivo **bailar**. Busca esta frase y traza un círculo a su alrededor. Luego escribe tres oraciones parecidas usando **gustar** con un infinitivo para decir tres cosas que te guste hacer.

Las respuestas van a variar y deben empezar con **Me gusta**.

MÁRCALO ORTOGRAFÍA
Haz un círculo alrededor de todos los verbos de la primera página de esta lectura que tengan la letra **i**. Luego escribe los infinitivos de los verbos.

comunicar, empezar, ir

DESAFÍO ¿Por qué crees que a los niños taínos les gusta oír al **bohique** contar cuentos a través de canciones? **(Sacar conclusiones)**

Las respuestas van a variar. Respuesta modelo: Las canciones eran entretenidas y fáciles de recordar.

Vocabulario de la lectura

Palabras clave

el loro papagayo, pájaro con plumaje colorado
el pueblo personas de una misma nacionalidad
el tambor instrumento de percusión con una membrana de piel

Completa cada oración con la forma correcta de una de las **palabras clave**.

1. El bohique sabe la historia de su ___pueblo___.

2. Los niños taínos enseñan a hablar a los ___loros___.

3. Les gusta bailar cuando oyen los ___tambores___.

Pronunciación y ortografía

La vocal **i** se pronuncia como la combinación *ee* de la palabra *seek* en inglés.

A. Completa las siguientes palabras de la lectura con **i**. Luego, escribe la palabra completa y pronúnciala al escribirla.

1. ta___í___nos **1.** ___taínos___

2. canc___i___ón **2.** ___canción___

3. boh___i___que **3.** ___bohique___

4. comun___i___ca **4.** ___comunica___

5. d___i___cen **5.** ___dicen___

B. Busca la palabra apropiada de la lectura para completar cada oración. Luego, escríbela mientras la pronuncias. Enfoca en los sonidos **a, e, i**.

1. El bohique es una persona ___importante___.

2. El bohique sabe toda la ___historia___ de su pueblo.

3. Tocan los tambores y las maracas ___también___.

4. El bohique ___empieza___ a contar un areito.

5. El bohique dice que los taínos son las ___primeras___ personas.

¿Comprendiste?

1. ¿Dónde están los niños taínos?

Están en la playa.

2. ¿Qué hacen?

Enseñan a hablar a los loros.

3. ¿Qué hace el bohique?

Comunica la historia a su pueblo.

4. ¿Qué aprenden los niños gracias al bohique?

Los niños aprenden de la vida de su pueblo.

Conexión personal

No hay maestros sólo en la escuela. Los niños de la lectura aprenden la historia del **bohique**. ¿Quiénes son los maestros importantes de tu vida? En los recuadros siguientes, menciona dos. Describe algunas cosas que hayas aprendido de cada uno. Aquí tienes un ejemplo.

Abuela		
Me dice la historia de nuestra familia. También me enseña canciones.		

Para leer *Una leyenda taína*

Estrategia de lectura

LEER POR ENCIMA Leer por encima una lectura antes de empezar puede darte una información valiosa sobre lo que vas a leer. Lee por encima este fragmento y escribe lo que has sabido mirando estas cosas.

Mirar	Saber
título	
dibujos	
texto	

Datos para tener en cuenta

Cuando los exploradores españoles llegaron al Nuevo Mundo, los **taínos** habitaban Cuba, Jamaica, Puerto Rico y la isla la Española, que es ahora Haití y la República Dominicana. La religión tenía un papel central en la cultura **taína**, y los **taínos** adoraban a varios dioses y espíritus. Los **taínos** tenían muchos mitos y leyendas, como la que vas a leer, que explica el mundo a alrededor de ellos. Después de llegar a la Española, Cristóbal Colón encargó a un estudioso español vivir con los **taínos** para recoger sus mitos. Muchos mitos y leyendas **taínos** son todavía una parte de la tradición cultural del Caribe.

The audio is on CD 1 of ***Lecturas para hispanohablantes,*** Track 23.

Una leyenda taína

En las islas del Caribe los bohiques cuentan una leyenda de la creación del mundo. Dicen que de las primeras personas, los taínos, el sol crea todo el mundo.

Los taínos viven en **cuevas** en las montañas. En una de las cuevas vive un hombre que se llama Marocael. Marocael cuida la cueva de su gente.

Un día el sol le habla a Marocael: —Marocael, Marocael, ¡te invito a mi casa!

Marocael está **aterrorizado** y contesta: —Muchas gracias, pero tengo que cuidar la cueva de mi gente.

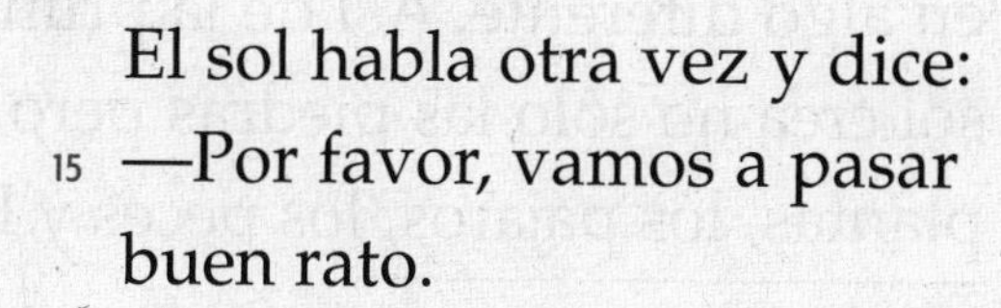

El sol habla otra vez y dice: —Por favor, vamos a pasar buen rato.

—No, muchas gracias —contesta Marocael—. Estoy muy contento en mi cueva.

PALABRAS CLAVE

la cueva hueco natural en la roca

aterrorizado(a) con miedo

ESTRATEGIA DEL BUEN LECTOR Esta leyenda es un mito, una historia antigua que sirve para explicar el origen natural de las cosas. A medida que leas, intenta imaginar cómo se desarrolla la historia. ¿A qué preguntas les da respuesta?

MÁRCALO > GRAMÁTICA Traza un círculo alrededor del pronombre de objeto directo de la oración encuadrada de la página siguiente. Luego subraya el nombre al que sustituye.

En esta página, los estudiantes deben trazar un círculo alrededor de **te** y subrayar **Marocael**. En la página siguiente, los estudiantes deben trazar un círculo alrededor de **lo** y subrayar **Marocael**.

DESAFÍO ¿Qué pueden aprender los historiadores acerca de una civilización anterior estudiando sus mitos y leyendas? **(Ampliar)**

Las respuestas van a variar. Respuesta modelo: Los mitos y las leyendas pueden proporcionar una mejor comprensión de los dioses de la civilización, de las creencias religiosas, del medio ambiente y de la estructura social.

CONSEJO PARA LA LECTURA
Recuerda el vocabulario para animales que ya sabes, como **pájaro** y **pez**.

MÁRCALO **PRONUNCIACIÓN**
En las líneas 20 a 23 de la lectura, haz un círculo alrededor de todas las palabras con combinaciones de vocales. Luego pronuncia cada palabra.

A pensar...

1. Escribe los números 1, 2, 3, 4 y 5 para indicar el orden en que suceden las cosas siguientes. **(Secuencia de sucesos)**
   - 4 El sol convierte a Marocael en una piedra.
   - 3 El sol se pone furioso y se lleva a Marocael.
   - 2 Marocael está aterrorizado y prefiere quedarse en su cueva.
   - 5 La gente de la cueva se convierte en plantas, pájaros y árboles.
   - 1 El sol invita a Marocael a su casa.

2. ¿Qué indica esta leyenda del papel del sol en la cultura taína? **(Inferir)**

   Las respuestas van a variar. Respuesta modelo: El sol les inspiraba miedo y respeto. Posiblemente se considerara un dios o un poder sobrenatural.

20 Y Marocael empieza a regresar a su cueva cuando el sol, **furioso,** habla fuerte y dice: —¡Ahora vienes conmigo, Marocael!— Y el sol lleva a Marocael de la cueva a su casa.

Cuando la gente de la cueva se despierta[1], 25 busca a Marocael pero no lo encuentra[2]. El sol convierte a Marocael en una de las primeras **piedras** de la **tierra.** Y cuando la gente sale de la cueva, el sol convierte a cada uno de ellos en algo diferente. Así de la primera gente, el 30 sol crea no sólo las piedras pero también las plantas, los pájaros, los peces y los árboles.

[1] deja de dormir [2] no lo ve

PALABRAS CLAVE
furioso(a) enojado
la piedra roca
la tierra el planeta

Vocabulario de la lectura

Palabras clave

aterrorizado(a) con miedo
la cueva hueco natural en la roca
furioso(a) enojado
la piedra roca
la tierra el planeta

Completa cada oración con la forma correcta de una de las **palabras clave**.

Marocael está ___aterrorizado___ cuando el sol lo invita a su casa. Dice que está muy contento en su ___cueva___. ___Furioso___, el sol convierte a Marocael en una de las primeras ___piedras___ de la ___tierra___.

Pronunciación y ortografía

La vocal **o** se pronuncia como la *o* de la palabra *open* en inglés. La **u** se pronuncia como la *oo* de la palabra *boot* en inglés. La **u** no tiene sonido cuando sigue las consonantes **g** y **q**. La combinación **gu** se pronuncia con una **g** dura como en la palabra **gustar**, y la vocal después de la **u** es la vocal pronunciada. La combinación **qu** se pronuncia como la *k* en inglés y la vocal después de la **u** es la vocal pronunciada.

A. Completa cada palabra de la lectura con la vocal necesaria. Luego, escríbela mientras la pronuncias.

1. s__o__l
2. m__u__chas
3. m__u__nd__o__
4. f__u__ri__o__s__o__
5. b__u__sca

B. Escoge una palabra de la lectura para completar cada oración. Pronuncia cada palabra mientras la escribes. Enfoca en todas las vocales y combinaciones.

1. Los ___bohiques___ cuentan una leyenda de la creación del mundo.

2. Los taínos viven en ___cuevas___.

3. Marocael está ___aterrorizado___ cuando el sol le habla.

4. El sol está ___furioso___ cuando Marocael no quiere ir a su casa.

5. El sol ___convierte___ a las personas en plantas, pájaros, peces y árboles.

¿Comprendiste?

1. ¿Dónde tiene lugar la leyenda?

Tiene lugar en una isla del Caribe.

2. Según la leyenda, ¿dónde viven los taínos?

Los taínos viven en cuevas.

3. ¿Quién cuida la cueva?

Marocael cuida la cueva.

4. ¿Qué le dice el sol al señor?

Dice: —¡Te invito a mi casa!

5. ¿Qué hace el sol con el señor?

El sol lo convierte en una de las primeras piedras de la tierra.

Conexión personal

El sol jugaba un papel muy importante en la vida de los **taínos**. ¿Influye mucho el sol en tu vida? Usando el vocabulario que has aprendido para describir el tiempo, menciona algunas cosas que te gusta hacer cuando hace sol.

Cuando hace sol, me gusta...

Literatura adicional

En esta sección vas a encontrar una selección de lecturas literarias en español. Hay poemas, partes de novelas y cuentos. Cada lectura tiene una biografía del autor e información relacionada con el tema de la selección. Como las lecturas culturales de **En voces,** las lecturas literarias presentan estrategias, consejos y apoyo para la lectura, preguntas para razonar, actividades para practicar el vocabulario, preguntas de comprensión y una actividad de escritura, que te ayudarán a entender cada selección. También encontrarás la sección **Márcalo,** que te servirá para hacer el análisis literario de las lecturas.

Términos literarios

Español – inglés

detalles sensoriales/sensory details
palabras descriptivas relacionadas con los sentidos (vista, oído, olfato, gusto, tacto)

hipérbole/hyperbole
descripción exagerada de una persona o cosa

metáfora/metaphor
comparación directa entre cosas diferentes que tienen alguna característica en común

paralelismo/parallelism
ideas relacionadas que expresan el mismo concepto

personificación/personification
uso de características humanas para describir un animal o un objeto

repetición/repetition
uso continuado de sonidos, palabras o frases para dar énfasis

Términos literarios

Inglés – español

sensory details/detalles sensoriales
descriptive words that appeal to the senses (sight, hearing, smell, taste, touch)

hyperbole/hipérbole
exaggerated description of a person or thing

metaphor/metáfora
direct comparison between two unlike things

parallelism/paralelismo
related ideas phrased in similar ways

personification/personificación
use of human characteristics to describe an animal or an object

repetition/repetición
recurring sounds, words, or phrases to give emphasis

LITERATURA ADICIONAL

Para leer *El cuento del cafecito*

Estrategia de lectura

ENTENDER LOS PASOS DE UN PROCESO Organizar los eventos de una historia te puede ayudar a recordar la secuencia en que ocurren. Por ejemplo, al leer esta lectura vas a encontrar una descripción detallada del proceso de criar y elaborar el café. A medida que leas, completa la tabla de abajo para ayudarte a entender los pasos de este proceso.

El café

Paso	Lo que se hace
1. preparar la tierra	hacer terrazas bajo la sombra de árboles
2. sembrar las plantas	

Datos para tener en cuenta

El café, que se cultiva mejor en las montañas de lugares con un clima cálido, se encuentra en varios países hispanohablantes. La manera tradicional de producir el café en pequeñas granjas individuales bajo la sombra de los árboles ya no es muy común. Las compañías cafeteras son dueñas de grandes terrenos de café que puede crecer a pleno sol y a altitudes más bajas. Estas compañías pagan poco por el café, que requiere mucho trabajo para ser elaborado–sembrar, alimentar, cosechar, secar y tostar. La autora de esta lectura, Julia Álvarez, fundó la Finca Alta Gracia en la región montañosa de la Cordillera Central en la República Dominicana. Ahí se produce café natural, sin cortar los árboles que proveen sombra y sin usar pesticidas. Además, Álvarez ayuda a la gente de la región a aprender a leer y escribir.

Sobre la autora

Julia Álvarez nació en Nueva York en 1950, pero vivió en la República Dominicana hasta 1960, cuando su familia volvió a Nueva York. Estudió escritura en varias escuelas y trabajó como profesora en Middlebury College, en Vermont, desde 1988. En 1991 Álvarez publicó *How the García Girls Lost Their Accents*, y ha publicado otros libros de ficción y de poesía. *El cuento del cafecito* se inspiró en las experiencias de Álvarez y su marido Bill Eichman en la Finca Alta Gracia.

El cuento del cafecito

Trabaja todo el día al lado de Miguel y sus hijos. Por la noche, mientras lee, levanta la cabeza y ve que la familia lo está mirando.

¿Qué dice el papel? Miguel quiere saber.

5 Son cuentos, explica Joe. Cuentos que me ayudan a comprender lo que significa vivir en esta tierra.

Miguel mira el libro en las manos de Joe con un respeto nuevo. Joe ha notado el
10 mismo afecto en la cara de Miguel mientras inspecciona las pequeñas plantas en su **vivero**.

Todos los días mientras trabajan juntos, Miguel le cuenta a Joe la historia del café.

CONSEJO PARA LA LECTURA
En esta historia, no se destaca el diálogo entre comillas o guiones. Presta atención a los signos de puntuación y los nombres para ayudarte a saber quién está hablando.

APUNTES

PALABRAS CLAVE
el vivero lugar donde se hacen crecer las plantas jóvenes

LITERATURA ADICIONAL

MÁRCALO GRAMÁTICA
En la página 70, subraya todas las palabras que indican la secuencia de los eventos. Luego escribe las palabras abajo, en orden cronológico.

Las respuestas van a variar.
Respuesta modelo:
Antes
primero
Mientras tanto, Entonces
luego, Después
Finalmente

APUNTES

Antes de sembrar café se debe preparar la
15 tierra en terrazas con árboles de distintos
tamaños para crear distintos niveles de
sombras: primero, los cedros; luego, las
guamas y los guineos.

Mientras tanto, Miguel comienza a germinar
20 las semillas de café. Los **retoños** se toman
alrededor de cincuenta días.

Del germinador, los pequeños transplantes
pasan al vivero por ocho meses. Finalmente,
cuando están fuertes y vigorosos, Miguel los
25 siembra en las terrazas.

Entonces hay que quitar la yerba y alimentar
las plantas con **abonos** hechos de lo que se
encuentre alrededor. Nosotros lo llamamos
orgánico, explica Miguel, porque usamos sólo
30 lo que la naturaleza nos brinda gratis.

Después de tres años, si Dios quiere, tenemos
nuestra primera cosecha. La recogemos cuatro
veces entre diciembre y marzo. Claro, sólo los
granos rojos.

35 Entonces comienza nuestra prisa: tenemos que
quitarle la pulpa a cada cereza [1] esa misma
noche o bien temprano la mañana siguiente.
La pulpa va a nuestra lombriguera [2] donde
producimos fertilizantes naturales.

[1] cáscara roja del grano de café
[2] lugar donde las lombrices hacen abono de los desechos orgánicos

PALABRAS CLAVE
el retoño planta que crece de la semilla
el abono material que se usa para alimentar a las plantas

40 Entonces cargamos los granos mojados al río. Deben lavarse con agua corriente por cerca de ocho horas—un proceso que requiere atención, porque debemos llevar las semillas al punto en que los granos están lavados
45 pero no se fermentan. No es muy distinto al momento en que una mujer se enamora—dice Miguel, sonriendo y mirando en la dirección de las montañas.

Y entonces comienza el largo proceso de secar
60 al sol. Algunos de nosotros, que no tenemos un patio de concreto, usamos la carretera. Hay que voltear los granos cada cuatro horas. Por la noche, los apilamos y depositamos bajo cubierta. ¡Pobre de nosotros si llueve y no
55 logramos cubrir los granos a tiempo! El café mojado **se enmohece** y termina en la pila del abono.

Después, cerca de dos semanas si el tiempo es bueno, ensacamos el cafe—

60 Joe respira con alivio. ¡No sabía que una taza costaba tanto trabajo! confiesa.

No he terminado, continúa Miguel, levantando la mano. Después de ensacar el café, lo dejamos descansar. Unos cuantos días,
65 unas cuantas semanas. Solamente le hemos quitado la pulpa pero el grano todavía está

PALABRAS CLAVE
enmohecerse pudrirse, descomponerse

LITERATURA ADICIONAL

DESAFÍO ¿Te gustaría trabajar en una granja cafetera? ¿Por qué? **(Evaluar)**

Las repuestas van a variar.

APUNTES

MÁRCALO ORTOGRAFÍA
Recuerda que las letras **b** y **v** se pronuncian igual, pero hay que tener cuidado al escribir las palabras con este sonido para no equivocarse en el deletreo. Haz un círculo alrededor de todas las palabras en las líneas 75 a 95 que tengan la letra **b**, y haz un recuadro alrededor de las palabras que tengan la **v**.

APUNTES

dentro del pergamino[3]. Así es que, después del descanso, halamos los sacos hasta el beneficio[4] para que les quiten el pergamino.
70 Más tarde, cuidadosamente, separamos los granos uno a uno, a mano, ya que un grano fermentado puede dañar el sabor del grano para el comprador. La trilla[5] o los de segunda categoría los dejamos para nosotros.

75 ¿Me quieres decir que este fantástico café que he estado bebiendo es de segunda? pregunta Joe, meneando la cabeza.

Miguel asiente. El grado de exportación es, naturalmente, para exportar.

80 Pero tu café es mucho mejor que cualquiera de los que he probado en cafeterías de lujo en Omaha, explica Joe.

Eso es porque—como usted mismo me ha dicho—es un hijo de agricultores, explica
85 Miguel. Saborea con todo el cuerpo y el alma.

Hasta ese momento, cuando lo dijo Miguel, Joe no se había dado cuenta de que eso era verdad. Él recuerda a su padre sembrando maíz en hileras tan derechas como si el mismo
90 Papá Dios las hubiera trazado con una regla. Mientras trabajaba, el padre de Joe silbaba una

[3] cáscara del café que queda después de lavar y secar los granos
[4] lugar donde se prepara el café para la venta
[5] parte inútil

pequeña melodía como si conversara con una manada invisible de aves.

A veces, mientras Joe trabaja al lado de Miguel, se encuentra a sí mismo silbando esa misma melodía.

¡No puedes vender tu terreno! le dice Joe a Miguel una noche. Debes seguir sembrando café a la antigua. Debes salvar este trocito del planeta para tus hijos y para todos ustedes. Tienes que convencer a tus vecinos antes de que sea muy tarde.

Anjá[6], eso es fácil para usted, dice Miguel, que no tiene que vivir esta lucha.

Esa noche Joe se decide.

A la mañana siguiente, baja en la camioneta con campesinos y pollos y chivos y cerdos. En el pueblo, entra en la estación de Codetel[7] y marca el número del lugar que antes llamaba su hogar.

Joe compra una parcela al lado de Miguel. Hacen un pacto. No van a alquilar sus parcelas a la compañía ni cortarán sus árboles. Van a cultivar a la antigua. Van a producir un café mejor.

[6] ¡cómo!, pues (interjección)
[7] compañía telefónica

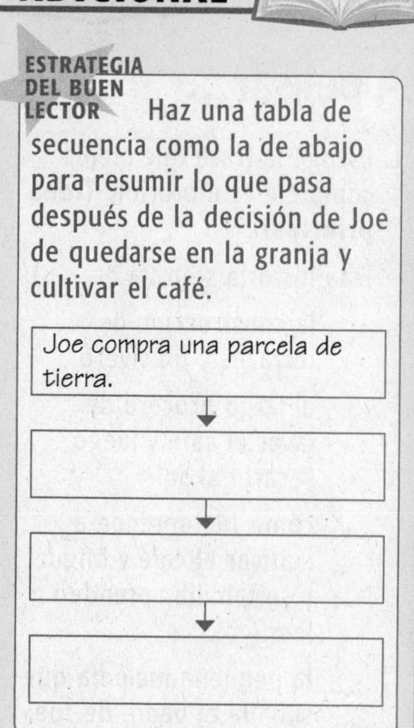

A pensar...

¿Por qué va Joe a la estación de Codetel en el pueblo? ¿Qué tiene que ver esto con la decisión de Joe?

Las respuestas van a variar. Respuesta modelo: Probablemente Joe va para llamar a su familia, o al banco para sacar su dinero. Joe decidió quedarse y necesita informarles a sus familiares y amigos, y también obtener el dinero para comprar la parcela de tierra.

LITERATURA ADICIONAL

A pensar...

1. Escoge la frase que mejor complete esta oración. **(Idea principal)**

Esta historia se trata de...

___ la construcción de terrazas y un vivero.

___ el largo proceso de lavar el café y luego secarlo al sol.

_✓_ cómo Joe aprende a cultivar el café y Miguel y su familia aprenden a leer.

___ la pequeña melodía que silbaba el padre de Joe.

2. ¿Crees que Miguel y Joe tendrán éxito al cultivar el café a la antigua? ¿Por qué? **(Predecir)**

Las respuestas van a variar. Respuesta modelo:
Sí, porque trabajan juntos y cuidadosamente. Van a producir un producto de alta calidad y esto les va a traer éxito.
No, porque va a ser muy difícil ganarse la vida de esta manera. Van a trabajar mucho y no saben quién va a comprar el café que producen.

Y ustedes van a aprender el alfabeto, añade Joe. Yo mismo les enseñaré.

Todos los días, bajo el **tutelaje** suave de Miguel, Joe aprende a cultivar el café. Ellos
120 hacen terrazas y siembran árboles.

Todas las noches, bajo la luz de una lámpara de aceite, Miguel y su familia aprenden el abecedario. Escriben letras y leen palabras.

Ya cuando Miguel y Carmen y sus hijos han
125 aprendido a escribir su nombre, las semillitas han retoñado. Cuando los árboles han crecido un pie, la familia ha logrado escribir una oración. Todos pueden leer una página cuando los árboles le llegan a la rodilla a Miguel. Y
130 cuando el café es tan alto como la pequeña Miguelina, han progresado hasta los capítulos. En tres años, para la primera cosecha del café sembrado por Joe, Miguel y Carmen y sus hijos pueden leer libritos enteros.

135 Es sorprendente lo bien que crece el café cuando le cantan las aves o cuando a través de una ventana abierta le llega una voz humana que lee las palabras en el papel que todavía guarda el recuerdo de haber sido árbol.

PALABRAS CLAVE
el tutelaje enseñanza, instrucción

Vocabulario de la lectura

Palabras clave

el abono material que se usa para alimentar a las plantas
enmohecerse pudrirse, descomponerse
el retoño planta que crece de la semilla
el tutelaje enseñanza, instrucción
el vivero lugar donde se hacen crecer las plantas jóvenes

Completa cada frase con una **palabra clave**.

1. El ___tutelaje___ de mi padre me ayudó mucho con mi tarea de matemáticas.

2. Josefina dejó el queso en la mesa del patio, y pronto el queso empezó a ___enmohecerse___.

3. Es buena idea alimentar las plantas del jardín con ___abono___ orgánico.

4. Hay que poner las pequeñas plantas en el ___vivero___ antes de sembrarlas en el jardín.

5. Vimos los primeros ___retoños___ sólo treinta días después de sembrar las semillas.

Pronunciación y ortografía

Las letras **b** y **v** generalmente tienen la misma pronunciación en español, el sonido suave de la **b** en la palabra **abuelita**. No hay otra distinción, así tienes que memorizar el deletreo de las palabras con estas dos letras para no confundirlas.

A. Completa cada palabra de la lectura con la **b** o **v** que falta y, luego, pronúnciala.

1. sa__b__er **2.** le__v__anta **3.** __v__i__v__ero

4. sem__b__rar **5.** de__b__en

B. Escribe la palabra correspondiente a cada definición. Todas las palabras están en la lectura.

1. limpiar con agua ___lavarse___ **2.** fertilizante ___abono___

3. las personas que viven cerca ___vecinos___ **4.** tomar por primera vez ___probar___

5. plantas altas que dan sombra ___árboles___

¿Comprendiste?

1. ¿Por qué Miguel mira a Joe con respeto cuando Joe está leyendo?

   Miguel no puede leer.

2. ¿Qué pasa si llueve y los trabajadores no logran cubrir los granos de café? ¿Si un grano fermentado está en los sacos que venden al comprador?

   Si el café se moja, se enmohece y sólo vale para abono. Un grano fermentado puede dañar el sabor del café para el comprador.

3. ¿Cómo es el pacto que hacen Joe y Miguel?

   Joe y Miguel prometen no alquilar su tierra a la compañía cafetera ni cortar los árboles, sino cultivar café a la antigua.

4. ¿Qué les enseña Joe a Miguel y su familia? ¿Qué le enseña Miguel a Joe?

   Joe les enseña a leer y escribir, y Miguel le enseña a Joe a cultivar el café.

Conexión personal

¿Tienes conocimiento especial de algo que puedas enseñarle a otra persona? ¿Hay algo que tú quieras aprender? Imagina que haces un pacto con un(a) amigo(a), que los dos van a enseñarle algo al otro. En la tabla, escribe lo que tu puedes enseñar y lo que quieres aprender de tu amigo(a).

Yo puedo enseñar...

Quiero aprender...

Para leer *Todos los días / Trabaja / Economía doméstica*

Estrategia de lectura

CLASIFICAR DESCRIPCIONES Muchos poemas tienen descripciones vívidas o detalles que ayudan a los lectores a formar imágenes mentales. Pueden ser imágenes de los personajes, del ambiente o de los eventos del poema, y siempre evocan por lo menos uno de los cinco sentidos. Los tres poetas de esta lectura utilizan descripciones que nos permiten entender sus sentimientos. En la tabla de abajo, escribe descripciones de los poemas e identifica los sentidos (vista, oído, gusto, tacto u olfato) que evocan.

Descripción	Sentido
una alacena huele a espliego	olfato

Datos para tener en cuenta

Los tres poemas de esta lectura tienen que ver con la vida doméstica, es decir la vida en casa. Los tres poetas nacieron en diferentes países latinoamericanos, uno al final del siglo XIX, una al principio del siglo XX y una al final. Los poemas de Calixto Pompa y Castellanos tratan de los quehaceres de la casa y los pensamientos de los protagonistas sobre los quehaceres como símbolo para la vida, pero el poema de Delgado no incluye referencias a los quehaceres sino a las actividades fuera de casa. Mientras leas los poemas, piensa en cómo cambia en el siglo XX el papel de los mujeres, y qué impacto puede tener esto en la vida diaria de la mujer latinoamericana y en la poesía.

LITERATURA ADICIONAL

There is no audio for this selection.

ESTRATEGIA DEL BUEN LECTOR Como muchos poemas contemporáneos, los poemas de esta lectura están escritos en **verso libre**, un estilo de poesía en que los versos no riman. Aun así, como toda poesía, estos poemas tienen un ritmo que se escucha al leerlo. Lee los poemas en voz alta y escucha al ritmo.

Sobre la autora

Nicole Cecilia Delgado nació en Río Piedras, Puerto Rico, en 1980. Estudia Literatura Comparada en la Universidad de Puerto Rico en Mayagüez, donde es miembro del grupo Poesía Zurde y editora de la revista *Zurde*. A Delgado le interesan las diferentes comunidades puertorriqueñas, tanto las de los pueblos y ciudades de la isla como las de otros lugares como Nueva York.

A pensar...

En la línea 13 de «Todos los días», ¿por qué crees que la poetisa usa palabras inglesas para hablar de su teléfono celular? **(Analizar)**

Respuesta modelo: La poetisa es puertorriqueña y vive en un lugar bilingüe donde la gente usa los dos idiomas juntos para hablar. También el teléfono celular es una invención moderna, y tal vez aún no hay bastantes términos en español para describirlo.

Todos los días

soñar paraísos o soñar pesadillas
pelear con el despertador **arrebatándome**
el sueño
cinco minutitos más entre las sábanas
el radio reloj disparando canciones mañaneras
5 cinco minutitos más
saltar de la cama porque se hizo tarde
lavarme los dientes y la cara
salir siempre de prisa

PALABRAS CLAVE
arrebatarse quitar con fuerza

caminar por el pueblo si hace fresco
10 montarme en el carro si no hay brisa
ir al trabajo, ir a las clases, revisar el email
contestar el celular cada vez que escucho el
timbre
ponerlo en silent mode para ignorarlo

pensar poesía en el camino
15 pensar poesía que no escribo porque no da
tiempo
porque no tengo la libreta cerca
porque se me olvida la poesía al contacto con
el lápiz

darme un baño de agua tibia de regreso a casa
comer pan y comer queso y comer uvas
20 ver las noticias por televisión
no todas las imágenes son ciertas
ir a la cama, quedarme dormida
el radio reloj susurrando melodías

todos los días.

LITERATURA ADICIONAL

DESAFÍO ¿En qué se parece o diferencia el día descrito en «Todos los días» a un día típico tuyo? Usa el diagrama de Venn de abajo para escribir tu respuesta. Donde los círculos están separados, escribe las diferencias. En el espacio de la intersección de los círculos, escribe las semejanzas. **(Comparar y contrastar)**

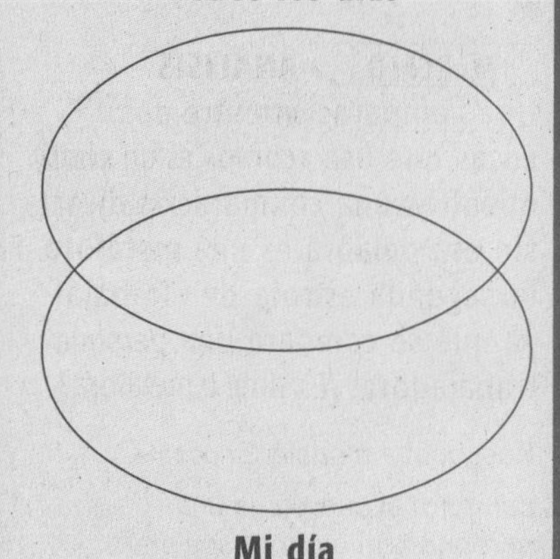

MÁRCALO ANÁLISIS
Repetición es un recurso literario en el que se repiten palabras, frases o versos para dar énfasis. Haz un círculo alrededor de ejemplos de repetición en «Todos los días». ¿Por qué repite la poetisa estas palabras o frases?

Respuesta modelo: La poetisa quiere enfatizar que ella hace las mismas cosas casi todos los días.

CONSEJO PARA LA LECTURA
Los poemas de esta lectura se tratan de la vida doméstica. A medida que leas cada poema, busca palabras y frases que te ayuden a entender los sentimientos de los poetas. Piensa en el ambiente creado por las descripciones de cada uno.

MÁRCALO > ANÁLISIS
Una comparación entre dos cosas que usa «como» es un **símil**, mientras una comparación directa sin esa palabra es una **metáfora**. En la segunda estrofa de «Trabaja» ¿a qué se compara una persona trabajadora? ¿Es símil o metafora?

Respuesta modelo: El poema compara el cuerpo de una persona trabajadora con un árbol fuerte y dice que el árbol se enoja porque esa persona es más fuerte. Es una metáfora.

A pensar...
¿A quién se dirige la voz poética? ¿Con qué motivo? ¿De qué habla?

Respuesta modelo: Se dirige a una persona joven con el motivo de hacerle trabajar con empeño. El poeta cree que através del trabajo, se vive libremente y con honor.

There is no audio for this selection.

Sobre el autor

Elías Calixto Pompa nació en Guatire, Venezuela, en 1837. A pesar de una formación humilde y autodidáctica, llegó a ser poeta, dramaturgo, periodista y luego, político. Vivió exiliado en los Estados Unidos durante el gobierno autocrático de Antonio Guzmán Blanco. En esa época publicó un libro de poesía entitulado *Versos de K. Listo,* del cual proviene este soneto.

Trabaja

Joven, trabaja, sin cesar trabaja,
La frente honrada que en sudor se moja
Jamás ante otra frente se sonroja[1]
Ni se rinde[2] servil a quien la ultraja[3]:

5 Tarde la nieve de los años cuaja
Sobre quien lejos la indolencia arroja[4],
Su cuerpo al roble[5], por lo fuerte, enoja,
Su alma orgullosa al lodazal no baja.

El pan que da el trabajo es más sabroso
10 Que la escondida miel que con empeño
Liba[6] la abeja en el rosal frondoso;

Si comes ese pan, serás tu dueño,
Mas si del ocio ruedas al abismo
Todos serlo podrán, menos tú mismo!

[1] hace salir los colores al rostro a causa de vergüenza [2] se da por vencido [3] menosprecia [4] echa, despide de sí [5] árbol muy grande, de madera buena [6] Chupa

PALABRAS CLAVE
empeño esfuerzo, dedicación

Sobre la autora

Rosario Castellanos (1925–1974), poetisa mexicana, nació en la Ciudad de México. Trabajó para varias organizaciones culturales en el estado de Chiapas, fue profesora en la Universidad Nacional Autónoma de México y también fue embajadora de México en Israel de 1971 a 1974. Castellanos escribió poesía (*Poesía no eres tú*, obra completa), novelas (*Balún Canán, Oficio de tinieblas*), cuentos (*Ciudad real, Los convivados de agosto*) y una obra de teatro *(El eterno femenino)*.

Economía doméstica 

He aquí la regla de oro, el secreto del orden:
Tener un sitio para cada cosa
y tener
cada cosa en su sitio. Así arreglé mi casa.
5 Impecable anaquel el de los libros:
Un apartado para las novelas,
otro para el ensayo
y la poesía en todo lo demás.

Si abres una alacena huele a espliego [1]
10 y no confundirás los manteles de lino
con los que se usan cotidianamente.
Y hay también la vajilla de la gran ocasión
y la otra que se usa, se rompe, se repone
y nunca está completa.
15 La ropa en su cajón correspondiente.

[1] planta olorosa, también conocida como lavanda

CONSEJO PARA LA LECTURA
Los versos de poesía, en especial los de verso libre, pueden ser cortos o largos. Fíjate que en estos poemas, las palabras aisladas escritas abajo de un verso forman parte de ese mismo verso.

MÁRCALO **ORTOGRAFÍA**
Subraya todas las palabras que tengan la **ll** en «Economía doméstica». Pronúncialas en voz alta. ¿Cuántas hay en total?

Hay cinco palabras en el poema con ll.

A pensar...

¿Qué desazona a la narradora y por qué?

Respuesta modelo: Las ideas y emociones que ella provisionalmente pone en varios lugares la desazona, porque ella dice que mañana las va a sacar, pero no lo hace.

APUNTES

Y los muebles guardando las distancias
y la composición que los hace armoniosos.
Naturalmente que la superficie
(de lo que sea) está pulida[2] y limpia.

20 Y es también natural
Que el polvo no se esconda en los rincones.
Pero hay algunas cosas
que **provisionalmente** coloqué aquí y allá
o que eché en el lugar de los trebejos[3].
25 Algunas cosas. Por ejemplo, un llanto
que no se lloró nunca;
una nostalgia de que me distraje,
un dolor, un dolor del que se borró el nombre,
un juramento no cumplido, un ansia[4].

30 Que se desvaneció[5] como el perfume
de un frasco mal cerrado
y retazos[6] de tiempo perdido en
cualquier parte.
Esto **me desazona**. Siempre digo: mañana...
y luego olvido. Y muestro a las visitas,
35 orgullosa, una sala en la que **resplandece**
la regla de oro que me dio mi madre.

[2] bien arreglado
[3] instrumento, utensilio
[4] inquietud, preocupación
[5] evaporarse, desaparecer
[6] pedazos, fragmentos de algo

PALABRAS CLAVE

provisionalmente no permanentemente
desazonarse disturbar, molestar
resplandecer brillar, distinguirse

Vocabulario de la lectura

Palabras clave

provisionalmente no permanentemente

desazonarse disturbar, molestar

resplandecer brillar, distinguirse

arrebatarse quitar con fuerza

empeño esfuerzo, dedicación

Completa el crucigrama con las **palabras clave** correctas.

Verticales

1. Julia empieza a... cuando escucha las malas noticias.
2. Manolo trata de... el papel de las manos de su amigo.

Horizontales

3. Elena trabaja con mucho...
4. El vicepresidente gobierna el país..., hasta que vuelva el presidente.
5. Es impresionante el gran... del palacio del gobierno.

1 d e s a z o n a r s e

2 a r r e b a t a r s e

3 e m p e ñ o

4 p r o v i s i o n a l m e n t e

5 r e s p l a n d e c e r

Pronunciación y ortografía

La l se pronuncia como la **l** en inglés. La pronunciación más común de la **ll** es el sonido de la *y* de la palabra *yes* en inglés. En algunos países de Latinoamérica, la **ll** tiene el sonido /zh/ de la *s* en la palabra *vision* en inglés, o de la *j* de *job* en inglés. En España, la **ll** se pronuncia como la *ll* de *million* en inglés.

A. Escribe la(s) letra(s) que falta(n) de las siguientes palabras de las lecturas. Pronuncia cada palabra.

1. orgu__ll__osa **2.** __l__ino **3.** __ll__anto

4. a__ll__á **5.** natura__l__mente

B. Escribe la palabra correspondiente a cada definición mientras la pronuncias. Todas las palabras están en los poemas.

1. un juego de platos vajilla

2. con mucho brillo pulido

3. un sueño malo pesadilla

4. un teléfono portátil celular

5. un instrumento para medir el tiempo reloj

¿Comprendiste?

1. ¿Cómo se encuentra la narradora de «Todos los días» al principio y al final del poema?

   Se encuentra dormida.

2. ¿Qué hace la narradora de «Todos los días» por la noche?

   Se baña, come, ve la televisión y luego se duerme.

3. Según el poeta de «Trabaja», ¿por qué es tan importante trabajar?

   Si uno trabaja duro, entonces se puede ganar la vida. Por ser independiente, nadie le puede ser dueño.

4. En el segundo verso de «Economía doméstica», ¿qué es lo que nunca está completa?

   La vajilla que se usa diario nunca está completa, a diferencia de la vajilla de gran ocasión.

5. Según «Economía doméstica», ¿cuál es la regla de oro?

   La regla de oro es tener un sitio para cada cosa y tener cada cosa en su sitio.

Conexión personal

¿Qué haces tú en casa? ¿Tienes que limpiar tu cuarto u otra parte de la casa? ¿En qué piensas mientras limpias? ¿Qué más haces en casa y por qué? Escribe tu respuesta en el cuaderno.

En casa, yo...

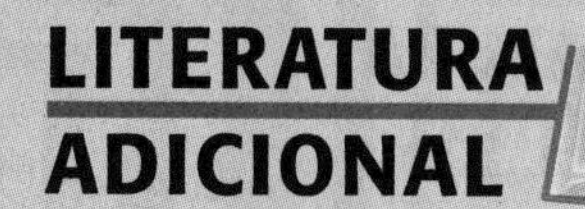

Para leer *Cajas de cartón: El juego de la patada*

Estrategia de lectura

RELACIONAR CON TU PROPIA VIDA Cuando lees, puedes relacionar los sucesos o las acciones de un personaje con tu propia vida. Mientras lees este extracto de *Cajas de cartón*, intenta pensar en experiencias parecidas que hayas tenido en tu vida. Usa la tabla para relacionar el ambiente, los sucesos y lo que Francisco Jiménez dice y hace con tus propias experiencias.

Lo que Francisco y yo tenemos en común	En qué somos diferentes Francisco y yo
Las respuestas van a variar.	

Datos para tener en cuenta

Esta lectura es del libro *Cajas de cartón* (2002), de Francisco Jiménez. El libro es una autobiografía, una historia personal escrita por esta misma persona, y se trata de las experiencias de la niñez de Jiménez. En este extracto, Panchito trabaja en el campo durante las vacaciones del verano. Los trabajadores migratorios, como la familia de Panchito, se mudan frecuentemente para seguir las cosechas de frutas y verduras en los campos. Es difícil que los niños migratorios reciban una buena educación porque en general no estudian en una escuela sino en varias. Jiménez nos relata qué aprende él fuera de escuela al trabajar en la cosecha de fresas, uvas y algodón durante un verano en California.

ESTRATEGIA DEL BUEN LECTOR Abajo haz una lista de todas las personas mencionadas en esta lectura. Luego escribe cómo se relaciona cada persona con Panchito: si son de la familia de Panchito o no.

señorita Logan: no
Papá: sí, familia
Carlos: no
Trampita, Torito y Rubén: sí, familia
Manuelito: no sabemos
Roberto: sí, familia
Ito: no
señor Díaz: no
Gabriel: no

CONSEJO PARA LA LECTURA
Francisco Jiménez usa diminutivos en esta lectura, principalmente en los nombres de las personas. Por ejemplo, el narrador se llama Panchito, para distinguirse de su papá Pancho. A medida que leas, busca los diminutivos y escríbelos abajo.

libretita
Panchito
Trampita
Torito
Manuelito
solito
Carcachita
taquitos
dinerito

Sobre el autor

Francisco Jiménez, que nació en 1943, inmigró con su familia a California desde Tlaquepaque, México, cuando tenía cuatro años. Siendo niño trabajó en los campos de California; su libro autobiográfico *Cajas de cartón* narra la historia de esos años. Se graduó de la escuela secundaria y luego de la Universidad de Santa Clara. Recibió su maestría y su doctorado en la Universidad de Columbia en Nueva York. Actualmente enseña lenguas y literatura en la Universidad de Santa Clara, donde es director del programa de estudios étnicos. Vive en Santa Clara, California, con su esposa y sus tres hijos.

Cajas de cartón: El juego de la patada

Yo estaba de mal humor. Era el último día de clases antes de salir de vacaciones de verano. Sabía que ese día se aproximaba pero trataba de no pensar en ello porque me ponía triste. Sin embargo, para mis compañeros de clase era un día feliz.

En la última hora, la señorita Logan solicitó voluntarios para compartir con el grupo lo que iban a hacer durante el verano. Muchos levantaron la mano. Unos hablaron de irse de viaje y otros de irse a un campamento de verano. Tratando de no escuchar, yo crucé los brazos debajo del pupitre y bajé la cabeza. Después de un rato logré desconectarme de lo

15 que decían y sólo escuchaba vagamente las voces que venían de diferentes partes del salón.

De regreso a casa en el autobús de la escuela, saqué mi libretita y mi lápiz del bolsillo de mi

20 camisa y comencé a sacar cuentas de cuánto tiempo faltaba para volver a empezar las clases —de mediados de junio hasta la primera semana de noviembre, cerca de cuatro meses y medio. Diez semanas **pizcando** fresas

25 en Santa María y otras ocho semanas cosechando uvas y algodón en Fresno. Conforme sumaba el número de días, me comenzó a doler la cabeza y mirando por la ventana me dije a mí mismo: «Ciento treinta y

30 dos días más después de mañana».

Tan pronto llegué a casa, me tomé dos aspirinas de Papá y me acosté. Apenas había cerrado los ojos cuando escuché a Carlos, nuestro vecino, gritar afuera: —¡Ándale,

35 Panchito, vamos a comenzar el juego!

El juego se llamaba *kick-the-can*. Lo jugaba con mis hermanos más chicos, Trampita, Torito y Rubén en días de clase cuando no tenía tarea, y los fines de semana cuando no llegaba tan

40 cansado de trabajar en los campos.

—¡Apúrate o me la pagas! —gritó Carlos impacientemente.

PALABRAS CLAVE

pizcar cosechar, recoger

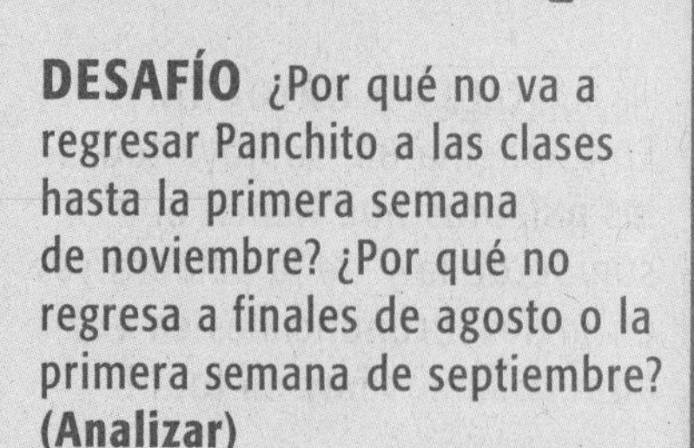

DESAFÍO ¿Por qué no va a regresar Panchito a las clases hasta la primera semana de noviembre? ¿Por qué no regresa a finales de agosto o la primera semana de septiembre? **(Analizar)**

Respuesta modelo: Aunque las clases empiezan a principios del otoño, Panchito tiene que trabajar hasta completar la cosecha en noviembre.

APUNTES

MÁRCALO › ORTOGRAFÍA En la página 88, subraya todas las palabras que tienen el sonido de la *y* de la palabra *yes* en inglés. Pronúncialas en voz alta. ¿Cuántas hay en total?

Hay cuatro palabras en la página con el sonido de la y de la palabra yes.

A pensar...

¿Qué dice Carlos cuando Panchito quiere que Manuelito juegue? ¿Por qué? ¿Crees que hay otras razones por las cuales Carlos dice eso? **(Analizar)**

Respuesta modelo: Carlos dice que Manuelito no puede jugar porque es demasiado lento. Carlos es el chico dominante y tiene que mantener su poder de esta manera.

Me gustaba el juego, pero no me divertía jugando con Carlos. Él era mayor que yo y a cada rato me lo recordaba, especialmente cuando no me ponía de acuerdo con él. Si queríamos jugar, teníamos que seguir sus reglas. Nadie podía jugar a menos que él quisiera. Vestía pantalón de mezclilla[1] ajustado y una camiseta blanca con las mangas remangadas para mostrar sus músculos y guardar ahí su cajetilla de cigarros.

—¡Ándale, Panchito! —gritó Trampita—. No nos hagas esperar más.

Salí a jugar. Quería olvidar lo de los próximos 133 días.

—Ya era hora —me dijo Carlos, dándome un golpe en el hombro derecho—. Tú serás el guardia —dijo, señalando a Rubén—. Trampita, tú haz la base. Torito, tú trae el bote. Cuando Carlos daba las órdenes, vi a Manuelito parado cerca de los botes de basura. En cada juego, él se paraba solito cerca de ahí porque Carlos no lo dejaba jugar.

—Deja que Manuelito juegue —le dije a Carlos.

—¡No! —me gritó enojado—. Ya te he dicho muchas veces que él no puede jugar. Es demasiado lento.

[1] jeans

—Ándale, Carlos, déjalo jugar —insistí.

—¡Que no! —volvió a gritar, dándonos a Manuelito y a mí una mirada amenazante.

—Ándale, Panchito, vete a jugar —me dijo
75 Manuelito tímidamente—. Sólo me pararé aquí para mirar.

Empezamos el juego y mientras jugábamos, me iba olvidando de mis problemas. Incluso mi dolor de cabeza desapareció y así seguimos
80 jugando hasta que anocheció.

El reloj despertador sonó muy temprano a la mañana siguiente. Eché un vistazo por la ventana. Estaba aún obscuro afuera. Cerré los ojos, tratando de dormir un poco más. Pero
85 Roberto, mi hermano mayor, saltó de la cama y jaló las cobijas.

—¡Es hora de levantarse! —dijo. Cuando lo vi ponerse su ropa de trabajo, recordé que teníamos que ir a trabajar y no a la escuela.
90 Sentí los hombros muy pesados.

De camino al trabajo, Papá encendió las luces de la Carcachita [2] para ver a través de la espesa niebla que soplaba de la costa. La niebla cubría el valle todas las mañanas como
95 una sábana gris muy grande.

[2] carro viejo

MÁRCALO ANÁLISIS
Recuerda que un símil es la comparación de dos cosas, usando la palabra **como**. Traza un recuadro alrededor del símil en esta página.

APUNTES

MÁRCALO > ANÁLISIS
Una metáfora es una comparación directa entre cosas diferentes que tienen alguna característica en común. Busca un ejemplo de metáfora en esta página y subráyala.

APUNTES

Ito, el **aparcero**, ya nos estaba esperando cuando llegamos. Luego una camioneta negra apareció. Podíamos verla a través de la muralla de neblina, no lejos de donde nos habíamos estacionado. El conductor se paró detrás de nuestra Carcachita y en un perfecto español ordenó al que viajaba en la tina[3] de la camioneta que se bajara.

—¿Quién es? —le pregunté a Papá, señalando con el dedo.

—No señales —me dijo Papá—. Es mala educación. Ése es el señor Díaz, el contratista. Dirige el campamento de **braceros** para la granja Sheehey. El hombre que está con él es un bracero.

En su español mocho[4], Ito nos presentó a Gabriel, el hombre que acompañaba al contratista.

Gabriel parecía pocos años mayor que Roberto. Vestía un pantalón holgado[5] de color marrón y una camisa de color azul descolorido. Su sombrero de paja lo traía ligeramente inclinado hacia la derecha. Tenía un par de largas y obscuras patillas bien recortadas que bajaban hasta la mitad de su

[3] espacio para cargar cosas en un vehículo
[4] incompleto, malo [5] demasiado grande

PALABRAS CLAVE
el (la) aparcero(a) persona que cultiva tierra de otro a cambio de una porción de la cosecha
el (la) bracero(a) persona que trabaja por día, sin contrato

cuadrada quijada[6]. Su cara estaba **curtida** y las grietas[7] profundas de sus talones eran tan negras como las suelas de sus guaraches.

Gabriel se quitó el sombrero y nos dimos la mano. Se veía nervioso, pero se relajó cuando lo saludamos en español.

Después de irse el contratista, marchamos en línea al final del campo, seleccionamos nuestro **surco** y comenzamos a trabajar. A Gabriel le tocó estar entre Papá y yo. Ya que era la primera vez que Gabriel cosechaba fresas, Ito le pidió a Papá que le enseñara cómo pizcar. —Es fácil, don Gabriel —le dijo Papá—. Lo principal es que la fresa esté madura y no magullada o podrida. Y cuando se canse de estar en cuclillas, puede pizcar de rodillas. Gabriel aprendía rápido mirando e imitando a Papá.

A las doce, Papá invitó a Gabriel a comer juntos en nuestra Carcachita. Él se sentó a mi lado en el asiento trasero, mientras Roberto y Papá se sentaron en el asiento delantero. De su bolsa de papel sacó una Coca-Cola y tres sándwiches: uno de mayonesa y dos de jalea. —¡Otra vez! Siempre nos da el mismo almuerzo ese Díaz —protestó Gabriel—. Estoy harto de esto.

[6] mandíbula [7] línea poco profunda en la piel

PALABRAS CLAVE

curtido(a) bronceado, oscurecido por el sol

el surco zanja en la tierra

LITERATURA ADICIONAL

A pensar...

1. ¿Por qué crees que Gabriel se veía nervioso cuando conoció a Panchito, Roberto y Papá? **(Inferir)**

   Respuesta modelo: Gabriel no sabía si Panchito y los demás hablaban español o no, y también estaba nervioso porque era el primer día en ese trabajo.

2. ¿Dónde almuerzan Panchito, Roberto, Papá y Gabriel? ¿Por qué crees que comen ahí? **(Sacar conclusiones)**

   Respuesta modelo: Comen en la Carcachita porque están en el campo y no hay otro lugar en que puedan sentarse y relajarse un poco. No hay cafetería ni otros servicios para los braceros.

A pensar...

¿A Gabriel le gusta el señor Díaz, el contratista? ¿Cómo lo sabes? **(Inferir)**

No, a Gabriel no le gusta el señor Díaz. Gabriel se queja del almuerzo que le da Díaz y del dinero que Gabriel paga por alojamiento, comida y transporte.

APUNTES

—Puede comerse uno de mis taquitos —le dije.

—Gracias, pero sólo si aceptas este sandwich de jalea —me respondió, acercándomelo. Miré la cara de Papá y cuando vi su sonrisa, lo tomé y le di las gracias.

—¿Tiene familia, don Gabriel? —le preguntó Papá.

—Sí, y la extraño mucho —le contestó con una mirada distante—. Especialmente a mis tres hijos.

—¿Qué edad tienen? —inquirió Papá.

—El más grande tiene cinco, el mediano tiene tres, y el más pequeño, que es una niña, tiene dos.

—¿Y usted don Pancho? ¿Cuántos tiene?

—Un puñado —le contestó Papá sonriendo—. Cinco muchachos y una niña. Todos viven en casa, gracias a Dios.

—Es usted afortunado. Los puede ver todos los días —dijo Gabriel—. A los míos no los he visto desde hace meses. Continuó como si estuviera pensando en voz alta. —Yo no quería dejarlos solitos, pero no tenía otra alternativa. Tenemos que comer, usted sabe. Les envío un dinerito para la comida y otras necesidades. Quisiera mandarles más, pero después de pagarle a Díaz el alojamiento, 175 comida y transporte, poco me queda. Este Díaz es un ladrón. Nos cobra demasiado por todo—. Después de una pausa agregó: —Ese sinvergüenza no sabe con quién se mete.

En ese momento escuchamos el sonido del 180 claxon de un coche. Era Ito, indicando que era hora de regresar a trabajar. Nuestro descanso de media hora para almorzar había terminado.

Aquella tarde y por varios días después, cuando regresábamos a casa del trabajo, estaba 185 muy cansado para jugar afuera; me iba directo a la cama después de cenar. Pero cuando me acostumbré a la pizca de la fresa, volví a jugar *kick-the-can.* El juego era siempre lo mismo: jugábamos con las reglas de Carlos. Y él nunca 190 dejaba participar a Manuelito.

El trabajo también era siempre lo mismo. Pizcábamos desde las siete de la mañana hasta las seis de la tarde. Sin embargo, a pesar de que los días eran largos, ansiaba ver a Gabriel 195 y almorzar con él todos los días. Yo disfrutaba escuchándole contar historias y pláticas sobre México. Se sentía tan orgulloso de ser del estado de Morelos como Papá de haber nacido en Jalisco.

A pensar…

¿Por qué Panchito y los otros chicos juegan a kick-the-can? ¿Por qué no juegan al tenis o al baloncesto? **(Evaluar)**

Respuesta modelo: No hay canchas de tenis ni de baloncesto donde viven, y tienen que jugar con las cosas que encuentran en el campo, como una lata.

APUNTES

Vocabulario de la lectura

Palabras clave

pizcar cosechar, recoger
el (la) aparcero(a) persona que cultiva tierra de otro a cambio de una porción de la cosecha
el (la) bracero(a) persona que trabaja por día, sin contrato
curtido(a) bronceado, oscurecido por el sol
el surco zanja en la tierra

Completa cada frase con una **palabra clave**.

1. Después de trabajar todo el verano de salvavidas en la piscina municipal, la piel de mi hermana está ___curtida___.
2. Julio trabaja todo el día para ___pizcar___ todas las fresas.
3. Los trabajadores migratorios son también conocidos como ___braceros___.
4. Mi papá es ___aparcero___ y tiene que compartir los tomates que cultiva con el dueño de la tierra.
5. Hoy Carla tiene que cosechar las uvas de cuatro ___surcos___ del campo.

Pronunciación y ortografía

En español la pronunciación más común de **ll** y de la letra **y** es el sonido de la *y* en inglés como en la palabra *yes*. En algunos países la **ll** y la **y** se pronuncian con los sonidos /zh/ o /j/ como en las palabras *vision* o *job* en inglés. Recuerda que la **y** también tiene el sonido de la vocal **i** cuando está sola o en combinación con otras vocales como en las palabras **y** o **hay**. Ya que **ll** e **y** en muchas palabras tienen la misma pronunciación, tienes que memorizar el deletreo de las palabras que tienen ese sonido.

Completa las siguientes oraciones con palabras de la lectura. Luego, lee cada oración en voz alta.

1. Tratando de no escuchar, ___yo___ crucé los brazos debajo del pupitre.
2. Saqué mi libretita ___y___ mi lápiz del ___bolsillo___ de mi camisa.
3. Ito ___ya___ nos estaba esperando cuando ___llegamos___.
4. Cuando se canse de estar en ___cuclillas___ puede pizcar de ___rodillas___.
5. ___Aquella___ tarde, cuando regresamos a casa del trabajo, estaba muy cansado.

¿Comprendiste?

1. ¿Por qué Panchito está de mal humor el último día de clases?

Él tiene que trabajar todo el verano mientras sus compañeros se van de viaje o a un campamento de verano.

2. ¿Qué cosechan Panchito y su familia y dónde?

Cosechan fresas en Santa María, y uvas y algodón en Fresno.

3. ¿Por qué no se divierte Panchito al jugar al *kick-the-can*?

El juego es siempre lo mismo: su vecino Carlos no deja que juegue Manuelito.

4. Según Papá, ¿cómo se pizcan las fresas?

Hay que pizcar sólo las fresas maduras y no las magulladas o podridas.

5. ¿Por qué la familia de Gabriel está lejos de él? ¿Dónde están los demás miembros de la familia?

Gabriel se fue de casa para buscar trabajo y les envía dinero. Es probable que su familia esté en el estado de Morelos.

Conexión personal

Al principio de la lectura, los compañeros de clase de Panchito hablan de sus planes para las vacaciones de verano. ¿Qué esperas hacer tú el próximo verano? ¿Te vas a ir de viaje, a un campamento de verano, a trabajar o algo diferente? Escribe tu respuesta en el cuaderno de al lado.

Durante el verano, yo...

LITERATURA ADICIONAL

Para leer *Cumpleaños*

Estrategia de lectura

HACERSE PREGUNTAS Hacerte preguntas sobre una obra literaria mientras lees es una manera de entender mejor el fragmento. Usa las cinco palabras, quién, qué, dónde, cuándo, por qué, para ayudarte a hacer las preguntas. En la tabla siguiente, escribe preguntas y las respuestas que encuentras mientras lees "Cumpleaños" de Carmen Lomas Garza y miras las ilustraciones.

"Cumpleaños"

¿Quién habla?	una joven
¿Qué describe?	una fiesta de cumpleaños
¿Dónde pasa la historia?	afuera en el patio
¿Cuándo es la fiesta?	en el sexto cumpleaños de la joven y el cuarto cumpleaños de su hermano
¿Por qué no pueden los niños ver la piñata?	Tienen los ojos vendados con un pañuelo.

Datos para tener en cuenta

"**Cumpleaños**" es un cuento del libro de Carmen Lomas *Cuadros de familia*. Este libro describe sus recuerdos de cuando vivía en Kingsville, Texas, cerca de la frontera de México. Por medio de viñetas ilustradas de algunas actividades familiares desde hacer tamales hasta recoger nopales, *Cuadros de familia* narra aspectos de la historia y cultura méxicoamericanas. En "**Cumpleaños**", Carmen Lomas Garza recuerda la celebración de su sexto cumpleaños.

The audio is on CD 1 of ***Lecturas para hispanohablantes,*** Track 28.

Sobre la autora

Carmen Lomas Garza, artista chicana, nació en Kingsville, Texas, en 1948. Empezó a estudiar arte a la edad de trece años. Sus pinturas, inspiradas en su niñez en el sur de Texas, son escenas típicas de la vida méxicoamericana.

Cumpleaños

Ésa soy yo, pegándole a la piñata en la fiesta que me dieron cuando cumplí seis años. Era también el cumpleaños de mi hermano, que cumplía cuatro años. Mi madre nos dio una
5 gran fiesta e invitó a muchos primos, vecinos y amigos.

Cumpleaños de Lala y Tudi by Carmen Lomas Garza, 1989

LITERATURA ADICIONAL

MÁRCALO › PRONUNCIACIÓN
Todas las palabras de más de una sílaba tienen una sílaba que se pronuncia más fuerte. Por ejemplo, en "amigo", se pronuncia "mi" más fuerte—es el acento o *golpe*. En la primera oración de la lectura, subraya las sílabas acentadas en las palabras.

MÁRCALO › ANÁLISIS
Este cuento tiene descripciones vivas, detalles que ayudan al lector a formarse una imagen mental clara. Escribe abajo las palabras o frases del cuento que te ayudan a visualizar en la mente la actividad y el entusiasmo de la fiesta de cumpleaños.

Las respuestas van a variar y pueden ser una gran fiesta; muchos primos, vecinos y amigos; los ojos cubiertos; pegarle a la piñata; rompiéndola; los caramelos caerán; los niños correrán.

ESTRATEGIA DEL BUEN LECTOR A medida que leas, busca representaciones del vocabulario en el dibujo. Primero identifica a la muchacha que cuenta el cuento y a su padre. Luego busca lo siguiente: **la cuerda, el palo, el pañuelo, la piñata.**

A pensar...

1. ¿De quién es el cumpleaños el día de la fiesta? **(Clarificar)**

   Es el cumpleaños de ambos, de la narradora y de su hermano.

2. ¿Qué detalles de la cultura méxicoamericana se describen en el cuento? **(Idea principal)**

   Las respuestas van a variar. Respuesta modelo: El cuento describe una típica celebración de cumpleaños méxicoamericana y la tradición de la **piñata.**

DESAFÍO ¿En qué se parece y en qué se diferencia la fiesta de cumpleaños descrita en "Cumpleaños" con las fiestas de cumpleaños de tu niñez o con las celebraciones de cumpleaños a las que ibas? Usa el diagrama de Venn para escribir las respuestas. Escribe las diferencias en las partes donde no coinciden los círculos. Escribe las semejanzas en la parte donde coinciden. **(Comparar y contrastar)**

"Cumpleaños"

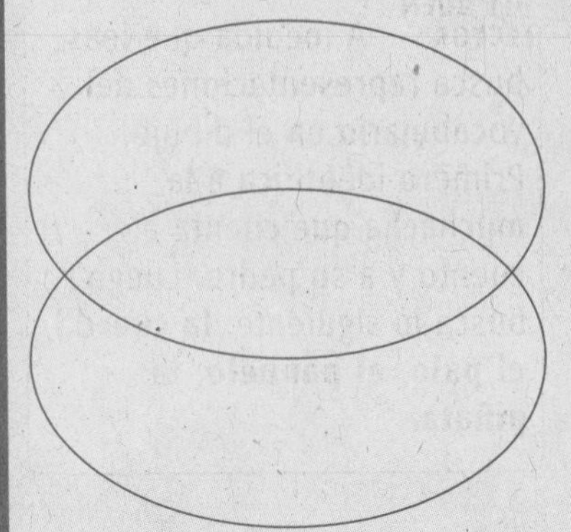

Cumpleaños que recuerdo

No puedes ver la piñata cuando le estás dando[1] con el **palo,** porque tienes los ojos cubiertos por un **pañuelo.** Mi padre está
10 tirando[2] de la **cuerda** que **sube** y **baja** la piñata. Él se encargará[3] de que todos tengan por lo menos una oportunidad de pegarle a la piñata. Luego alguien acabará rompiéndola[4], y entonces todos los caramelos que tiene
15 dentro caerán y todos los niños correrán a cogerlos.

[1] le pegas [2] halando [3] va a estar seguro [4] la va a quebrar

PALABRAS CLAVE

el palo pieza de madera larga
el pañuelo tela pequeña
la cuerda hilo fuerte
subir ir para arriba
bajar ir para abajo

Vocabulario de la lectura

Palabras clave

bajar ir para abajo
la cuerda hilo fuerte
el palo pieza de madera largo
el pañuelo tela pequeña
subir ir para arriba

Escoge dos **palabras clave** y escribe una oración sobre "Cumpleaños" usando cada una.

____

____

____

____

Pronunciación y ortografía

Recuerda que cada palabra se pronuncia con una sílaba más fuerte que las otras. En palabras que terminan en vocal, **n** o **s**, la sílaba más fuerte es la penúltima sílaba, como en las palabras **año, escriben** y **hermanos**. En palabras que terminan en consonante, excepto **n** y **s**, la sílaba fuerte es la última, como en las palabras **cumplir** y **oportunidad**. Cuando la pronunciación de una palabra rompe estas reglas, se escribe con un acento sobre la sílaba fuerte para indicar la pronunciación correcta, como en las palabras **hablé, sílaba** y **lápiz**.

Lee las siguientes palabras de la lectura en voz alta, siguiendo con atención la pronunciación de sílabas fuertes indicada por acentos. Escribe el número de la regla que la palabra rompe (1 ó 2).

1. pegándole 1
2. cumplí 1
3. también 1
4. dátil 2
5. invitó 1
6. estás 1
7. fácil 2
8. acabará 1
9. rompiéndola 1
10. correrán 1

¿Comprendiste?

1. ¿Cuántos años tiene la narradora?

Tiene seis años.

2. ¿Cuántos años tiene el hermano de la narradora?

Tiene cuatro años.

3. ¿Quiénes asistieron a la fiesta?

Asistieron muchos primos, vecinos y amigos.

4. ¿Por qué los niños no pueden ver la piñata cuando le pegan?

No la pueden ver porque tienen los ojos cubiertos por un pañuelo.

5. ¿Qué hay dentro de la piñata?

Hay caramelos.

Conexión personal

¿Recuerdas bien alguna de las celebraciones familiares de tu niñez? Elige un cumpleaños, una fiesta u otra celebración que recuerdes y escribe algunos detalles en la red siguiente.

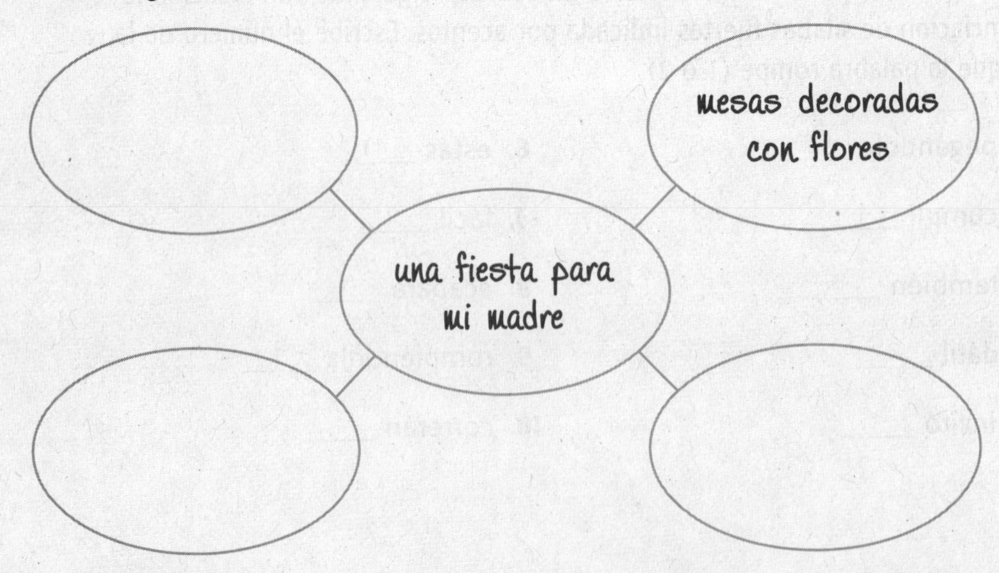

Para leer *La exclamación / En Uxmal*

Estrategia de lectura

CLARIFICAR EL SIGNIFICADO DE UN POEMA Se llama clarificar al proceso de dejar de leer mientras examinas rápidamente lo que ha pasado y buscas respuestas a las preguntas que puedas tener.
Completa la tabla siguiente haciendo lo siguiente:

- **Lee el título y las dos primeras líneas del poema.**
- **Deja de leer para clarificar esas líneas.**
- **Resume con tus propias palabras las ideas de las líneas en uno de los recuadros.**
- **Continúa leyendo y clarifica el resto del poema de la misma manera.**

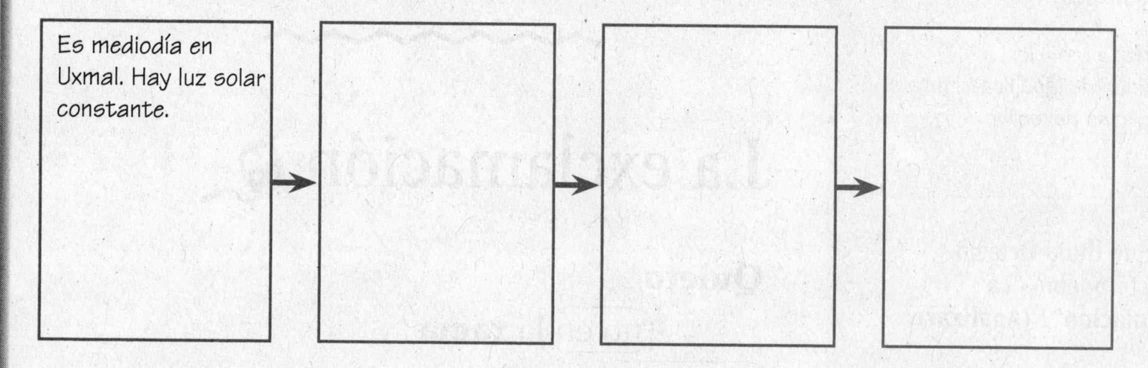

Datos para tener en cuenta

En su discurso del Nobel, Octavio Paz hizo las siguientes declaraciones:

Los españoles encontraron en México no sólo una geografía sino una historia. Esa historia está viva todavía: no es un pasado sino un presente. El México precolombino, con sus templos y sus dioses, es un montón de ruinas pero el espíritu que animó ese mundo no ha muerto. Nos habla en el lenguaje cifrado de los mitos, las leyendas, las formas de convivencia, las artes populares, las costumbres. Ser escritor mexicano significa oír lo que nos dice ese presente –esa presencia.

La poesía está enamorada del instante y quiere revivirlo en un poema; lo aparta de la sucesión y lo convierte en presente fijo.

Piensa en cómo estas ideas se reflejan en los siguientes poemas.

LITERATURA ADICIONAL 

The audio is on CD 1 of ***Lecturas para hispanohablantes,*** Track 29.

ESTRATEGIA DEL BUEN LECTOR No te preocupes si no puedes entender los poemas todo de una vez. Enfócate en lo que entiendes y parte de ahí.

A pensar...

1. La **forma** es la colocación de las líneas del poema en la página. ¿Qué significa la manera en que se organizan las líneas en la página de **"La exclamación"**? **(Sacar conclusiones)**

   Respuesta modelo: La colocación de las líneas imita el vuelo rápido del colibrí.

2. ¿Por qué titula Octavio Paz este poema **"La exclamación"**? **(Analizar)**

   Respuesta modelo: Está comparando los movimientos del colibrí con una exclamación porque los dos suceden de repente y duran poco.

MÁRCALO ANÁLISIS
La **repetición** es una técnica literaria en la que los sonidos, las palabras, las frases o las líneas se repiten para dar énfasis. Vuelve a leer **"La exclamación"** y traza un círculo alrededor de las frases que aparezcan más de una vez. ¿Por qué crees que el poeta repite estas frases una después de otra?

Respuesta modelo: Quiere enfatizar lo rápido que se mueve el pájaro de un lugar a otro.

Sobre el autor

Octavio Paz (1914–1998), poeta y ensayista que ganó el Premio Nóbel de Literatura en 1990, nació en la Ciudad de México. Durante los años cincuenta publicó *El laberinto de soledad (The Labyrinth of Solitude),* una colección de ensayos sobre la identidad mexicana, y *Libertad bajo palabra (Liberty Under Oath),* que contiene el poema «Piedra de sol» («Sunstone»). Inspirado en el calendario azteca, «Piedra de sol» es tal vez su obra más famosa. Desde 1962 hasta 1968 Octavio Paz fue embajador de México en India. Vivió en varios países y su escritura refleja una perspectiva internacional. Paz escribió sobre muchos temas, incluso sobre política, filosofía y amor.

La exclamación

Quieto
no en la **rama**
en el aire
No en el aire
5 en el instante
el **colibrí**

PALABRAS CLAVE
quieto(a) que no se mueve
la rama parte extrema del árbol
el colibrí pájaro pequeño que vuela rápido

En Uxmal

Mediodía

La luz no **parpadea,**
el tiempo se vacía[1] de minutos,
se ha detenido[2] un pájaro en el aire.

5 *Pleno sol*

La hora es transparente:
vemos, si es invisible el pájaro,
el color de su **canto.**

[1] dejaba vacío [2] ha parado

PALABRAS CLAVE
parpadear cerrar y abrir los ojos **el canto** acción de cantar

CONSEJO PARA LA LECTURA
Uxmal, ubicado en la península de Yucatán en México, es el lugar de una antigua civilización maya.

MÁRCALO ANÁLISIS
La **personificación** es una figura retórica que consiste en dar características humanas a un objeto, animal o idea. Traza un círculo alrededor de la línea que tiene una personificación en "**En Uxmal**". ¿Qué se personifica?

Se personifica la luz. En el poema la luz tiene la habilidad de parpadear como las personas.

A pensar...

Ten en cuenta que el poema fue inspirado por las ruinas de una civilización antigua. ¿Qué piensas que el poeta quiere decir cuando dice que un pájaro se ha detenido en el aire? **(Analizar)**

Respuesta modelo: A medida que el narrador mira las ruinas de Uxmal, ve una parte del pasado. El tiempo se ha congelado, como el pájaro se ha detenido en el aire.

MÁRCALO PRONUNCIACIÓN
En las líneas 3 y 4 del poema, haz un recuadro alrededor de las palabras que tengan el sonido /s/. Recuerda que hay 3 letras que tienen el sonido /s/.

Vocabulario de la lectura

Palabras clave

el canto acción de cantar
el colibrí pájaro pequeño que vuela rápido
parpadear cerrar y abrir los ojos
quieto(a) que no se mueve
la rama parte extrema del árbol

Completa cada analogía con una de las **palabras clave**. Recuerda que en una analogía, las dos últimas palabras tienen que estar relacionadas de la misma manera en que las dos primeras palabras están relacionadas.

1. CABEZA : PELO : : árbol : rama
2. LEER : LIBRO : : cantar : canto
3. PUERTA : CERRAR : : ojo : parpadear
4. BEBIDA : REFRESCO : : pájaro : colibrí
5. FELIZ : ALEGRE : : tranquilo : quieto

Pronunciación y ortografía

En Latinoamérica la **c** suave (seguida de **e, i**), la **s** y la **z** tienen el mismo sonido que la *s* de *stone* en inglés. Las palabras **cenar, sala** y **zapato** tienen el sonido /s/ aunque se escriben con consonantes distintas. La **c** dura (seguida de **a, o, u**) y la **q** (que siempre va seguida de **u** y otra vocal) tienen el mismo sonido de la *k* de *kitten* en inglés.

Lee los dos poemas en voz alta y escribe cada palabra con las letras **c, q, s** o **z**. Luego, indica si se pronuncia la letra con el sonido /s/ o /k/. Si una palabra tiene letras repetidas o dos de las letras, indica el sonido de cada letra en orden.

exclamación, k, s	vacía, s	si, s
quieto, k	minutos, s	invisible, s
instante, s	sol, s	color, k
colibrí, k	es, s	su, s
luz, s	transparente, s	canto, k
se, s	vemos, s	

¿Comprendiste?

1. ¿Qué tipo de pájaro se describe en **«La exclamación»**?

Se describe el colibrí.

2. ¿En qué tres lugares se encuentra el colibrí?

Se encuentra en la rama, en el aire y en el instante.

3. ¿A qué hora empieza el primer verso de **«En Uxmal»**?

Empieza al mediodía.

4. En el segundo verso de **«En Uxmal»**, ¿qué palabra usa el poeta para describir la hora?

Usa la palabra **transparente.**

5. ¿Qué palabra usa el poeta para describir el pájaro de **«En Uxmal»**? Si el pájaro es invisible, ¿cómo sabemos que existe?

Usa la palabra **invisible.** Su canto nos dice que el pájaro existe.

Conexión personal

Si fueras poeta, ¿de qué te gustaría escribir? ¿Sería de algo de la naturaleza, de un lugar donde has estado, u otro tema? En el centro de la red escribe un tema para tu poema. Luego escribe las palabras que asocies con él.

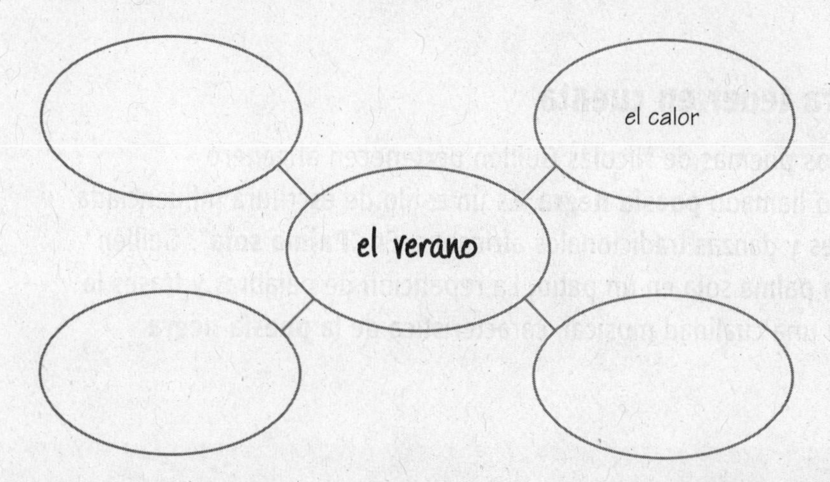

Para leer *Palma sola*

Estrategia de lectura

AMBIENTE El ambiente de un poema o un cuento es el tiempo y el lugar donde pasa la acción. El ambiente puede ser un telón de fondo, sin ningún efecto en lo que pasa, o puede ser importante para el significado del poema. Usa la tabla siguiente para escribir las líneas de "Palma sola" que indican el ambiente.

Tiempo/Lugar	Significado
bajo la luna y el sol	muestra el paso del tiempo
en el patio	indica que la palma está presa
el patio sellado	indica que el patio está en un espacio cerrado
guardián del atardecer	enfatiza que la palma está sola

Datos para tener en cuenta

Muchos de los poemas de Nicolás Guillén pertenecen al género afro-caribeño llamado **poesía negra**. Es un estilo de escritura influenciada por canciones y danzas tradicionales africanas. En "**Palma sola**", Guillén describe una palma sola en un patio. La repetición de palabras y frases le da al poema una cualidad musical, característica de la **poesía negra**.

Sobre el autor

El Poeta Nacional de Cuba, Nicolás Guillén (1902–1989) es uno de los escritores latinos más conocidos. Su poesía celebra la herencia africana de la gente cubana y la historia étnica de la isla. Guillén admiró la literatura española y la poesía clásica española. Sus poemas combinan elementos de la poesía española con el lenguaje común de los cubanos. En muchas de sus obras se puede ver el ritmo de *son,* un tipo de música de origen africano y español.

Palma sola

La palma que está en el patio
nació sola;
creció sin que yo la viera[1],
creció sola;
5 bajo la luna y el sol,
vive sola.

Con su largo cuerpo fijo[2],
palma sola;
sola en el patio sellado[3],
10 siempre sola,
guardián del atardecer,
sueña sola.

[1] vi [2] sin mover [3] sin salida

PALABRAS CLAVE
crecer hacer más grande

CONSEJO PARA LA LECTURA
La poesía es como tener palabras y música envueltas en el mismo paquete. El ritmo, el patrón de acentos fuertes y débiles, es una de las maneras en que los poetas añaden la cualidad musical. A medida que leas "**Palma sola**" observa como Guillén repite ciertas palabras para dar ritmo al poema.

MÁRCALO **ANÁLISIS**
Recuerda que la **personificación** es un recurso literario que da características humanas a algo que no sea humano. Traza un círculo alrededor de las líneas del poema que contengan personificación.

A pensar…

1. ¿Qué frases usa el poeta para describir la existencia solitaria de la palma? **(Clarificar)**

   Las respuestas van a variar y pueden ser **palma sola; nació sola; creció sin que yo la viera; creció sola; vive sola; siempre sola; sueña sola; palma sola soñando.**

2. ¿En qué se diferencia la palma del poema de una palma que se encuentre en la naturaleza? **(Comparar y contrastar)**

   Respuesta modelo: La planta del poema tiene sus raíces en una maceta en vez de en la tierra. Vive en un patio en vez de en su entorno natural. Está aislada y separada de otros seres vivos.

LITERATURA ADICIONAL

ESTRATEGIA DEL BUEN LECTOR Presta atención a los detalles descriptivos del poema. Haz un dibujo de cómo te imaginas la palma.

MÁRCALO > PRONUNCIACIÓN En las líneas 13 a 22 del poema, haz un recuadro alrededor de las palabras que tengan el sonido /r/ o /rr/. Pronúncialas al leer las palabras.

MÁRCALO > ANÁLISIS Una **metáfora** es una comparación implícita entre dos cosas. En **"Palma sola"**, **Guardián del atardecer** es una metáfora: la palma se compara con un guardián. Lee el último verso del poema para encontrar otra metáfora. Subraya la metáfora y di las dos cosas que se comparan.

Los estudiantes deben subrayar ***cazadora de las nubes****. La palma se compara con una cazadora. Al decir que la palma caza las nubes, el poeta enfatiza la altura del árbol.*

DESAFÍO ¿De qué maneras la palma está cautiva? ¿De qué maneras es libre? **(Evaluar)**

Respuesta modelo: La palma está cautiva porque está confinada en una maceta en un patio. Es libre porque crea sus propios sueños.

La palma sola **soñando,**
palma sola,
15 que va libre por el viento,
libre y sola,
suelta[4] de **raíz** y **tierra,**
suelta y sola;
cazadora de las nubes,
20 palma sola,
palma sola,
palma.

[4] no atada

PALABRAS CLAVE

soñar imaginar durante el sueño
el raíz (pl. raíces) parte de una planta debajo la tierra
la tierra suelo natural

Vocabulario de la lectura

Palabras clave

crecer hacer más grande
el raíz parte de una planta debajo la tierra
soñar imaginar durante el sueño
la tierra suelo natural

Escoge tres **palabras clave** y escribe una oración con cada una.

____

____

____

____

____

____

____

____

Pronunciación y ortografía

La **r** entre vocales se pronuncia con un solo golpe de la lengua como la *d* de *ladder* en inglés. En cambio, la **r** inicial de palabra y la **r** seguida de consonante tienen el mismo sonido que la **rr** y se pronuncian con varios golpes rápidos de la lengua.

Lee el poema en voz alta, enfocando en las palabras con **r** y **rr**. Indica si las palabras tienen el sonido /r/ o /rr/.

1. viera ___/r/___

2. siempre ___/rr/___

3. raíz ___/rr/___

4. tierra ___/rr/___

5. cazadora ___/r/___

¿Comprendiste?

1. ¿Qué es una palma?

Es un tipo de árbol.

2. ¿Dónde está la palma del poema?

Está en el patio.

3. ¿Es el patio abierto o sellado?

Es sellado.

4. ¿Con qué dos cosas compara la palma Nicolás Guillén?

La compara con un guardián del atardecer y una cazadora de las nubes.

5. ¿Qué dos palabras se repiten frecuentemente en el poema?

Se repiten **palma** y **sola**.

Conexión personal

Nicolás Guillén elige una palma en un patio para representar el concepto de **la soledad**. Si fueras poeta, ¿qué usarías para explicar la situación de estar solo? Usa la red de palabras para escribir tus ideas. Se dan algunas palabras de ejemplo.

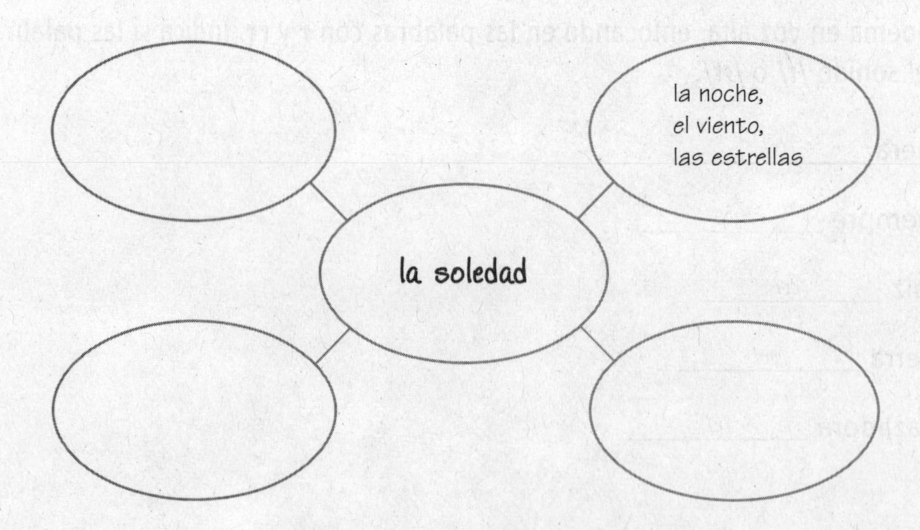

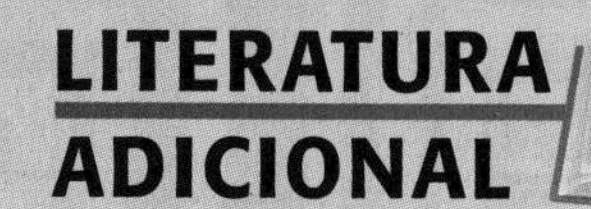

Para leer *Como agua para chocolate*

Estrategia de lectura

RELACIONAR CON TU PROPIA VIDA Puedes relacionar el tema de una lectura con tu propia vida. Mientras lees la receta de Como agua para chocolate, piensa en comidas y recetas que tengan un significado especial para ti. Compara la receta de Laura Esquivel para hacer chocolate con una de tus propias recetas.

Chocolate	Mi receta
sólo dos ingredientes	muchos ingredientes

Datos para tener en cuenta

Esta lectura es una receta de la novela *Como agua para chocolate* de la escritora mexicana Laura Esquivel. El libro tiene forma de entregas mensuales con comida y remedios caseros que se usan para describir la vida y los amores de la protagonista. Es una receta para el chocolate, que se hace de las semillas, o granos, de cacao. La palabra **cacao** viene de la palabra náhuatl *cacahuatl*. El cacao era tan apreciado por los aztecas que las semillas se usaban como una forma de moneda. Los aztecas también molían las semillas para producir la rica bebida de chocolate.

LITERATURA ADICIONAL

CONSEJO PARA LA LECTURA
Recuerda el vocabulario que has aprendido relacionado con la comida y su preparación: **libras, azúcar, aceite, caliente, cuchillo**.

MÁRCALO > **ANÁLISIS**
Esta lectura contiene **detalles sensoriales**, palabras descriptivas que tienen que ver con los sentidos. Vuelve a leer la receta y marca las frases o las partes que se relacionan con la vista, el gusto y el tacto. Luego escríbelas en la categoría apropiada de la tabla siguiente.

Las respuestas van a variar. A continuación se dan posibles respuestas.

la vista	«aspecto descolorido»
el gusto	«acrimonia y aspereza»
el tacto	«Con las manos se moldean las tablillas.»

APUNTES

The audio is on CD 1 of ***Lecturas para hispanohablantes,*** Track 32.

Sobre la autora

Laura Esquivel nació en México en 1950. Empezó su carrera de escritora como guionista *(scriptwriter)* de películas. En 1989 publicó la novela *Como agua para chocolate,* que ganó mucha popularidad tanto en Latinoamérica como en Estados Unidos. En 1992, la película basada en la novela tuvo mucho éxito y Esquivel ganó el premio Ariel (de la Academia Mexicana de Ciencias y Artes Cinematográficas) al mejor guión.

Como agua para chocolate

Ingredientes chocolate:

2 libras Cacao Soconusco
2 libras Cacao Maracaibo
2 libras Cacao Caracas
Azúcar entre 4 y 6 libras según el gusto

Manera de hacerse:

La primera operación es tostar el cacao. Para hacerlo es conveniente utilizar una charola de hojalata[1] en vez del comal[2], pues el aceite que se desprende de los granos se pierde entre los poros del comal. Es importantísimo poner cuidado en este tipo de indicaciones, pues la bondad del chocolate depende de tres cosas, a saber: de que el cacao que se emplee esté sano y no averiado[3], de que se mezclen en su **fabricación** distintas clases de cacao y, por último, de su grado de tueste[4].

El grado de tueste aconsejable es el del momento en que el cacao comienza a despedir su aceite. Si se retira antes, aparte de presentar un **aspecto** descolorido y desagradable, lo hará indigesto[5]. Por el contrario, si se deja más tiempo sobre el fuego, el grano quedará quemado en gran parte y contaminará de acrimonia y aspereza al chocolate[6].

(···)

[1] *charola de hojalata* cacerola de lata
[2] disco de metal usado para tostar
[3] deteriorado
[4] tostado
[5] que no se puede comer
[6] *contaminará de acrimonia y aspereza* hará un sabor malo

PALABRAS CLAVE
la fabricación elaboración **el aspecto** apariencia

ESTRATEGIA DEL BUEN LECTOR Mientras lees, haz una lista a continuación de los utensilios de cocina que se usan en la receta. Luego escribe el verbo de la receta que indica para qué se usa cada utensilio.

charola de hojalata: tostar
cedazo: separar
metate: moler
mazo: machacar
cuchillo: señalar

APUNTES

DESAFÍO ¿Piensas que sería fácil o difícil usar esta receta? ¿Por qué? **(Evaluar)**

Las respuestas van a variar. Respuesta modelo: Creo que sería difícil porque se necesitan los utensilios para tostar, moler y machacar el cacao. También hay que tostar los granos de cacao durante un tiempo determinado.

LITERATURA ADICIONAL

A pensar...

1. Escribe los números 1, 2, 3, 4 y 5 para indicar el orden de los pasos de la receta. **(Orden cronológico)**
   - 5 Dividir la masa en trozos
   - 2 Separar las cáscaras con un cedazo
   - 4 Añadir el azúcar y machacar la mezcla
   - 1 Tostar los granos en una charola de hojalata
   - 3 Moler los granos en un metate

2. ¿De qué tres cosas depende la bondad del chocolate? Traza un círculo alrededor de las respuestas correctas. **(Identificar idea principal y detalles)**
   - el amargor de los granos de cacao
   - (la mezcla de diferentes clases de granos)
   - (la condición óptima de los granos)
   - el uso de una plancha de yeso para tostar los granos
   - (el grado de tueste del cacao)

3. ¿Qué pasa cuando el cacao no se tuesta suficiente tiempo y cuando se ha tostado mucho? **(Causa y efecto)**

   Cuando no se tuesta suficiente tendrá un aspecto descolorido y desagradable y será indigesto. Cuando se tuesta demasiado, se quemará y se volverá amargo y agrio.

20 Cuando el cacao ya está tostado como se indicó, se limpia utilizando un cedazo[7] para separar la cáscara[8] del grano. Debajo del metate[9] donde se ha de **moler**[10], se pone un cajete[11] con buena lumbre[12] y cuando ya 25 está caliente el metate, se procede a moler el grano. Se mezcla entonces con el azúcar, **machacándolo** con un mazo[13] y moliendo las dos cosas juntas. En seguida se divide la masa en **trozos.** Con las manos se moldean 30 las tablillas[14], redondas o alargadas[15], según el gusto, y se ponen a orear[16]. Con la punta de un cuchillo se le pueden señalar las divisiones que se deseen.

[7] red para filtrar [8] parte exterior [9] piedra para moler
[10] aplastar [11] cazuela [12] fuego
[13] martillo de madera [14] pieza, tableta [15] largas
[16] tomar el aire

PALABRAS CLAVE
moler aplastar
machacar golpear para aplastar
el trozo pieza

Vocabulario de la lectura

Palabras clave

el aspecto *apariencia*
la fabricación *elaboración*
machacar *golpear para aplastar*
moler *aplastar*
el trozo *pieza*

Completa cada oración con una de las **palabras clave**.

1. La fabricación de chocolate necesita tiempo e ingredientes buenos.

2. El cacao presenta un aspecto descolorido si se retira antes.

3. Hay que dividir la masa de chocolate en trozos antes de orearlo.

4. Se procede a moler el grano con un metate.

5. Hay que machacar el grano y el azúcar con un mazo.

Pronunciación y ortografía

Has aprendido a usar el acento escrito con palabras que rompen las reglas de pronunciación. El acento escrito también se usa para marcar palabras interrogativas y se escribe sobre la vocal fuerte de la sílaba fuerte.

¿Quién(es)?	¿Cuándo?	¿Cuál(es)?
¿Qué?	¿Dónde?	¿Cuánto(a)?
¿Por qué?	¿Adónde?	¿Cuántos(as)?
¿Cómo?	¿De dónde?	

1. ¿Cuál es la primera operación en la preparación de chocolate?

2. ¿Qué utensilio recomienda la narradora para tostar el cacao?

3. ¿Por qué es importante poner cuidado en las ingredientes y la preparación del chocolate?

4. ¿Cómo sabes que el cacao está tostado?

5. ¿Cuántos ingredientes hay en la receta?

¿Comprendiste?

1. ¿Cuántas libras de cacao necesitas para preparar la receta?

Necesitas seis libras.

2. ¿Cuál es el otro ingrediente?

Es azúcar.

3. ¿Qué haces primero?

Primero, tuestas el cacao.

4. ¿Cuándo procedes a moler el grano?

Procedes a moler el grano cuando el metate está caliente.

5. ¿Cómo se moldean las tablillas?

Se las moldean con las manos.

Conexión personal

¿Te gusta el chocolate? ¿Qué otras comidas te gustan? Escríbelas en la tabla y escribe algunos adjetivos para describir cada una.

Comida	Descripción
chocolate	dulce, marrón

Para leer *Don Quijote de la Mancha*

Estrategia de lectura

ENTENDER LOS MOTIVOS DE LOS PERSONAJES Los motivos son las emociones, los deseos o las necesidades que hacen que un personaje actúe o reaccione de una manera determinada. Mientras lees esta adaptación del principio de *Don Quijote de la Mancha*, usa la tabla siguiente para entender las acciones de don Quijote. Al lado de cada acción, describe la razón, o motivo, que tuvo para hacerla.

Acción	Razón
1. Quiere recorrer el mundo en busca de aventuras.	Quiere ser como los heroicos caballeros andantes de las novelas de caballerías.
2. Añade el nombre de su región, la Mancha, a su propio nombre.	Quiere que la Mancha sea famosa.
3. Limpia la armadura que perteneció a su bisabuelo.	Cree que va a luchar en batallas y por lo tanto necesita una armadura y armas.
4. Nombra Rocinante a su caballo.	Decide que el caballo de un caballero andante debe tener un nombre admirable.
5. Imagina que Aldonza Lorenzo es una dama noble.	Como caballero andante, tiene que tener una dama a quién dedicarle sus heroicas hazañas.

Datos para tener en cuenta

El siguiente fragmento es una adaptación del primer capítulo de ***El ingenioso hidalgo don Quijote de la Mancha***. Es la famosa novela de Miguel Cervantes. Las novelas de caballerías, los libros que "secaron" el cerebro de don Quijote, fueron lecturas populares entre la Edad Media y el Renacimiento. Los caballeros andantes eran héroes frecuentes de las novelas de caballería. Andaban errantes en busca de aventuras para probar su valentía, honor y cortesía con las mujeres.

LITERATURA ADICIONAL

ESTRATEGIA DEL BUEN LECTOR En esta selección, don Quijote entra a un mundo de fantasía. Lee cada párrafo. Anota las cosas que ocurren en la imaginación del personaje y lo que hace para hacerlas realidad.

APUNTES

MÁRCALO > ORTOGRAFÍA
En español, hay una letra que se escribe pero casi nunca se pronuncia. En el primer párrafo de la lectura, haz un círculo alrededor de todas las palabras que tengan esa letra. Si encuentras casos especiales, explica qué ocurre.

En las palabras **Mancha, muchísimos** y **noches**, la letra **h** aparece después de la letra c. En ese caso, las dos letras juntas producen el sonido **/ch/** como en la palabra inglesa champion.

The audio is on CD 1 of ***Lecturas para hispanohablantes,*** Track 33.

Sobre el autor

Miguel de Cervantes Saavedra (1547–1616) nació en Alcalá de Henares, España. Fue soldado y luchó en Lepanto, donde perdió el uso de la mano izquierda. Más tarde fue capturado por piratas y pasó cinco años prisionero. Escribió en todos los géneros. Algunas de sus obras son *Viaje del Parnaso* (poesía); *Comedias y entremeses* (drama); y su obra más famosa, *Don Quijote de la Mancha,* que se publicó en dos partes y puede ser la novela más importante de la literatura universal. Aunque *Don Quijote* fue un éxito inmediato, Cervantes fue pobre toda la vida.

El famoso hidalgo don Quijote de la Mancha

Había una vez un **hidalgo** pobre en un lugar de España que se llama la Mancha. En su casa había muchísimos libros de **caballería** porque el pasatiempo favorito de este señor era leer y leer, especialmente libros de caballería. Se pasaba las noches completas sin dormir, leyendo hasta el amanecer, y lo mismo durante el día.

PALABRAS CLAVE

el (la) hidalgo(a) persona de clase noble y distinguida
la caballería soldados de la Edad Media que montaban a caballo

Leyó tantos y tantos libros que un día se le
10 secó el cerebro[1] y perdió el juicio[2]. Se imaginó
todo tipo de situaciones: batallas, desafíos,
encantamientos, heridas, amores, tormentas y
muchas otras cosas imposibles. Para él todas
estas cosas eran reales, tan reales como su
15 casa, el ama[3] de cuarenta años, su sobrina de
diecinueve años, su **rocín** flaco y el mozo[4].

Un día resuelve hacerse **caballero andante.**
Decide ir por todo el mundo con sus armas y
caballo a buscar aventuras. Desea pelear por
20 la justicia como los caballeros andantes de las
novelas que le gustan. Se va por el mundo a
buscar honra y fama.

Primero limpia las armas que fueron de su
bisabuelo. Después decide que el rocín de
25 un caballero andante tiene que tener un
nombre impresionante. «Rocinante te voy a
llamar», le dice a su rocín. Luego cambia su
propio nombre para incorporar el nombre de
su región y hacerla famosa. De esa forma se
30 convierte en don Quijote de la Mancha.

[1] *se le secó el cerebro* se volvió loco [2] la razón
[3] sirviente [4] joven sirviente

CONSEJO PARA LA LECTURA

Esta lectura tiene muchos juegos de palabras. **Quijote,** además del nombre del personaje, es una parte de la armadura. **Rocinante** viene de **rocín** (caballo de tiro) y **ante** (antes), es decir que "antes era un caballo de trabajo". **Dulcinea**, el nombre de la dama, viene de **dulce**.

MÁRCALO ANÁLISIS

Una **hipérbole** es una figura retórica *(figure of speech)* que consiste en exagerar una expresión para darle énfasis. Un ejemplo es "Este libro pesa una tonelada". En el segundo párrafo de la lectura, busca la hipérbole y subráyala.

APUNTES

PALABRAS CLAVE

el rocín caballo de trabajo
el caballero andante persona que anda a caballo buscando aventuras

A pensar...

1. Numera las siguientes oraciones del 1 al 4 para indicar en qué orden ocurrieron. **(Orden cronológico)**

   __3__ Don Quijote le pone el nombre "Rocinante" a su caballo.

   __2__ Don Quijote limpia las armas de su bisabuelo.

   __4__ Don Quijote decide llamar a Aldonza Lorenzo con el nombre de "Dulcinea del Toboso".

   __1__ A don Quijote se le secó el cerebro por leer libros de caballería.

2. ¿Qué motivos tiene don Quijote para hacerse caballero andante? **(Aclarar)**

   Respuesta modelo: A Quijote le gusta los heroicos caballeros andantes en los libros de caballería que ha estado leyendo.

DESAFÍO Según Cervantes, ¿cómo son los libros de caballería? En la lectura, busca partes que justifiquen tu respuesta. **(Inferir)**

Las respuestas van a variar. Respuesta modelo: Cervantes sugiere que los libros de caballería son peligrosos para algunas personas. Don Quijote los lee toda la noche sin dormir. Cervantes también se burla de los libros—es por leer tantos que don Quijote se vuelve loco.

Por último, como buen caballero andante, necesita una enamorada a quien dedicarle sus grandes **hazañas.** En Toboso, un lugar cerca de
35 la Mancha, hay una moza labradora[5], Aldonza Lorenzo, de la que antes estuvo enamorado. En su imaginación Aldonza se convierte en la dama de sus sueños. Es así como nace la figura de Dulcinea del Toboso, porque así se llama el
40 lugar donde ella vive.

[5] *moza labradora* muchacha que trabaja en el campo

PALABRAS CLAVE
la hazaña acción heroica

Vocabulario de la lectura

Palabras clave

la caballería soldados de la Edad Media que montaban a caballo
el caballero andante persona que anda a caballo buscando aventuras
la hazaña acción heroica
el (la) hidalgo(a) persona de clase noble y distinguida
el rocín caballo de trabajo

Completa el siguiente párrafo con las **palabras clave** correctas.

Don Quijote es un ___hidalgo___ que vive en la Mancha. Se volvió loco por leer tantos libros de ___caballería___. Un día, decide hacerse ___caballero andante___. A su ___rocín___ le pone el nombre "Rocinante" y se va por el mundo a realizar muchas ___hazañas___.

Pronunciación y ortografía

Ya sabes que en español la letra **h** no tiene sonido. Por eso debes tener cuidado y no olvidarte de escribirla. Completa las definiciones con palabras que tengan la letra **h**. Si necesitas ayuda, búscalas en la lectura. ¡Atención! Algunas palabras no aparecen en la lectura.

1. persona de clase noble h i d a g l o
2. alimento que dan las gallinas h u e v o
3. partes duras de los brazos y las piernas h u e s o s
4. fama, buena opinión que se recibe de los demás h o n r a
5. tormenta de viento muy fuerte h u r a c á n
6. objeto para acostarse a descansar; generalmente está atada a un árbol

   h a m a c a
7. acto de valentía h a z a ñ a
8. convertirse en h a c e r s e

¿Comprendiste?

1. ¿Quién es don Quijote?

Don Quijote es un hidalgo pobre de una región de España que se llama la Mancha.

2. ¿Qué tipo de libros le gusta leer?

Le gusta leer libros de caballería.

3. ¿Por qué se le secó el cerebro?

Se le secó el cerebro porque leyó muchísimos libros de caballería.

4. ¿Qué resuelve hacerse don Quijote?

Resuelve hacerse caballero andante.

5. ¿Cómo se llama su caballo?

Su caballo se llama Rocinante.

6. ¿Quién es Aldonza Lorenzo? ¿Qué nombre le da don Quijote?

Aldonza Lorenzo es una moza labradora. Don Quijote le da el nombre de Dulcinea del Toboso.

Conexión personal

Muchas historias de aventuras tratan de una búsqueda, un viaje que un personaje hace para alcanzar una meta determinada. Piensa en personajes de libros, de películas o de programas de televisión que van en busca de algo. Escríbelos en la tabla siguiente.

Personaje	Libro, película, etc.	Lo que quiere lograr
don Quijote	Don Quijote de la Mancha	pelear por la justicia

Para leer *Oda al tomate*

Estrategia de lectura

ELEGIR DE PALABRAS Los escritores eligen las palabras con cuidado para decir claramente lo que piensan. Así, un escritor puede hacer que los lectores sientan de una manera determinada o puede ayudarlos a visualizar una imagen. ¿Cómo te afectan las palabras de "Oda al tomate"? Usa el cuadro siguiente para escribir palabras y frases interesantes, y las ideas o los sentimientos que te transmiten.

Palabras y frases	Ideas y sentimientos que transmiten
"el tomate invade las cocinas"	expresa la abundancia de tomates
"su color fogoso"	transmite una imagen del color rojo brillante

Datos para tener en cuenta

Esta lectura es el poema "Oda al tomate", del libro *Odas elementales* (1954) del poeta chileno Pablo Neruda (1904–1973). Las odas son poemas largos y líricos, en que el autor analiza ciertos temas, normalmente de naturaleza seria o reflexiva. De manera diferente a la mayoría de las odas, las de Pablo Neruda hablan de lo ordinario y lo cotidiano, desde los tomates y las alcachofas hasta el aire o la lluvia.

LITERATURA ADICIONAL

CONSEJO PARA LA LECTURA
Lee el poema en voz alta. Fíjate en la puntuación para que sepas dónde detenerte o hacer una pausa. ¿Cuántas oraciones hay en el poema? Todas las oraciones empiezan con letra mayúscula. Escribe la respuesta en la línea siguiente.

Hay cuatro oraciones.

MÁRCALO › ANÁLISIS
Recuerda que la **personificación** es el uso de características humanas para describir a un objeto, un animal o una idea. Pablo Neruda usa la personificación para dar vida a los alimentos. Haz un círculo alrededor de los ejemplos de personificación que encuentres en el poema. ¿Qué alimentos se personifican? Escribe la respuesta en las líneas siguientes.

Se personifican el tomate, la cebolla, el aceite, el perejil y el asado.

DESAFÍO ¿Por qué estaría la calle llena de tomates? **(Sacar conclusiones)**

Las respuestas van a variar. Respuesta modelo: Un mercado de frutas podría estar en esta calle.

There is no audio for this selection.

Sobre el autor

Pablo Neruda nació en Parral, Chile. Su verdadero nombre era Ricardo Neftalí Reyes. Estudió pedagogía en francés en la Universidad de Chile. Allí conoció a Albertina Azócar. A ella le dedicó los primeros poemas de *Veinte poemas de amor y una canción desesperada* (1924). Para Neruda, todo puede ser poesía. En sus famosas *Odas elementales* escribió versos para el tomate, el átomo, un reloj, la pobreza y la soledad. Pablo Neruda fue diplomático en varios países de Europa y en México. En 1971 obtuvo el Premio Nóbel de Literatura.

Oda al tomate

La calle
se llenó de tomates,
mediodía,
verano,
5 la luz
se parte
en dos
mitades
de tomate,
10 corre
por las calles
el jugo.

En diciembre
se desata
15 el tomate,
invade
las cocinas,
entra por los almuerzos,
se sienta
20 reposado[1]
en los aparadores[2],
entre los vasos,
las mantequilleras,
los saleros[3] azules.
25 Tiene
luz propia,
majestad benigna.
Debemos, por desgracia,
asesinarlo:
30 se hunde[4]
el cuchillo
en su pulpa **viviente,**
en una roja
víscera,
35 un sol
fresco,
profundo,

[1] relajado [2] estantes en una cocina [3] recipientes para la sal
[4] penetra

PALABRAS CLAVE
viviente que vive

ESTRATEGIA DEL BUEN LECTOR A medida que leas, señala con un marcador los alimentos que se mencionan en el poema. Clasifícalas en grupos de tu propia elección y escríbelas a continuación.

Se deben señalar las palabras **tomates, ensaladas, cebolla, aceite, pimienta, sal, perejil, papas, asado.** Las agrupaciones de los estudiantes van a variar: por orden alfabético, tipos de comida, colores, preferencias de los estudiantes, valor nutritivo, grado de preparación, etc.

APUNTES

DESAFÍO ¿Por qué es diciembre y todavía es verano en el poema? **(Evaluar)**

Es verano en diciembre porque el poema se escribió en Chile, que está en el hemisferio sur y tiene las estaciones al contrario que los países del hemisferio norte.

A pensar...

1. ¿Por qué crees que el poeta compara el tomate con el sol? **(Sacar conclusiones)**

   Las respuestas van a variar. Respuesta modelo: Los compara porque los dos son redondos y el sol puede estar rojo como un tomate.

2. ¿Qué crees que quiere decir la frase **la cintura del verano**? **(Analizar)**

   Las respuestas van a variar. Respuesta modelo: Significa la mitad del verano, como la cintura está en la mitad del cuerpo.

APUNTES

inagotable[5],
llena de ensaladas
40 de Chile,
se casa alegremente
con la clara cebolla,
y para celebrarlo
se deja
45 caer
aceite,
hijo
esencial del olivo,
sobre sus hemisferios entreabiertos[6],
50 **agrega**
la pimienta
su fragancia,
la sal su magnetismo:
son las bodas
55 del día,
el perejil
levanta
banderines[7],
las papas
60 hierven vigorosamente,
el asado
golpea

[5] sin fin [6] separados [7] banderas pequeñas

PALABRAS CLAVE
agregar añadir

con su aroma
en la puerta,
65 es hora!
vamos!
y sobre
la mesa, en la cintura
del verano,
70 el tomate,
astro de tierra,
estrella
repetida
y **fecunda,**
75 nos muestra
sus circunvoluciones[8],
sus canales,
la insigne plenitud[9]
y la abundancia
80 sin hueso[10],
sin coraza[11],
sin escamas[12] ni espinas,
nos entrega
el regalo
85 de su color **fogoso**
y la totalidad de su **frescura.**

[8] espirales [9] integridad [10] semilla dura de algunas frutas, carozo
[11] cáscara [12] láminas que cubren el cuerpo de los peces

PALABRAS CLAVE

fecundo(a) fértil
la frescura cualidad de fresco
fogoso(a) color de fuego, rojo

MÁRCALO ANÁLISIS
El **paralelismo** es un recurso literario que consiste en relacionar ideas y frases de maneras parecidas. Un ejemplo es *tiempo para reír, tiempo para llorar.* Busca y subraya un ejemplo de paralelismo casi al final del poema. ¿Qué palabra se usa en cada línea? Escribe la palabra en la línea siguiente.

sin

APUNTES

MÁRCALO ORTOGRAFÍA
En las líneas 75 a 86 del poema, haz un recuadro alrededor de las palabras que tengan el sonido /s/. Recuerda que hay 3 letras que tienen el sonido /s/.

APUNTES

Vocabulario de la lectura

Palabras clave

agregar añadir
fecundo(a) fértil
fogoso(a) color de fuego, rojo
la frescura cualidad de fresco
viviente que vive

En el espacio en blanco que aparece al lado de cada par de palabras, escribe si las palabras son sinónimos o antónimos. Los sinónimos son palabras que significan lo mismo o que tienen significados semejantes. Los antónimos son palabras que tienen significados diferentes.

1. calor—frescura antónimos
2. adicionar—agregar sinónimos
3. fértil—fecundo sinónimos
4. ardiente—fogoso sinónimos
5. muerto—viviente antónimos

Pronunciación y ortografía

En Latinoamérica la **c** suave (antes de las vocales **e** o **i**), la **s** y la **z** tienen el mismo sonido: la **s** de la palabra *say* en inglés. Por eso, es importante memorizar el deletreo de las palabras con estas letras. En España, la **c** suave y la **z** tienen el sonido de la combinación *th* de la palabra *think* en inglés.

A. Completa las siguientes palabras de la lectura con la(s) letra(s) que falta(n). Pronuncia cada palabra.

1. di_c_iembre
2. almuer_z_os
3. maje_s_tad
4. _c_intura
5. e_s_en_c_ial

B. Identifica la palabra de la lectura correspondiente a cada definición. Pronuncia la palabra mientras la escribes.

1. carne a la brasa asado
2. una verdura que te hace llorar cuando la cortas cebolla
3. recipientes para beber agua vasos
4. una buena cantidad de algo abundancia
5. iluminación luz

¿Comprendiste?

1. ¿En qué mes ocurre el poema?

Ocurre en diciembre.

2. ¿Qué tiene el tomate?

Tiene luz propia, majestad benigna.

3. ¿Qué no tiene el tomate?

No tiene hueso, coraza, escamas, ni espinas.

4. ¿Cuáles son los ingredientes de la ensalada?

Los ingredientes de la ensalada son tomates, cebolla, aceite, pimienta y sal.

Conexión personal

¿Escribirías una oda sobre algo simple? Elige un tema para tu oda y escribe una lista de palabras y frases que usarías para describirlo en el cuaderno de la derecha. Incluye por lo menos un ejemplo de personificación.

Oda a ______________

Academic and Informational Reading

En esta sección aprenderás estrategias que te ayudarán a leer todo tipo de material informativo. Encontrarás muchos ejemplos, desde revistas y libros de texto hasta horarios de autobuses. Al emplear estas sencillas y efectivas técnicas podrás entender todos los textos que ves a diario.

Academic and Informational Reading Terms

application aplicación

boldface negrita

caption leyenda

chart tabla

content area materia

fact hecho

feature característica

focus enfoque

goal objetivo

graph gráfica

heading encabezamiento

indented sangría

italics cursiva

label rótulo

legend referencia

link enlace

main idea idea principal

map mapa, plano

paragraph párrafo

pie chart gráfica circular

primary source fuente principal

public notice notificación pública

purpose propósito

quotation cita

quotation marks comillas

reason razón

safety guidelines instrucciones de seguridad / precauciones

scan leer rápidamente

schedule horario

subject tema

subtopic subtema

supporting detail detalle de apoyo

table tabla

technical directions instrucciones técnicas

topic tema

typeface tipo de letra

Venn diagram diagrama de Venn

visuals fotos e ilustraciones

Analyzing Text Features

Reading a Magazine Article

A magazine article is designed to catch and hold your interest. You will get the most from your reading if you recognize the special features of a magazine page and learn how to use them. Look at the sample magazine article as you read each strategy below.

A Read the **title** to get an idea of what the article is about. Scan any other **headings** to see how information in the article is organized.

B As you read, notice any **quotations.** Who is quoted? Is the person a reliable source on the subject?

C Notice information set in special type, such as **italics** or **boldface**. For example, look at the caption in the article that is set in italic type.

D Study **visuals**, such as charts, graphs, pictures, maps, and bulleted lists. Visuals add important information and bring the topic to life.

Analizar las características del texto

Leer un artículo de una revista

Un artículo de una revista se diseña para captar y mantener el interés. Sacarás el mayor provecho de la lectura si reconoces las características especiales de una página de una revista y aprendes a usarlas. Fíjate en el artículo de la revista del ejemplo a medida que leas las estrategias siguientes.

A Lee el **título** para tener una idea de lo que trata el artículo. Lee rápidamente los otros **subtítulos** para ver cómo se organiza la información del artículo.

B A medida que lees, fíjate en las **citas**. ¿De quién es la cita? ¿Es la persona una fuente confiable con respecto al tema?

C Fíjate en la información escrita con letra diferente, como **cursiva** o **negrita**. Por ejemplo, fíjate que la leyenda gráfica del artículo está escrita en cursiva.

D Observa los **datos visuales**, como tablas, gráficas, fotografías, mapas y listas. Los datos visuales añaden información importante y dan vida al tema.

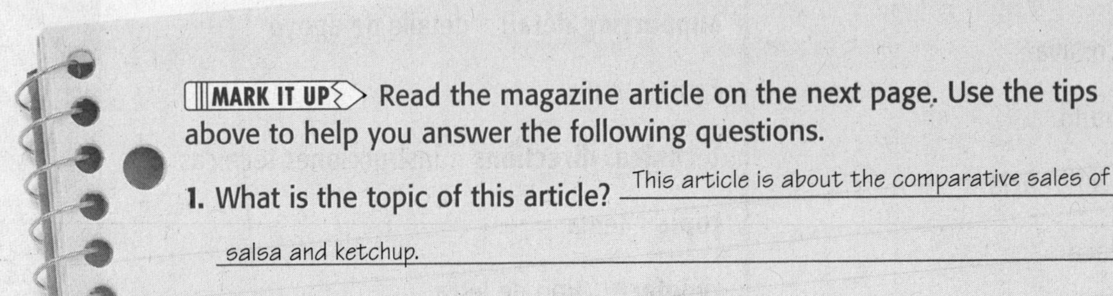

MARK IT UP Read the magazine article on the next page. Use the tips above to help you answer the following questions.

1. What is the topic of this article? *This article is about the comparative sales of salsa and ketchup.*

2. Underline the name and title of the person who speaks for Marcus Condiments.

3. Do you think the spokesperson for Restivo Tomato Products is a reliable source of information on salsa? Why or why not?

   Yes, because she's a marketing manager for a major salsa maker.

4. Circle the caption set in italic type.

5. Draw a box around the visual that compares the sales of ketchup and salsa.

A

SALSA AND KETCHUP BATTLE IT OUT FOR TOP SAUCE

When you want to add a little spice to your snack or supper, do you reach for the salsa or the ketchup? Until recently, sales figures showed that more people grabbed the ketchup bottle, slathering the tomato sauce on their hamburgers, hot dogs, French fries, mashed potatoes, scrambled eggs, green beans, and almost anything else you can imagine. Elvis Presley even used it as a topping for sweet potato pie.

In 1996, however, salsa moved into number one position, replacing ketchup as the nation's top tomato sauce. Since then, the two condiments have been battling it out, with ketchup frantically trying to play catch-up. And it seems to have

B succeeded. "Salsa's popularity has peaked. Ketchup is back on top," boasts Peter Harrington, chief executive of the world's largest ketchup maker, Marcus Condiments.

D

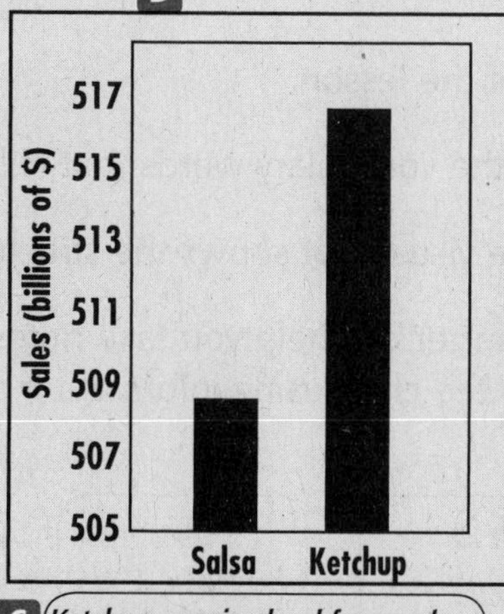

C *Ketchup regains lead from salsa.*

Salsa producers do not seem overly concerned, though. Mary Sullivan, a senior marketing manager for a leading salsa maker, Restivo Tomato Products, confidently noted that salsa is perfectly able to keep pace with ketchup. It's every bit as versatile a sauce, she says. "We're not limited to hamburgers and hot dogs." Every day, more people spoon more salsa over a whole alphabet of foods, from avocados to ziti.

To increase their slim lead over salsa, Marcus Condiments is focusing on research that shows families with children use three times more ketchup than childless households.

The salsa-ketchup war probably will not be decided any time soon. And maybe it shouldn't be. After all, to update an old saying, "Variety is the spice of life"—and of tomato sauce, too.

Analyzing Text Features

Reading a Textbook

The first page of a textbook lesson introduces you to a particular topic. The page also provides important information that will guide you through the rest of the lesson. Look at the sample textbook page as you read each strategy below.

A Preview the **title** and other **headings** to find out the lesson's main topic and related subtopics.

B Read the **key ideas** or **objectives** at the top of the page. Keep these in mind as you read. They will help you set a purpose for your reading.

C Look for a list of terms or **vocabulary words** at the start of each lesson. These words will be identified and defined throughout the lesson.

D Study **visuals** such as photographs and illustrations. Read the **captions.** Visuals can add information and interest to the topic.

Analizar las características del texto

Leer un libro de texto

La primera página de un libro de texto presenta un tema determinado. La página también da información importante que te guiará por el resto de la lección. Fíjate en la página del libro de texto del ejemplo a medida que leas las estrategias siguientes.

A Mira primero el **título** y los otros **subtítulos** para averiguar el tema principal de la lección y los temas que se relacionan.

B Lee las **ideas clave** o los **objetivos** en la parte superior de la página. Tenlos presentes a medida que lees. Te ayudarán a determinar un propósito para la lectura.

C Busca una lista de términos o **palabras de vocabulario** al principio de cada lección. Estas palabras se identificarán y definirán a lo largo de la lección.

D Observa los **datos visuales**, como fotografías y dibujos. Lee las **leyendas**. Los datos visuales añaden información importante y dan vida al tema.

MARK IT UP Read the sample textbook page. Then use the strategies above to help you answer the following questions.

1. What is the topic of this lesson? This lesson is about waves and erosion.

2. Circle the key idea of the lesson.

3. Draw a box around the vocabulary words that will be defined in the lesson.

4. Put a star next to the visual that shows the structure of a sea arch.

5. Using a graphic organizer can help you take notes on the textbook material you learn. Complete the chart using information on shoreline features from the lesson.

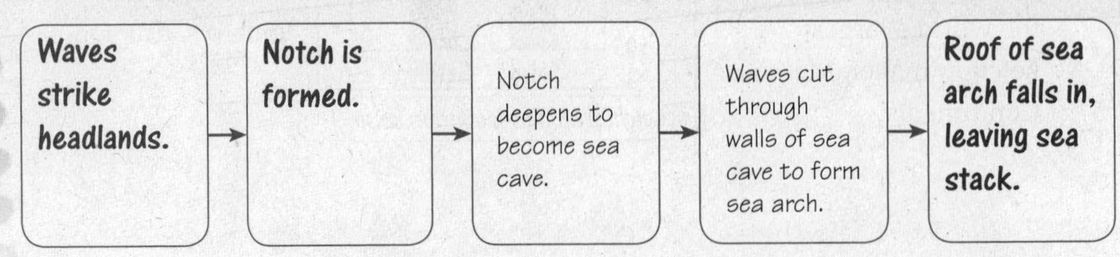

A Shoreline Features

Ocean waves change the shape of a shoreline by eroding rock materials and by depositing sediments.

Waves and Erosion

Breaking storm waves may strike rock cliffs with a force of thousands of kilograms per square meter. Such breakers easily remove large masses of loose sand and clay. Air and water driven into cracks and fissures may split bedrock apart. Sand and pebbles carried by the water abrade the bedrock. Waves pound loose rock and boulders into pebbles and sand. In addition, seawater dissolves minerals from rocks such as limestone.

When waves strike the headlands of a deep-water shoreline, they may cut away the rock up to the high-tide level, forming a notch. If the materials overhanging the notch collapse, a sea cliff results.

Cliffs made of soft materials such as soil and sand wear away very quickly. For example, waves washing up on Cape Cod in Massachusetts are carrying away materials from sand cliffs there so rapidly that the cliffs are receding at a rate of about one meter every year.

In cliffs made of harder rock materials, a notch may deepen until it becomes a sea cave. Waves may cut through the walls of sea caves to form sea arches. Arches may also form when waves cut through vertical cracks in narrow headlands. If the roof of a sea arch falls in, what remains is a tall, narrow rock island called a sea stack.

Sea caves, sea arches, and sea stacks can be seen on the coasts of California, Oregon, Washington, and Maine, on the Gaspé Peninsula of Canada, and in many parts of the Mediterranean Sea.

16.3

B **KEY IDEA**

Waves erode shorelines and deposit sediments in characteristic formations.

C **KEY VOCABULARY**

- beach
- sandbar
- fjord

BAJA PENINSULA Ocean waves have formed this sea stack and sea arch in Mexico.

D

Sea stack

Sea arch

★

Understanding Visuals

Reading a Table

Tables give a lot of information in an organized way. These tips can help you read a table quickly and accurately. Look at the example as you read each strategy in this list.

A Look at the **title** to find out the content of the table.

B Read the **introduction** to get a general overview of the information included in the table.

C Examine the **heading** of each row and column. To find specific information, locate the place where a row and column intersect.

Entender las ilustraciones

Leer una tabla

Las tablas dan mucha información de manera ordenada. Estos consejos pueden ayudarte a entender una tabla rápidamente y con exactitud. Fíjate en el ejemplo a medida que leas las estrategias de la lista.

A Fíjate en el **título** para saber el contenido de la tabla.

B Lee la **introducción** para tener una perspectiva general de la información que cubre la tabla.

C Fíjate en los **títulos** de cada fila y columna. Para averiguar un dato específico, localiza el lugar donde coinciden una fila y una columna.

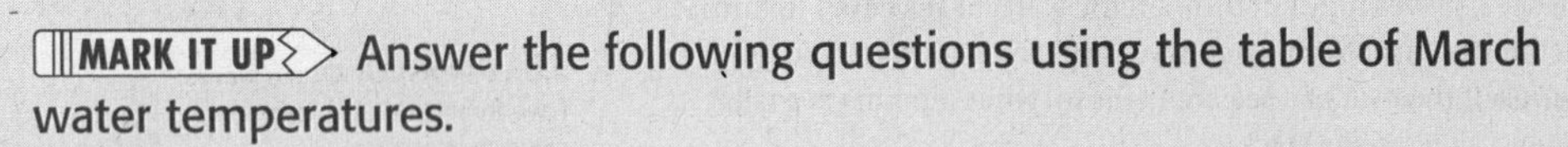

MARK IT UP Answer the following questions using the table of March water temperatures.

1. Which two beaches have the same water temperature? Circle the answers in the table.

2. What units are used to measure the water temperatures?

   degrees Fahrenheit

3. If you were planning a swimming vacation in March, what two beaches might you consider visiting?

   Veracruz, Mexico, or Honolulu, HI

B Water temperatures vary widely along the coasts of North America. This table shows the temperature of the water in March at eight beaches.

A **Average March Water Temperature at Eight Beaches (°F)**

C

Location	Temperature
Newport, RI	37
Ocean City, MD	42
Veracruz, Mexico	75
Freeport, TX	62
Oceanside, CA	58
Seattle, WA	46
Honolulu, HI	76
Juneau, AK	37

Understanding Visuals

Reading a Map

To read a map correctly, you have to identify and understand its elements. Look at the example below as you read each strategy in this list.

A Read the **title** to find out what the map shows.

B Study the **legend,** or **key,** to find out what symbols and colors are used on the map and what they stand for.

C Look at **geographic labels** to understand specific places on the map.

D Look at the **scale** to understand how distances on the map relate to actual distances.

E Locate the **compass rose,** or **pointer,** to determine direction.

Entender las ilustraciones

Leer un mapa

Para leer un mapa correctamente, tienes que identificar y entender sus elementos. Fíjate en el ejemplo siguiente a medida que leas las estrategias de la lista.

A Lee el **título** para saber lo que muestra el mapa.

B Estudia la **leyenda** o la **clave** para averiguar los símbolos y colores que se usan en el mapa y lo que representan.

C Fíjate en los **rótulos geográficos** para entender lugares específicos del mapa.

D Fíjate en la **escala** para entender la relación entre las distancias del mapa y las distancias reales.

E Localiza la **rosa de los vientos** o la **aguja**, para determinar la dirección.

MARK IT UP Use the map to answer the following questions.

1. What does this map show? It shows a sea route around South America and a sea route through the Panama Canal. It shows how the Panama Canal drastically cut the length of the sea trip from San Francisco to New Orleans.

2. How many miles is the sea route from San Francisco to New Orleans by way of the Strait of Magellan?

   15,594 miles

3. How many miles would you save by taking the Panama Canal from San Francisco to New Orleans rather than the route through the Strait of Magellan?

   10,205 miles

4. Draw a straight line from San Francisco to New Orleans. About how many miles apart are these cities by land?

   about 2,500 miles

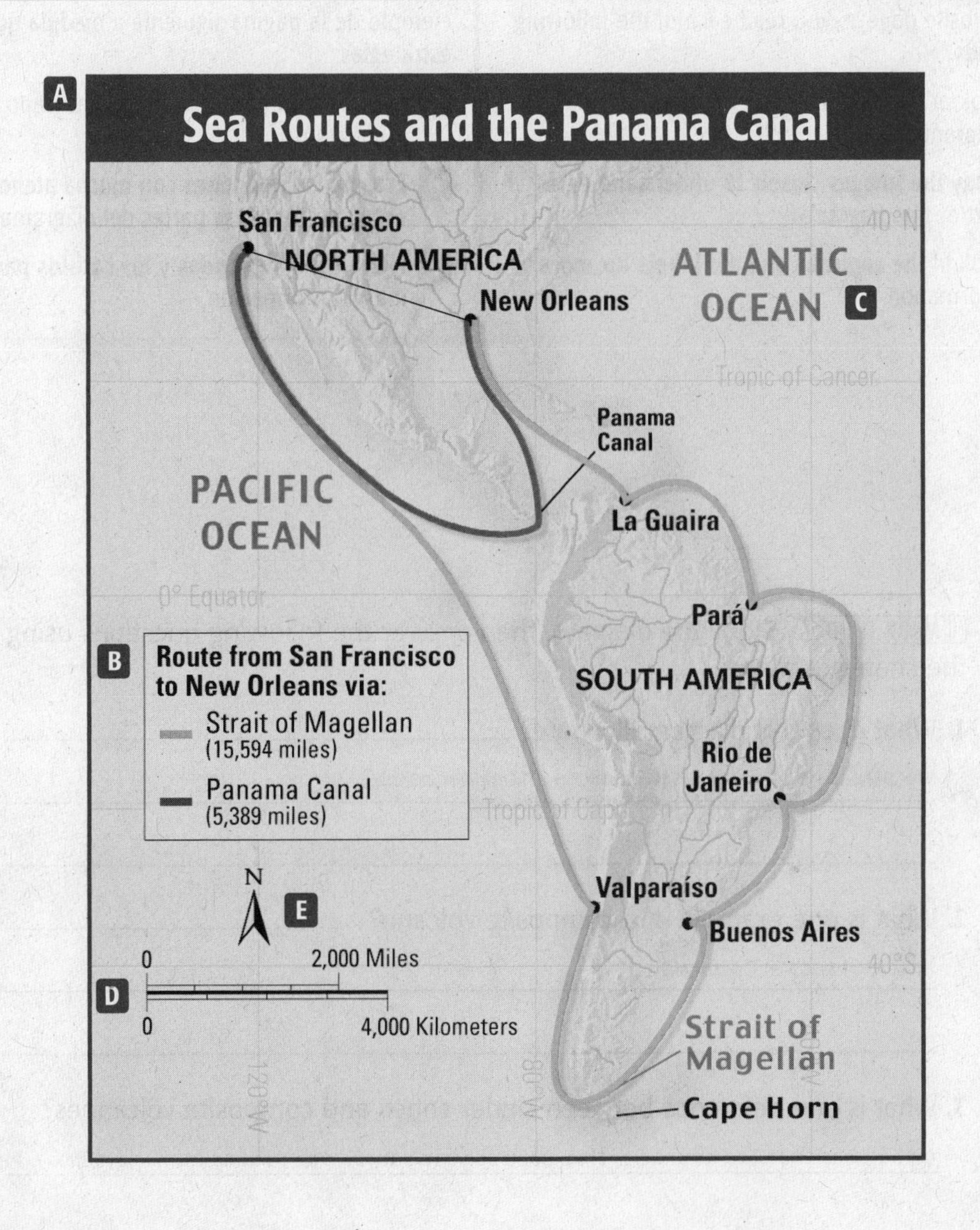
A
Sea Routes and the Panama Canal
San Francisco
NORTH AMERICA
New Orleans
ATLANTIC OCEAN
C
Tropic of Cancer
Panama Canal
PACIFIC OCEAN
La Guaira
0° Equator
Pará
B
Route from San Francisco to New Orleans via:
Strait of Magellan (15,594 miles)
Panama Canal (5,389 miles)
SOUTH AMERICA
Rio de Janeiro
Tropic of Capricorn
N
E
Valparaíso
Buenos Aires
0
2,000 Miles
D
0
4,000 Kilometers
40°S
Strait of Magellan
Cape Horn

Understanding Visuals

Reading a Diagram

Diagrams combine pictures with a few words to provide a lot of information. Look at the example on the opposite page as you read each of the following strategies.

A Look at the **title** to get an idea of what the diagram is about.

B Study the **images** closely to understand each part of the diagram.

C Look at the **captions** and the **labels** for more information.

Entender las ilustraciones

Leer un diagrama

Los diagramas combinan fotografías con algunas palabras para dar mucha información. Fíjate en el ejemplo de la página siguiente a medida que leas las estrategias.

A Lee el **título** para tener una idea de lo que trata el diagrama.

B Estudia las **imágenes** con mucha atención para entender todas las partes del diagrama.

C Fíjate en las **leyendas** y los **rótulos** para tener mayor información.

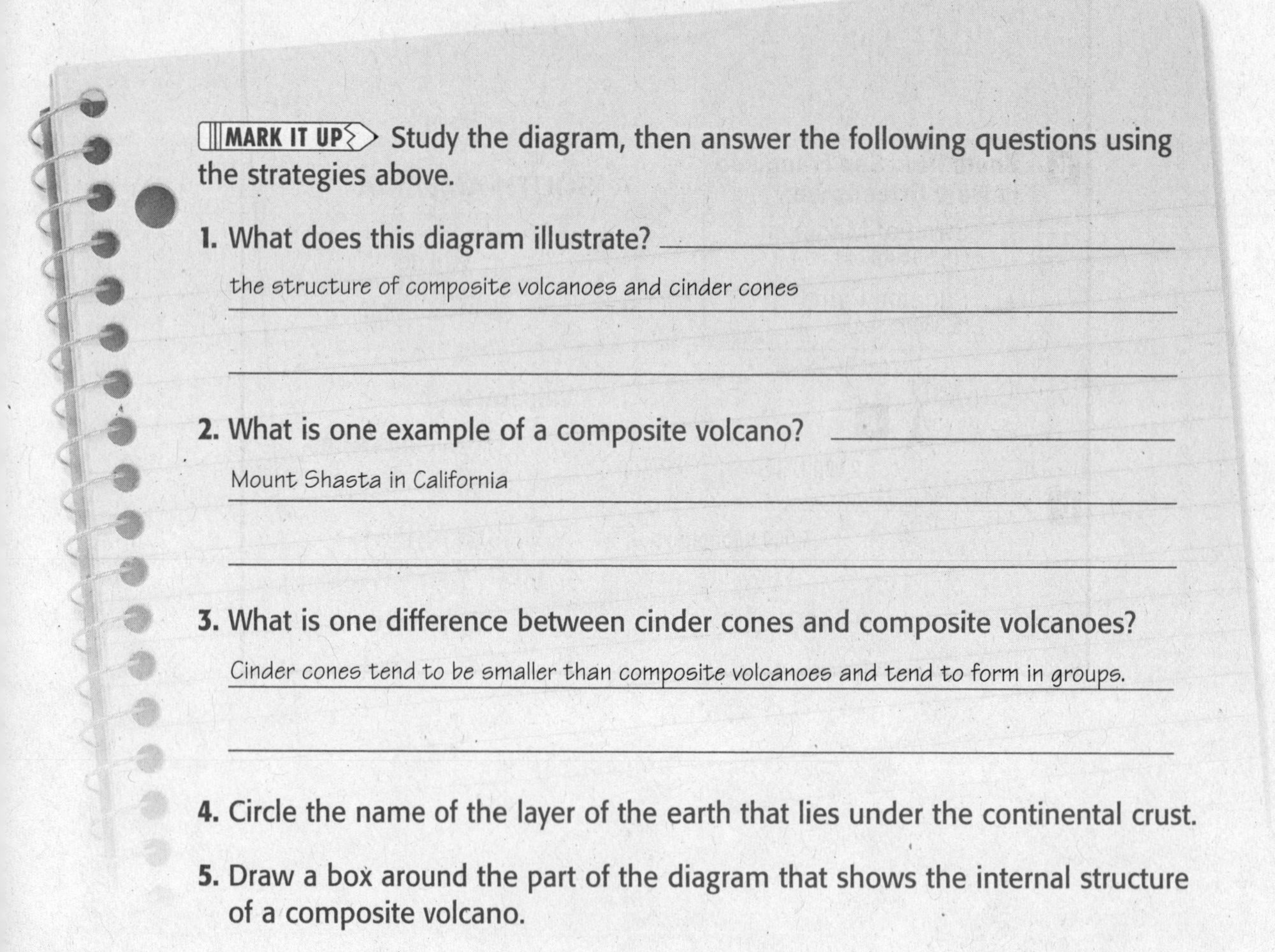

MARK IT UP Study the diagram, then answer the following questions using the strategies above.

1. What does this diagram illustrate? ____________________

   the structure of composite volcanoes and cinder cones

2. What is one example of a composite volcano? ____________________

   Mount Shasta in California

3. What is one difference between cinder cones and composite volcanoes?

   Cinder cones tend to be smaller than composite volcanoes and tend to form in groups.

4. Circle the name of the layer of the earth that lies under the continental crust.

5. Draw a box around the part of the diagram that shows the internal structure of a composite volcano.

A Volcanic Landforms

The shape and structure of a volcano are determined by the nature of its eruptions and the materials it ejects. A cinder cone, perhaps the simplest form of volcano, forms when molten lava is thrown into the air from a vent. Cinder cones, which tend to be smaller than other types of volcanoes, typically form in groups and on the sides of larger volcanoes. Composite volcanoes develop when layers of materials from successive eruptions accumulate around a vent. The diagram shows the structure of these two types of volcanoes.

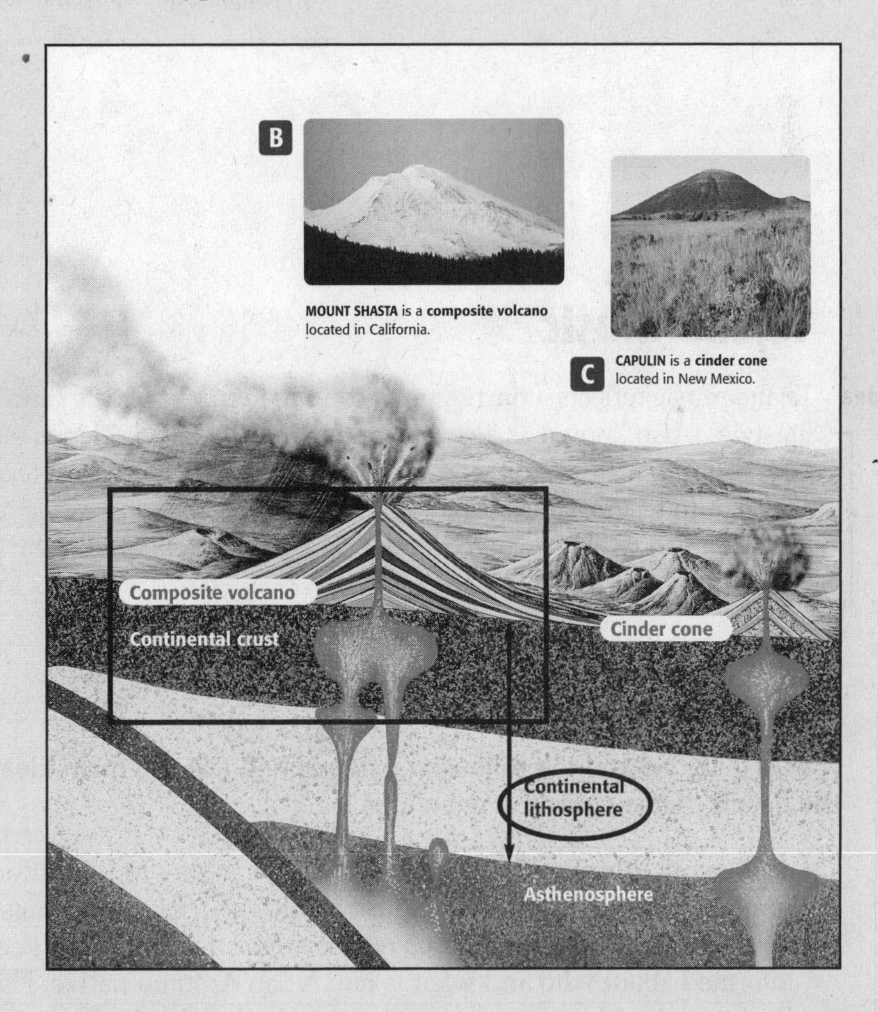

Recognizing Text Structures

Main Idea and Supporting Details

The *main idea* in a paragraph is its most important point. *Details* in the paragraph support the main idea. Identifying the main idea will help you focus on the main message the writer wants to communicate. Use the following strategies to help you identify a paragraph's main idea and supporting details.

- Look for the **main idea,** which is often the first sentence in a paragraph.
- Use the main idea to help you **summarize** the point of the paragraph.
- Identify specific **details,** including facts and examples, that support the main idea.

Reconocer las estructuras del texto

Idea principal y detalles de apoyo

La *idea principal* de un párrafo es lo más importante del párrafo. Los *detalles* del párrafo apoyan la idea principal. Identificar la idea principal te ayudará a centrarte en el mensaje principal que el autor quiere comunicar. Usa las siguientes estrategias para ayudarte a identificar la idea principal y los detalles de apoyo de un párrafo.

- Busca la **idea principal** que a menudo es la primera oración de un párrafo.
- Usa la idea principal para ayudarte a **resumir** lo más importante del párrafo.
- Identifica **detalles** específicos, incluyendo hechos y ejemplos, que apoyen la idea principal.

Tejano Music

Main idea

Details

Tejano music reflects a harmonious combination of Mexican and American lifestyles. Also known as Tex Mex or conjunto music, it blends elements of jazz, country, rock 'n' roll, and rhythm and blues. The typical tejano band, or conjunto tejano, consists of a guitar, an accordion, and a *bajo sexto*, or large Spanish twelve-stringed guitar. The performers often wear colorful sombreros and fringed jackets.

MARK IT UP Read the following paragraph. Circle the main idea. Then underline the details that support the main idea.

San Antonio, Texas, is a hub of tejano music. Many radio stations compete to bring listeners the latest recording artists and songs. On any given day, articles in numerous newspapers and magazines keep fans informed about who and what is hot. A San Antonio native, Flaco Jiménez, played an important role in spreading this lively art form around the world.

Recognizing Text Structures

Problem and Solution

Does the proposed solution to a problem make sense? In order to decide, you need to look at each part of the text. Use the following strategies to read the text below.

- Look at the beginning or middle of a paragraph to find the **statement of the problem.**
- Find **details** that explain the problem and tell why it is important.
- Look for the **proposed solution.**
- Identify the **supporting details** for the proposed solution.
- Think about whether the solution is a good one.

Reconocer las estructuras del texto

Problema y solución

¿Tiene sentido la solución propuesta para un problema? Para poder determinarlo, tienes que fijarte en todas las partes de un texto. Usa estas estrategias para leer el texto siguiente.

- Mira el principio o el medio de un párrafo para buscar el **enunciado del problema**.
- Busca **detalles** que expliquen el problema y digan por qué es importante.
- Busca la **solución propuesta**.
- Identifica los **detalles de apoyo** para la solución propuesta.
- Piensa si es una buena solución.

Lunchroom Language Tables Can Beef Up Students' Skills *by Tara Blum*

Statement of problem

Teachers, parents, administrators, and school board members are concerned that foreign language students are not getting enough practice actually using the language in conversation.

Details about the problem

In their foreign language classes, students read dialogs from their textbooks and respond to questions, but rarely get a chance to just communicate their thoughts.

Proposed solution

One way to address this problem would be to establish language tables in the lunchroom. Students taking a specific language would eat their lunch at a designated table one day a week. The only rule would be that they speak no English, just the foreign language.

Details about the solution

This plan has several advantages. First, it doesn't require any additional equipment or materials. Second, it wouldn't take time away from other classes or activities. Language students have to eat lunch just like everyone else. Finally, it would be a lot of fun.

MARK IT UP Use the text and strategies above to answer these questions.

1. Underline the proposed solution.

2. Circle one reason that supports this solution.
Answers will vary. A sample answer has been circled.

3. Explain why you think this is or is not a good solution to the problem.
This is a good solution because it would get students using foreign language without a teacher present in a fun setting. / This is not a good solution because kids would resent not eating with their friends and wouldn't follow the no-English rule.

Recognizing Text Structures	Reconocer las estructuras del texto

Sequence

Sequence is the order in which events happen. Whether you read a story or a social studies lesson, it is important for you to understand *when* things happen in relation to one another. The tips below can help you identify sequence in any type of text.

- Look for the **main steps** or **events** in the sequence.
- Look for **words and phrases that signal time**, such as *in 1845, two days later,* and *by fall of that year.*
- Look for **words and phrases that signal order**, such as *after, first,* and *meanwhile*.

Secuencia

La *secuencia* es el orden en que ocurren los sucesos. Tanto si lees un cuento como una lección de estudios sociales, es importante que entiendas *cuándo* suceden las cosas unas con respecto a otras. Los consejos siguientes pueden ayudarte a identificar la secuencia de cualquier tipo de texto.

- Busca los **principales pasos** o **sucesos** de la secuencia.
- Busca **palabras y frases que indiquen tiempo**, como *en 1845, dos días después* y *durante el otoño de ese año*.
- Busca **palabras y frases que indiquen orden,** como *después, primero* y *mientras tanto*.

MARK IT UP Read the passage about the war with Mexico on the next page. Then use the information from the article and the tips above to answer the questions.

1. Underline two words or phrases that signal time.
   Answers will vary. Possible answers have been underlined.
2. Circle two words or phrases that signal order.
   Answers will vary. Possible answers have been circled.
3. A time line can help you identify and understand a sequence of events. Use the information from the passage to complete this time line.

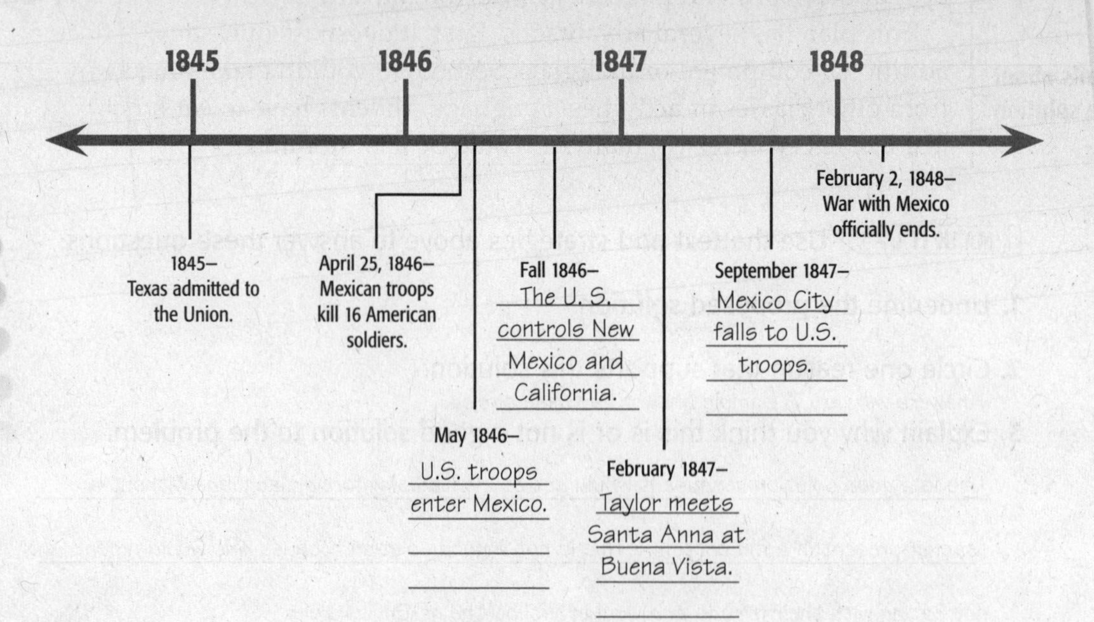

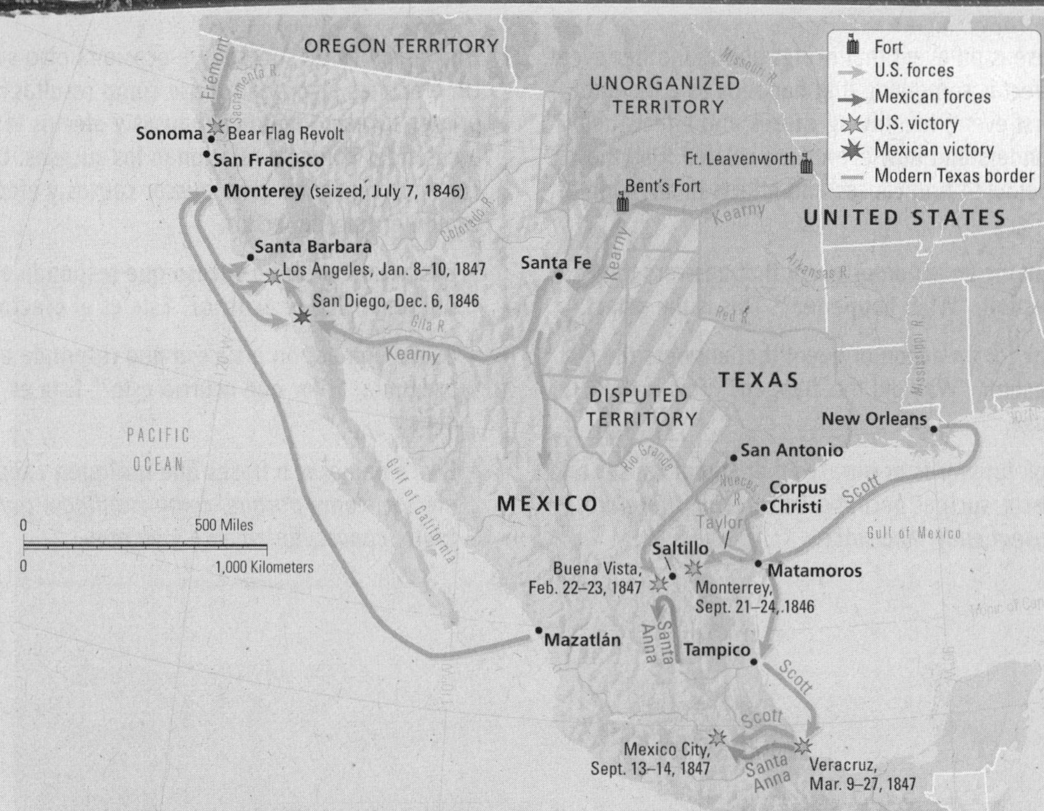

War with Mexico

In 1845, Congress admitted Texas to the Union as a slave state, despite Northern objections to the spread of slavery. However, Mexico still claimed Texas as its own. Mexico angrily viewed this annexation as an act of war.

In a diplomatic gesture, President Polk sent an ambassador to Mexico offering $25 million for Texas, California, and New Mexico. After Mexico refused, the U.S. sent troops to the northern bank of the Rio Grande. The Mexicans responded with troops on the southern bank. On April 25, 1846, a Mexican cavalry unit crossed the Rio Grande, ambushing an American patrol and killing 16 American soldiers. Two days later, Congress declared war.

U.S. troops entered Mexico in May 1846. About the same time, troops marched toward New Mexico. They took the territory without firing a shot. They then moved westward, and by fall of that year, Americans controlled all of New Mexico and California.

The defeat of Mexico proved far more difficult. The Mexican army was much larger, but the U.S. troops were led by well-trained officers. American forces invaded Mexico from two directions. First, General Taylor battled his way south from Texas toward Northern Mexico. In February 1847, his 4,800 troops met General Santa Anna's 15,000 Mexican forces at Buena Vista. Santa Anna retreated.

Meanwhile, a fierce battle for southern Mexico was raging. Seven months after Taylor's victory in the North, Mexico City fell to U.S. troops led by General Winfield Scott.

The war officially ended on February 2, 1848 with the signing of the Treaty of Guadalupe Hidalgo. This treaty gave the U.S. the present-day states of California, Nevada, Utah, most of Arizona, and parts of New Mexico, Colorado, and Wyoming. In return, the U.S. offered Mexico $15 million and protection of the 80,000 Mexicans living in the newly acquired territories.

Recognizing Text Structures

Cause and Effect

A *cause* is an event that brings about another event. An *effect* is something that happens as a result of the first event. Identifying causes and effects helps you understand how events are related. Use the tips below to find causes and effects in any kind of reading.

- Look for an action or event that answers the question, "What happened?" This is the **effect.**
- Look for an action or event that answers the question, "Why did this happen?" This is the **cause.**
- Look for words or phrases that **signal** causes and effects, such as *because, as a result, therefore, consequently,* and *since.*

Reconocer las estructuras del texto

Causa y efecto

Una *causa* es un suceso que ocasiona otro suceso. Un *efecto* es algo que sucede como resultado del primer suceso. Identificar causas y efectos te ayuda a entender cómo se relacionan los sucesos. Usa los consejos siguientes para buscar causas y efectos en cualquier tipo de lectura.

- Busca una acción o suceso que responda a la pregunta, "¿Qué ocurrió?" Éste es el **efecto**.
- Busca una acción o suceso que responda a la pregunta, "¿Por qué ocurrió esto?" Ésta es la **causa**.
- Busca palabras o frases que **indiquen** causas y efectos, como *porque, como resultado, por lo tanto, consecuentemente* y *ya que*.

MARK IT UP Read the cause-and-effect passage on the next page. Notice that the first cause and effect are labeled. Then use the strategies above to help you answer the following questions.

1. Circle words in the passage that signal causes and effects. The first one has been done for you.

2. Some causes may have more than one effect. What are two effects of the mosquito's saliva on the body of the victim?

   It prevents blood from clotting and triggers an allergic reaction.

3. Complete the following diagram showing the cause and effects of mosquito bites.

Cause: Female mosquito needs blood to nourish her eggs.

Effect: Punctures victim's skin

Effect: Injects saliva and sucks victim's blood.

Effect: Victim has allergic reaction to saliva and develops itchy bump.

Bzz! Slap!

If you spend any time outdoors in the summer, at some point you will probably find yourself covered with mosquito bites. The word *mosquito* means "little fly" in Spanish, but the impact these pesky insects have on people is anything but small.

Cause

Mosquitoes can transmit serious diseases such as yellow fever, encephalitis, and malaria. Usually, though, mosquito bites just cause people to develop raised, red bumps that itch like crazy.

Signal Word

Effect

This is what happens. Female mosquitoes need blood to nourish the eggs developing in their bodies. Consequently, they zero in on living things whose blood they can suck. Once they find a likely victim, the attack begins.

This attack is not really a bite, since a mosquito isn't able to open her jaws. Instead, she punctures the victim's skin with sharp stylets inside her mouth. The mosquito's saliva then flows into these puncture wounds. Because the saliva keeps the victim's blood from clotting, the mosquito can drink her fill. This can sometimes amount to 150 percent of the mosquito's weight.

Meanwhile, the mosquito's saliva sets off an allergic reaction in the

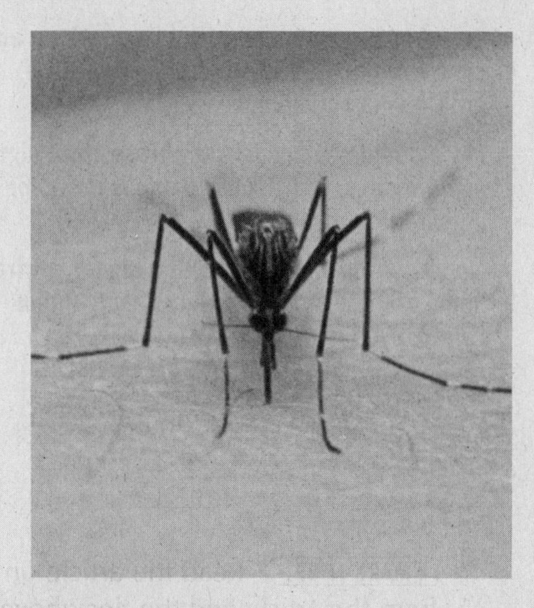

victim. As a result, the person develops the itchy swelling we call a mosquito bite. Ironically, if the mosquito finishes eating before the victim slaps or drives her off, there will be less saliva left in the skin. Therefore, the allergic reaction and itching will not be so severe.

Here are some steps you can take to help prevent mosquito bites or lessen their effect if you do get bitten.

- Don't go out at prime mosquito time—from dusk to dawn.
- Use insect repellent at all times.
- If you do get bitten, DON'T SCRATCH. Scratching just increases the allergic reaction.

Recognizing Text Structures

Comparison and Contrast

Comparing two things means showing how they are the same. **Contrasting** two things means showing how they are different. Comparisons and contrasts are important because they show how things or ideas are related. Use these tips to help you understand comparison and contrast in reading assignments such as the article on the opposite page.

- Look for **direct statements** of **comparison and contrast.** "These things are similar because..." or "One major difference is..."
- Pay attention to **words and phrases that signal comparisons**, such as *also, both, is the same as,* and *in the same way.*
- Notice **words and phrases that signal contrasts**. Some of these are *however, still, but,* and *in contrast.*

Reconocer las estructuras del texto

Comparación y contraste

Comparar dos cosas consiste en mostrar en qué se parecen. ***Contrastar*** dos cosas consiste en mostrar en qué se diferencian. Las comparaciones y los contrastes son importantes porque indican cómo se relacionan las cosas o las ideas. Estos consejos te ayudarán a entender la comparación y el contraste en las tareas de lectura como las del artículo de la página siguiente.

- Busca **enunciados** de **comparación y contraste.** "Estas cosas se parecen porque..." o "Una gran diferencia es..."
- Presta atención a **palabras y frases que indican comparaciones,** como *también, ambos, es igual que* y *de la misma manera.*
- Fíjate en **palabras y frases que indican contrastes.** Algunas de éstas son *sin embargo, todavía, pero* y *por el contrario.*

MARK IT UP Read the article on the next page. Then use the information from the article and the tips above to answer the questions.

1. Circle the words and phrases that signal comparisons. A sample has been done for you.
2. Underline the words and phrases that signal contrast. Notice the sample that has been done.
3. A Venn diagram shows how two subjects are similar and how they are different. Complete this diagram, which uses information from the article to compare and contrast *la quinceañera* and a sweet sixteen party. Add one or more similarities to the center of the diagram and one or more differences to each outer circle.

La Quinceañera	**Both**	**Sweet Sixteen Party**
takes place on girl's fifteenth birthday	mark a girl's passage to adulthood	takes place on girl's sixteenth birthday
usually includes thanksgiving Mass	include a lavish party	is more for friends than family

La Quinceañera and Sweet Sixteen

¡FELICIDADES!

Almost every culture has a ceremony to mark the passage of young people from childhood to adulthood. In the Latin culture, this rite of passage for girls is *la quinceañera*. For American girls, it is the sweet sixteen birthday party.

Comparison Although both *la quinceañera* and the sweet sixteen birthday party commemorate a girl's passage to **Contrast** adulthood, they differ in when, where, and how the occasion is celebrated. *Quinceañera* means "fifteenth birthday," and that's when the celebration is held. In contrast, a sweet sixteen party takes place when, as the name suggests, a girl turns sixteen.

The origin of *la quinceañera* is uncertain, although it may have roots in the Aztec, Maya, or Toltec cultures. It generally involves the celebration of a thanksgiving Mass followed by a lavish party for the extended family and friends. The *quinceañera* often dances a waltz with her father and other male relatives. In Mexico, girlfriends may give the celebrant a rag doll symbolizing her leaving childhood and its toys behind.

Sweet sixteen parties, on the other hand, do not include the religious component of *la quinceañera*. They

also tend to be designed for the girl's friends rather than for her family. Like *quinceañeras*, however, they often are held in hotels or reception halls and include live bands, plentiful food, and many-tiered birthday cakes.

Both *quinceañeras* and sweet sixteeners take advantage of the opportunity to look as adult as possible. They generally deck themselves out in long dresses. *Quinceañeras* often choose frilly frocks in white or pastel colors topped by hats or headdresses. Sweet sixteen dresses can run the gamut from frothy and frilly to sleek and sophisticated.

So whether a girl celebrates *la quinceañera* or her sweet sixteen, the message is the same—"Welcome to adulthood!"

Recognizing Text Structures

Persuasion

To be persuasive, an opinion should be backed up with reasons and facts. After you carefully read an opinion and the reasons and facts that support it, you will be able to decide if the opinion makes sense. As you read these tips, look at the sample persuasive essay on the next page.

- Look for words or phrases that **signal an opinion**, such as *I believe, I think,* and *in my opinion.*
- Identify reasons, facts, or expert opinions that **support** the position.
- Ask yourself if the opinion and the reasons that back it up **make sense.**
- Look for **errors in reasoning,** such as overgeneralizations, that may affect the presentation of the opinion.

Reconocer las estructuras del texto

Persuasión

Para persuadir, una opinión se debe respaldar con razones y hechos. Después de que leas atentamente una opinión y las razones y los hechos que la apoyan, podrás decidir si la opinión tiene sentido. A medida que leas estos consejos, fíjate en el ensayo persuasivo del ejemplo de la página siguiente.

- Busca palabras o frases que **indiquen una opinión**, como *creo, pienso* y *en mi opinión*.
- Identifica razones, hechos u opiniones expertas que **apoyen** la posición.
- Pregúntate si la opinión y las razones que la respaldan **tienen sentido**.
- Busca **errores de razonamiento**, como generalizar en exceso, que pueden afectar a la presentación de la opinión.

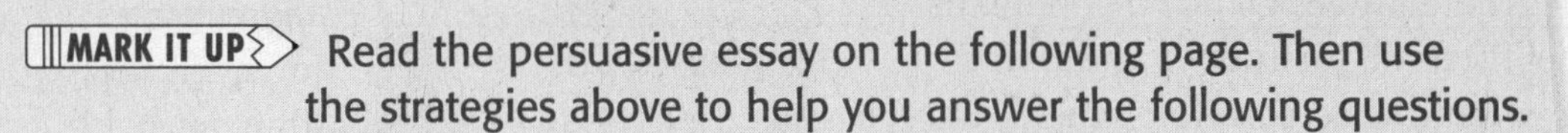

MARK IT UP Read the persuasive essay on the following page. Then use the strategies above to help you answer the following questions.

1. Underline any words or phrases that signal the writer's opinion.
2. Circle any words or phrases that signal the opinion of persons other than the writer.
3. The writer presents both sides of this debate. List the points supporting both sides in the chart below. One reason has been provided for you.

For swimming pool	Against swimming pool
1. The school has a responsibility to teach swimming. 2. Most students don't have money or time to take private swimming lessons. 3. Students' education is more important than building repairs. 4. Swimming is an excellent form of exercise.	1. Students can take swimming lessons at the health club. 2. Money must be used to repair school building.

Our School Needs to Get in the Swim *by Jorge Rojo*

This school needs a swimming pool. Swimming is an important life skill and I believe it is the responsibility of the school to provide this essential part of students' education.

The school's mission is to educate the whole person—mind and body—and to prepare students to be productive citizens. In addition to our academic subjects, we are taught how to eat right, budget our money, and drive a car. But we don't learn the water safety skills that could someday save our lives.

The community and school board obviously don't feel the way I do, however. They repeatedly have refused to fund the building of a pool. In the opinion of one board member, "Students can take swimming lessons at the local health club." Other school officials think that the school has more important needs—repairing the sagging gym floor and installing new lockers, for example.

In my opinion, these reasons are not valid. First, most students cannot afford lessons at the health club. Even those who have the money don't have the time. They're busy with homework and other activities during the school year and have to work or go to summer school during vacation.

I agree that the gym floor should be replaced and wouldn't mind having a new locker. But I believe that the educational needs of the students should come first. Swimming is one of the best forms of exercise there is. Even if knowing how to swim never saves your life, it can improve its quality. Isn't that what an education is all about?

Reading in the Content Areas

Social Studies

Social studies class becomes easier when you understand how your textbook's words, pictures, and maps work together to give you information. Following these tips can make you a better reader of social studies lessons. As you read the tips, look at the sample lesson on the right-hand page.

A Read the **title** of the lesson and other **headings** to find out what the lesson is about. Smaller headings may introduce subtopics that are related to the main topic.

B Read the **main ideas** or **objectives** listed on the first page of the lesson. These items summarize the lesson and help set a purpose for your reading.

C Look at the **vocabulary terms** listed on the lesson's first page. These terms will be boldfaced or underlined where they appear in the text.

D Notice **how information is organized.** In social studies lessons, ideas are often presented using sequence, cause and effect, comparison and contrast, and main idea and supporting details.

E Carefully examine **visuals** such as photographs, boxed text, maps, charts, bulleted lists, time lines, and diagrams. Think about how the visuals and the text are related.

Lecturas sobre diferentes materias

Estudios sociales

La clase de estudios sociales te resultará más fácil cuando entiendas cómo se combinan las palabras del texto, las fotografías y los mapas para dar información. Seguir estos consejos te ayudará a comprender mejor las lecciones de estudios sociales. A medida que leas los consejos, fíjate en la lección del modelo de la página de la derecha.

A Lee el **título** de la lección y otros **subtítulos** para saber de lo que trata la lección. Los subtítulos más cortos pueden presentar temas derivados que se relacionan con el tema principal.

B Lee la lista de las **ideas principales** o los **objetivos** de la primera página de la lección. Éstos resumen la lección y ayudan a determinar un propósito para la lectura.

C Fíjate en la lista de los **términos del vocabulario** de la primera página de la lección. Estas palabras estarán en negrita o subrayadas donde aparezcan en el texto.

D Observa **cómo se organiza la información**. En las lecciones de estudios sociales, las ideas se suelen presentar usando secuencia, causa y efecto, comparación y contraste, e idea principal y detalles de apoyo.

E Fíjate muy bien en los **datos visuales** como fotografías, textos encuadrados, mapas, tablas, listas, líneas del tiempo y diagramas. Piensa en cómo se relacionan los datos visuales y el texto.

MARK IT UP Carefully read the textbook page on the right. Use the information from the text and from the tips above to answer the questions.

1. What is the topic of this lesson? ______

   the struggle of Mexican Americans to gain equal rights

2. Circle the main idea of the lesson.

3. List two details about César Chávez's life. *Answers will vary. Sample answer: born in Yuma, Arizona, in 1927; started a union for farm workers in 1962*

4. Underline the sentence that tells what farm workers did to protest poor pay.

5. What information does the quotation in the tinted box add to the text?

   details about the poor wages farm workers like Chávez and his family earned

3 The Equal Rights Struggle Expands

C **TERMS & NAMES**
César Chávez
National Congress of American Indians
Betty Friedan
NOW
ERA

B **MAIN IDEA**
The African-American struggle for equality inspired other groups to fight for equality.

WHY IT MATTERS NOW
Nonwhites and women continue to fight for equality today.

ONE AMERICAN'S STORY

César Chávez was born in Yuma, Arizona, in 1927. In the 1940s, he and his family worked as migrant laborers in the California fields. (Migrant workers travel from place to place in search of work.) One time, they found work picking peas. The whole family, parents and six children, worked. Chávez described the poor pay for such hard work.

A VOICE FROM THE PAST

They [the managers] would take only the peas they thought were good, and they only paid you for those. The pay was twenty cents a hamper, which had to weigh in at twenty-five pounds. So in about three hours, the whole family made only twenty cents.
César Chávez, *César Chávez: Autobiography of* La Causa

In 1962, Chávez decided to start a union for farm workers. But the owners refused to recognize the union. Chávez used the example set by Martin Luther King, Jr., to change their minds.

D **Responding to Chávez's call, workers went on strike. Then Chávez asked people not to buy produce harvested by nonunion workers. The tactics worked. In 1970, 26 major California growers signed a contract with the union. It gave the workers higher wages and new benefits. The victory of Chávez and his union showed how the fight for equal rights spread beyond African Americans, as you will read in this section.**

E

César Chávez, head of the National Farm Workers Association, marches with striking grape pickers in the 1960s. (*Huelga* is the Spanish word for strike.)

A Mexican Americans Organize

The farm workers' struggle inspired other Mexican Americans. By the 1960s, most Mexican Americans lived in cities in the Southwest and California. In 1970, Mexican Americans formed *La Raza Unida* (lah RAH•sah oo•NEE•dah)—"the united people." *La Raza* fought for better jobs, pay, education, and housing. It also worked to elect Mexican Americans to public office.

Mexican-American students also began to organize. They wanted reform in the school system. The students demanded such changes as

Science

Reading a science textbook becomes easier when you understand how the explanations, drawings, and special terms work together. Use the strategies below to help you better understand your science textbook. Look at the examples on the opposite page as you read each strategy in this list.

A Preview the **title** and any **headings** to see what scientific concepts you will learn about.

B Read the **key ideas** or **objectives.** These items summarize the lesson and help set a purpose for your reading.

C Read the list of **vocabulary terms** that will be introduced and defined in the lesson.

D Notice the **boldfaced** and **italicized** terms in the text. Look for the definitions of these terms.

E Carefully examine any **pictures** or **diagrams.** Read the **captions** to see how the graphics help to illustrate the text.

Ciencias

Leer un libro de texto de ciencias te resultará más fácil cuando entiendas cómo se combinan las explicaciones, los dibujos y los términos especiales. Usa las estrategias siguientes para ayudarte a entender mejor el libro de ciencias. Fíjate en los ejemplos de la página siguiente a medida que leas las estrategias de la lista.

A Mira primero el **título** y los **subtítulos** para ver sobre qué conceptos científicos vas a aprender.

B Lee las **ideas clave** o los **objetivos**. Éstos resumen la lección y ayudan a determinar un propósito para la lectura.

C Lee la lista de **los términos de vocabulario** que se presentarán y definirán en la lección.

D Ten en cuenta los términos en **cursiva** y **negrita** del texto. Busca las definiciones de estos términos.

E Observa con mucha atención todos los **dibujos** o **diagramas**. Lee las **leyendas** para ver cómo las gráficas ayudan a ilustrar el texto.

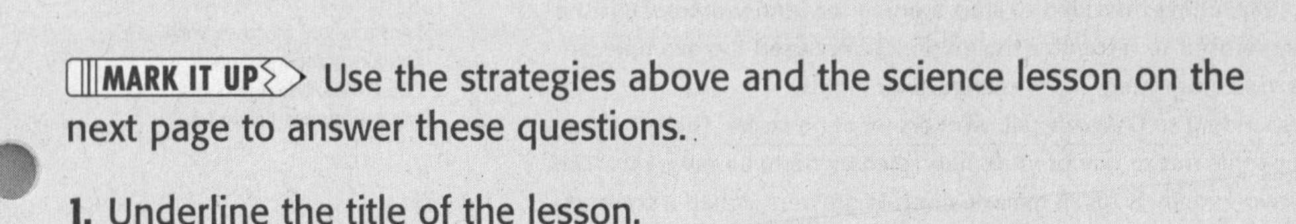

MARK IT UP Use the strategies above and the science lesson on the next page to answer these questions.

1. Underline the title of the lesson.

2. Circle the list of vocabulary words that will appear in the lesson.

3. Draw a box around one boldfaced term in the lesson.

4. Examine the graph and read the text directly above it. What idea does the graph illustrate?

   The graph illustrates how the elevation of the snow line changes in relation to a given latitude.

5. At what latitude is the elevation of the snow line lowest?

   at the North Pole

15.1

B **KEY IDEAS**

Glaciers are huge ice masses that move under the influence of gravity.

Glaciers form from compacted and recrystallized snow.

C **KEY VOCABULARY**

- glacier
- snow line
- firn
- valley glacier
- continental glacier
- ice cap

A What Is a Glacier?

About 75 percent of Earth's fresh water is frozen in glaciers. A **glacier** is a large mass of compacted snow and ice that moves under the force of gravity. A glacier changes Earth's surface as it erodes geological features in one place and then redeposits the material elsewhere thus altering the landscape.

Where Glaciers Form

Glaciers form in areas that are always covered by snow. In such areas, more snow falls than melts each year; as a result layers of snow build up from previous years. Climates cold enough to cause such conditions may be found in any part of the world. Air temperatures drop as you climb high above sea level and as you travel farther from the equator.

Even in equatorial areas, however, a layer of permanent snow may exist on high mountains at high elevation. Farther from the equator, the elevation need not be so high for a layer of permanent snow to exist. In the polar areas, permanent snow may be found even at sea level. The lowest elevation at which the layer of permanent snow occurs in summer is called **D** the **snow line.** If a mountain is completely covered with snow in winter but without snow in summer, it has no snow line.

In general, the snow line occurs at lower and lower elevations as the latitudes approach the poles. The snow line also changes according to total yearly snowfall and the amount of solar exposure. Thus, the elevation of the snow line is not the same for all places at a given latitude.

VISUALIZATIONS CLASSZONE.COM

Examine seasonal migration of snow cover.
Keycode: ES1501

E

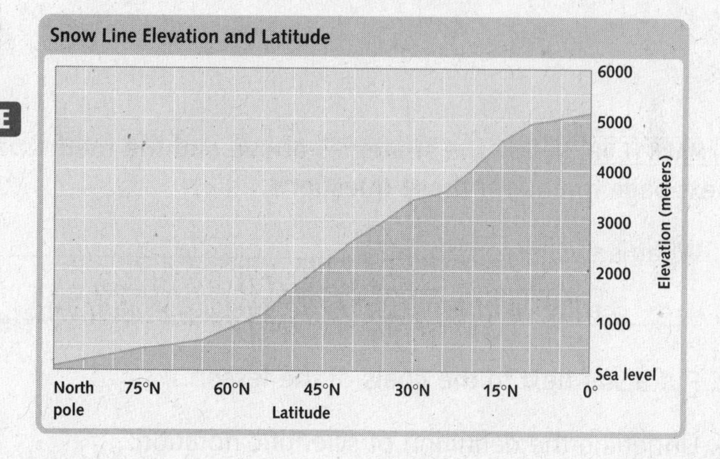

VOCABULARY STRATEGY

The word *firn* comes from a German word meaning "last year's snow." The word *névé* is related to a Latin word meaning "cooled by snow."

How Glaciers Form

Except for bare rock cliffs, a mountain above the snow line is always buried in snow. Great basins below the highest peaks are filled with snow that can be hundreds of meters thick. In these huge snowfields, buried snow becomes compressed and recrystallizes into a rough, granular ice material called **firn** (feern) or névé (nay-VAY).

Mathematics

Reading in mathematics is different from reading in history, literature, or science. A math lesson has few words, but instead illustrates math concepts using numbers, symbols, formulas, equations, diagrams, and word problems. Use the following strategies, and the lesson on the next page, to help you better understand your math textbook.

A Scan the **title** and **headings** to see which math concepts you will learn about.

B Look for **goals, objectives** or **key ideas**. These help focus your reading.

C Read **explanations** carefully. Sometimes a concept is explained in more than one way to make sure you understand it.

D Look for **special features** such as study or technology tips or connections to real life. These provide more help or information.

E Study any **worked-out solutions** to sample problems. These are the key to understanding how to do the homework assignment.

Matemáticas

Leer matemáticas es diferente de leer historia, literatura o ciencias. Una lección de matemáticas tiene pocas palabras. En su lugar los conceptos matemáticos se ilustran por medio de números, símbolos, fórmulas, ecuaciones, diagramas y problemas verbales. Usa estas estrategias, y la lección de la página siguiente, para ayudarte a entender mejor un libro de texto de matemáticas.

A Lee rápidamente el **título** y los **subtítulos** para ver qué conceptos matemáticos vas a aprender.

B Busca las **metas**, los **objetivos** o las **ideas clave**. Éstos te ayudan a centrarte en la lectura.

C Lee las **explicaciones** con mucha atención. Algunas veces un concepto se explica de más de una manera para asegurar la comprensión.

D Busca **características especiales** como consejos de estudio o tecnología o conexiones con el mundo real. Todo esto proporciona más ayuda o información.

E Estudia todas las **soluciones desarrolladas** de los problemas modelo. Son la clave para entender cómo hacer la tarea.

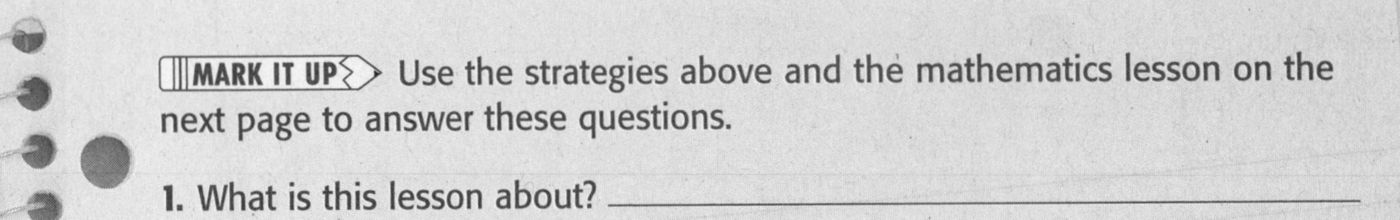

MARK IT UP Use the strategies above and the mathematics lesson on the next page to answer these questions.

1. What is this lesson about?

   using scientific notation

2. Put a star next to the goals of the lesson.

3. Underline the definition of scientific notation.

4. Circle the explanations of how to rewrite numbers in decimal form.

5. What practical application does scientific notation have in the real world?

   It is used to describe and solve problems that involve large numbers, such as the amount of water annually discharged by the Amazon River.

EXPLORING DATA AND STATISTICS

8.4 Scientific Notation A

GOAL 1 USING SCIENTIFIC NOTATION

A number is written in **scientific notation** if it is of the form $c \times 10^n$, where $1 \le c < 10$ and n is an integer. C

B *What you should learn*

GOAL 1 Use scientific notation to represent numbers.

GOAL 2 Use scientific notation to describe **real-life** situations, such as the price per acre of the Alaska purchase in **Example 6**.

D *Why you should learn it*

▼ To solve **real-life** problems, such as finding the amount of water discharged by the Amazon River each year in **Example 5**.

ACTIVITY Developing Concepts

Investigating Scientific Notation

1. Rewrite each number in decimal form.

   a. 6.43×10^4 b. 3.072×10^6 c. 4.2×10^{-2} d. 1.52×10^{-3}

2. Describe a general rule for writing the decimal form of a number given in scientific notation. How many places do you move the decimal point? Do you move the decimal point left or right?

EXAMPLE 1 *Rewriting in Decimal Form*

Rewrite in decimal form.

a. 2.834×10^2 b. 4.9×10^5 c. 7.8×10^{-1} d. 1.23×10^{-6}

SOLUTION E

a. $2.834 \times 10^2 = 283.4$ **Move decimal point right 2 places.**

b. $4.9 \times 10^5 = 490{,}000$ **Move decimal point right 5 places.**

c. $7.8 \times 10^{-1} = 0.78$ **Move decimal point left 1 place.**

d. $1.23 \times 10^{-6} = 0.00000123$ **Move decimal point left 6 places.**

EXAMPLE 2 *Rewriting in Scientific Notation*

a. $34{,}690 = 3.469 \times 10^4$ **Move decimal point left 4 places.**

b. $1.78 = 1.78 \times 10^0$ **Move decimal point 0 places.**

c. $0.039 = 3.9 \times 10^{-2}$ **Move decimal point right 2 places.**

d. $0.000722 = 7.22 \times 10^{-4}$ **Move decimal point right 4 places.**

e. $5{,}600{,}000{,}000 = 5.6 \times 10^9$ **Move decimal point left 9 places.**

Reading an Application

To get a part-time job or to register for summer camp or classes at the local community center, you will have to fill out an application. Being able to understand the format of an application will help you fill it out correctly.

A **Begin at the top.** Scan the application to understand the different sections.

B Look for special **instructions for filling out** the application.

C Note any **request for materials** or **special information** that must be included with the application.

D Watch for **sections you don't have to fill in** or **questions you don't have to answer.**

E Look for difficult or confusing words or abbreviations. Look them up in a dictionary or ask someone what they mean.

Leer una solicitud

Para solicitar un trabajo de medio tiempo, matricularte para un campamento de verano o para asistir a clase en un centro de la comunidad local, vas a tener que rellenar una solicitud. Poder entender el formato de una solicitud te ayudará a rellenarla correctamente.

A **Empieza desde el principio.** Lee rápidamente la solicitud para entender las diferentes secciones.

B Busca **instrucciones especiales para rellenar** la solicitud.

C Toma nota de cualquier **petición de documentos** o **información especial** que se tenga que entregar con la solicitud.

D Ten cuidado con **las secciones que no tienes que rellenar** o **las preguntas que no tienes que responder.**

E Busca palabras o abreviaciones que sean difíciles o confusas. Búscalas en el diccionario o preguntale a alguien lo que significan.

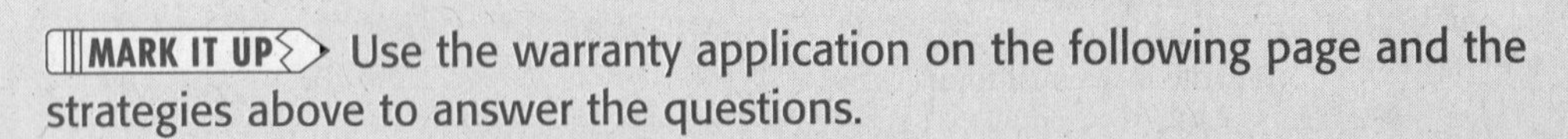

MARK IT UP Use the warranty application on the following page and the strategies above to answer the questions.

1. Why is it important to fill out and mail this warranty application?

   The completed warranty serves as confirmation of ownership in the event of theft and guarantees that the customer receives special offers and benefits.

2. Underline the phrase that tells when the application must be mailed.

3. What information about the product do you have to supply?

   date of purchase and retail price

4. Circle the part of the application that you do not have to fill out.

5. What document must you use to fill out this application? *sales receipt*

6. **ASSESSMENT PRACTICE** Circle the letter of the correct answer.
   What amount should you include in the box marked "retail price paid"?
   A. the total amount you paid for the product
   B. the total amount you paid minus the cost of the maintenance agreement
   (C.) the price marked on the product
   D. the cost of extra charges, such as delivery and installation

A Congratulations on investing in a Calvo product. Your decision will reward you for years to come. Please complete your Warranty Registration Card to ensure that you receive all the privileges and protection that come with your purchase.

Your completed Warranty Registration Card serves as confirmation of ownership in the event of theft.

Returning the attached card guarantees you'll receive all the special offers for which your purchase makes you eligible.

DETACH AND MAIL PORTION BELOW.

USA Limited Warranty Registration	
123456 XXXX	ABCDEFG7654321
MODEL NUMBER	SERIAL NUMBER

Registering your product ensures that you receive all of the benefits you are entitled to as a Calvo customer. Complete the information below in ink, and drop this card in the nearest mailbox.

B **IMPORTANT - RETURN WITHIN TEN DAYS**

Date of Purchase

Your Name
First
Initial
Last

Address
Street
Apt. #
City
State
ZIP Code

C **Retail Price Paid** **$** **.00**
(Excluding sales tax, maintenance agreement, delivery, installation, and trade-in allowance.) **E**

D **Your Phone Number** (optional)
Area Code
Phone Number

CALVO

Reading Beyond the Classroom

Reading a Public Notice

Public notices can tell you about events in your community and give you valuable information about safety. When you read a public notice, follow these tips. Each tip relates to a specific part of the notice on the next page.

A Read the notice's **title,** if it has one. The title often gives the main idea or purpose of the notice.

B See if there is a logo, credit, or other way of telling **who created the notice.**

C Ask yourself, **"Who should read this notice?"** If the information in it might be important to you or someone you know, then you should pay attention to it.

D Look for **contact information** that indicates where to get answers to questions.

Leer fuera del salón de clase

Leer un aviso público

Los avisos públicos te informan de acontecimientos de tu comunidad y te dan una información valiosa sobre la seguridad. Cuando leas un aviso público, sigue estos consejos. Cada pista se relaciona con una parte específica del aviso de la siguiente página.

A Lee el **título** del aviso, si lo tiene. El título suele dar la idea principal o el propósito del aviso.

B Fíjate si hay un logotipo, rótulo u otra manera de saber **quién redactó el aviso.**

C Pregúntate, **"¿Quién debe leer este aviso?"** Si la información del aviso puede ser importante para ti o para alguien que conoces, entonces debes prestarle atención.

D Busca la **información para ponerse en contacto** que indica dónde conseguir respuesta a cualquier pregunta.

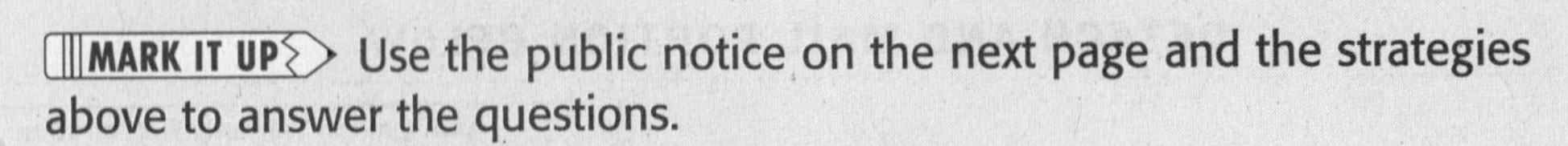

MARK IT UP Use the public notice on the next page and the strategies above to answer the questions.

1. What is the purpose of this notice?

to encourage people to get flu shots

2. Circle the name of the organization that created the notice.

3. Who does this notice apply to?

anyone who wants to prevent the flu

4. Make a star next to the contact information.

5. Who should get a flu shot earliest, health care workers or healthy people between the ages of 50 and 64?

health care workers

6. ASSESSMENT PRACTICE Circle the letter of the correct answer.
The best time to get a flu shot is

A. your doctor's decision
(B.) October or November
C. October
D. December

A

When should *YOU* get your flu shot?

C

	OCT / NOV	DEC or later
People at high risk of severe illness ✓ **65 years old or older**—Even in you're in great health ✓ **Children 6–23 months old**—Children younger than 2 years old have one of the highest rates of hospitalizations from influenza ✓ **Adults and children with a chronic health condition**—Such as heart disease, diabetes, kidney disease, asthma, cancer, and HIV/AIDS ✓ **More than 3 months pregnant during flu season**—Typically November through March	**Best Time**	**Not too late!**
People who can give the flu to those at high risk ✓ **Household contact or caregiver of someone at high risk** ✓ **Health care workers** ✓ **Household contact or caregiver of a child under 2 years old**—Infants younger than 6 months old can't get a flu shot, but they can get the flu	**Best Time**	**Not too late!**
Your child's very first flu shot ✓ **Children 6 months–8 years old** getting the very first flu shot need a booster shot one month after the first dose of vaccine	**Best Time**	**Not too late!**
Healthy people 50–64 years old	**Best Time** (NOV)	**Not too late!**
Anyone who wants to prevent the flu	**Best Time** (NOV)	**Not too late!**

A flu shot is your best protection against the flu.

For more information: Ask your health care provider or call the CDC Immunization Hotline.

English: 1-800-232-2522 ★ Español: 1-800-232-0233 www.cdc.gov/nip/flu

D

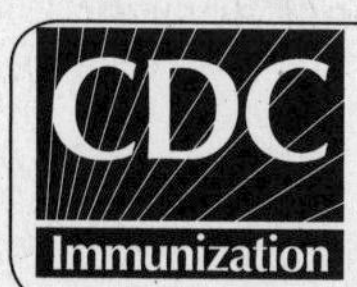

B

SAFER • HEALTHIER • PEOPLE

Fight the Flu

Reading a Web Page

When you research information for a report or project, you may use the World Wide Web. Once you find the site you want, the strategies below will help you find the facts and details you need. Look at the sample Web page on the right as you read each of the strategies.

A Notice the page's **Web address,** or URL. Write down the Web address or bookmark it if you think you might return to the page at another time or if you need to add it to a list of sources.

B Read the **title** of the page. The title usually tells you what topics the page covers.

C Look for **menu bars** along the top, bottom, or side of the page. These guide you to other parts of the site that may be useful.

D Notice any **links** to other parts of the site or to related pages. Links are often highlighted in color or underlined.

E Many sites have a link that allows you to **contact** the creators with questions or feedback.

F Use a **search feature** to find out quickly whether the information you want to locate appears anywhere on the site.

Leer una página web

Cuando buscas información para un informe o proyecto, puede que uses la Red. Una vez que has encontrado el sitio que quieres, las estrategias siguientes te ayudarán a encontrar los hechos y los detalles que necesitas. Mira el ejemplo de una página web de la derecha a medida que leas las estrategias.

A Fíjate en la **dirección de la página web** o URL. Anota la dirección de la página o guárdala en el archivo de favoritos si piensas que puedes usar la página otra vez o si necesitas añadirla a una lista de recursos.

B Lee el **título** de la página. El título normalmente indica qué temas cubre la página.

C Busca las **barras del menú** en la parte superior, inferior o lateral de la página. Éstas te llevarán a otras partes del sitio que pueden serte útiles.

D Fíjate en los **enlaces** con otras partes del sitio o páginas relacionadas. Los enlaces suelen estar marcados con otro color o subrayados.

E Muchos sitios tienen un enlace que te permite **ponerte en contacto** con los creadores para hacer preguntas o dar tu opinión.

F Utiliza el **sistema de búsqueda** para averiguar rápidamente si la información que quieres localizar aparece en alguna parte del sitio.

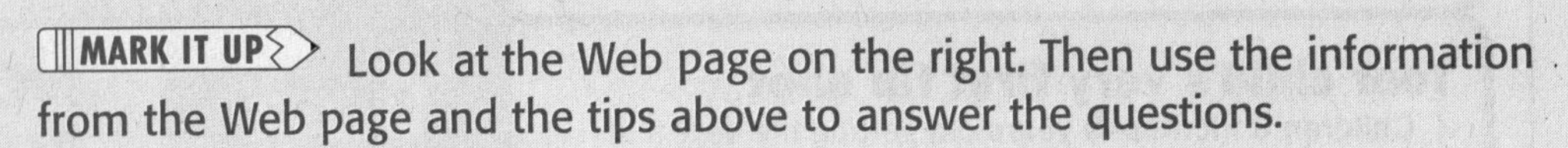

MARK IT UP Look at the Web page on the right. Then use the information from the Web page and the tips above to answer the questions.

1. Circle the Web address of this site.

2. Draw boxes around two places you can search the site to see if it contains the information you need.

3. What is the name of the president of NLN? Carlos Vásquez

4. Put a star by the link you should click on to make an online contribution to NLN.

5. **ASSESSMENT PRACTICE** Circle the letter of the best answer.
This site is designed to give information about
(A.) issues of interest to Latinos
B. Latino education
C. raising Latino children
D. politicians Latinos should vote for

L-Net
Back
Forward
Reload
Home
Images
Print
Security
Stop
L
Location:
http://www.natlatnet.org
A
C
About NLN
Resource Center
Contact Us
E
Search
National Latino Network
B
President's Corner
Carlos Vásquez
Policy Issues
Census
Civil Rights
Education
Farm Workers
Foreign Policy
Health
Housing & Development
Immigration
Social Security
Web site Features
What's New?
learning links
Quick clicks
NLN Mission
Job Opportunities
President's Bio
INSTITUTE FOR LATINO HEALTH
Affiliate Locator
Press Room
Headline News
Press Releases
Sign Up for NLN News
Support NLN
Join Online
Web site Search
F
The Archives
Special Events
NLN Awards
Southwest Conference
D

Reading Technical Directions

Reading technical directions will help you understand how to use the products you buy. Use the following tips to help you read a variety of technical directions.

A Look carefully at any **diagrams** or **other images** of the product.

B **Read all the directions** carefully at least once before using the product.

C Notice **headings** or **lines** that separate one section from another.

D Look for **numbers, letters,** or **bullets** that give the steps in sequence.

E Watch for **warnings** or **notes** with more information.

Leer instrucciones técnicas

Leer instrucciones técnicas te ayudará a entender a usar los productos que compras. Usa los consejos siguientes para ayudarte a leer una variedad de instrucciones técnicas.

A Fíjate muy bien en cualquier **diagrama** u **otras imágenes** del producto.

B **Lee todas las instrucciones** atentamente por lo menos una vez antes de usar el producto.

C Fíjate en los **títulos** o las **líneas** que separen una sección de otra.

D Busca **números, letras** o **símbolos** que ordenen los pasos en secuencia.

E Presta atención a las **advertencias** o **notas** que contengan más información.

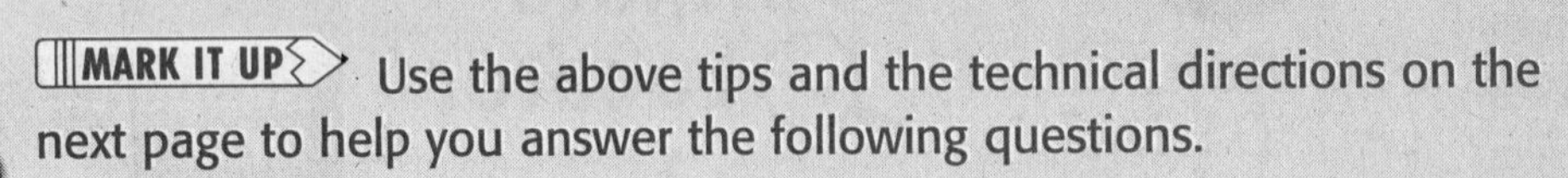

MARK IT UP Use the above tips and the technical directions on the next page to help you answer the following questions.

1. What kind of battery do you need for the clock?

   a 1.5 volt battery

2. How do you know if the time displayed is AM or PM? Circle the answer on the next page.

3. Underline the steps to follow in setting the alarm.

4. How long will the alarm sound if you don't turn it off?

   60 seconds

5. **ASSESSMENT PRACTICE** Circle the letter of the correct answer. Which of the following is NOT a safe place to set up the clock radio?

   A. on a stable, flat desk
   (**B.**) in the bathroom
   C. away from open windows
   D. on a bedside table

B **Alarm Clock Radio**
INSTRUCTIONS FOR USE

A

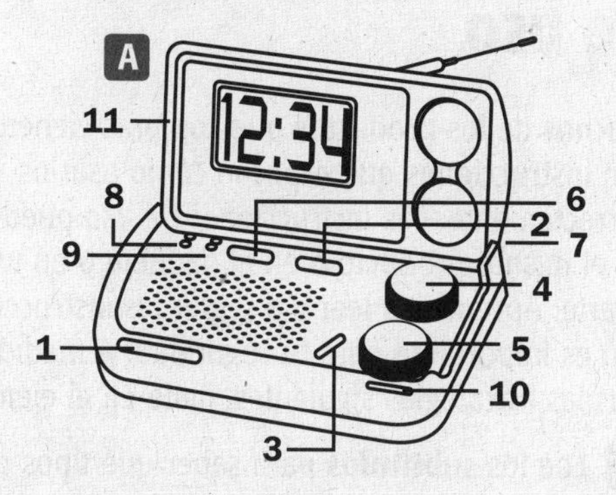

1. SNOOZE/LIGHT BUTTON
2. FUNCTION SWITCH
3. BAND SWITCH
4. TUNING CONTROL
5. VOLUME CONTROL
6. TIME/ALARM SET SWITCH
7. BATTERY DOOR (RADIO)
8. HOUR BUTTON
9. MINUTE BUTTON
10. EJECT BUTTON
11. BATTERY HOLDER (CLOCK)

BATTERIES
FOR RADIO:
To insert batteries, remove the BATTERY DOOR (7) and insert 2 AAA batteries, observing the correct position of the polarity.

FOR CLOCK:
Pull out the BATTERY HOLDER (11). Use a 1.5 volt battery and place with positive electrode facing front. Reinsert battery holder.

C **HOW TO PLAY THE RADIO**
- Press the EJECT BUTTON (10) to open lid.
- Turn the FUNCTION SWITCH (2) TO "ON" position.
- Use the BAND SWITCH (3) to select broadcasting band (AM or FM).
- Turn the TUNING CONTROL knob (4) to select the listening station.

D **TO SET THE TIME**
- Slide the TIME/ALARM SET SWITCH (6) to the "T.SET" position.
- Depress the HOUR BUTTON (8) until the correct hour is displayed. Be careful to set time to AM or PM as required. When PM time is registered, a "P" will apppear on the display.
- Depress the MINUTE BUTTON (9) until the correct minute is reached.

TO SET THE ALARM
- Slide the TIME/ALARM SET SWITCH (6) to the "AL.SET" position. "AL" indicator will appear on the display.
- Depress the HOUR BUTTON (8) until the desired alarm hour is displayed. Be careful to correctly set alarm to AM or PM as required. When PM time is registered, a "P" will appear on the display.
- Depress the MINUTE BUTTON (9) until the desired alarm time is reached.

WAKE TO ALARM
- Set the FUNCTION SWITCH (2) TO "ALARM" position. When the desired alarm time is reached, you will hear a sequential "BEEP" alarm for 60 seconds.
- To shut the alarm off temporarily, press the SNOOZE/LIGHT BUTTON (1) once. The alarm will stop for 4 minutes, then come on again.
- To stop the alarm completely, set the FUNCTION SWITCH (2) to "OFF" position.

WAKE TO MUSIC
- Set the FUNCTION SWITCH (2) TO "AUTO" position.
- The radio will turn on automatically at your desired alarm time.

SAFETY PRECAUTIONS **E**
- Do not place the unit near a moisture environment, such as a bathtub, kitchen, sink, etc. The unit should be well protected from rain, dew, condensation, or any form of dampness.
- Do not place the unit on surfaces with strong vibration. Place the unit only on flat, stable, and level surfaces.

Product Information: Directions for Use

Many of the products you buy come with instructions that tell you how to use them correctly. Directions for use may appear on the product itself, on its packaging, or on a separate insert. Learning to read and follow directions for use is important for your safety. As you read each strategy below, look at the sample.

A Read any **headings** to find out what kinds of information are given with the product.

B Read the directions, which usually tell you *why, how, when,* and *where* to use the product, *how much to use, how often,* and *when* to stop using it.

C Carefully read any **warnings** given with the product. The manufacturer will usually tell you what to do if you experience any problems.

D Look for any **contact information** that tells you where to call or write if you have a question about the product.

Información sobre el producto: Instrucciones de uso

Muchos de los productos que compras vienen con instrucciones que explican cómo usarlos correctamente. Las instrucciones de uso pueden venir en el mismo producto o en el paquete o en una hoja aparte. Aprender a leer y a seguir las instrucciones de uso es importante para tu seguridad. A medida que leas las estrategias siguientes, fíjate en el ejemplo.

A Lee los **subtítulos** para saber qué tipos de información se dan en el producto.

B Lee las instrucciones, las cuales normalmente explican *por qué, cómo, cuándo* y *dónde* usar el producto, y también *cuánto tiempo* se usa, *cuán a menudo* y *cuándo dejar* de usarlo.

C Lee con mucha atención cualquier **advertencia** que se dé con el producto. El fabricante usualmente explica qué hacer si surge algún problema.

D Busca cualquier **información para ponerte en contacto** que indique dónde llamar o escribir si tienes alguna pregunta acerca del producto.

MARK IT UP Use the product directions to help you answer these questions.

1. How do you use the product to cleanse your mouth? mix it with an equal amount of water and use as a gargle or rinse

2. Circle the active ingredient in this product.

3. What should you do if someone accidentally swallows this product? Underline the answer.

4. Draw a box around the number you should call if you have questions about the product.

5. **ASSESSMENT PRACTICE** Circle the letter of the correct answer. When should you stop using this product?
   - **A.** when the temperature drops below 59° F
   - (**B.**) if pain and swelling increase
   - **C.** if you have a minor abrasion
   - **D.** ten days after you buy it

Solution of Hydrogen Peroxide 3% U.S.P.

Active ingredient: Hydrogen peroxide 3% **A**

Inactive ingredients: 0.001% Phosphoric Acid as a stabilizer and purified water

Indications: For topical use to help prevent infection in minor cuts, burns, and abrasions, or to cleanse the mouth.

Directions: Apply locally to affected areas. To cleanse the mouth, dilute with an equal amount of water and use as a **B** gargle or rinse. Do not use in excess of ten consecutive days.

Warnings: **C**

- FOR EXTERNAL USE: Topically to the skin and mucous membranes. KEEP OUT OF EYES.
- If redness, irritation, swelling, or pain persists or increases or if infection occurs, discontinue use and consult a physician.
- KEEP THIS AND ALL DRUGS OUT OF THE REACH OF CHILDREN. **In case of accidental ingestion, seek professional assistance or contact a Poison Control Center immediately**.

Storage: Keep bottle tightly closed and at controlled room temperature 59°–86° F (15°–30° C). Do not shake bottle.

Questions? (888) 555-1234 **D**

Reading a Bus Schedule

Knowing how to read a bus schedule accurately can help you get where you need to go—on time. Look at the sample bus schedule as you read the tips below.

A Look at the **title** to know what the schedule covers.

B Identify **labels** that show **dates** or **days of the week** to help you understand how the daily or weekly schedule works.

C Look at **place labels** to know what stops are listed on the schedule.

D Look for **expressions of time** to know what hours or minutes are listed on the schedule.

E Pay attention to the **organization** of the information. Read across the row to see when a bus will reach each location.

Leer un horario de autobús

Saber leer un horario de autobús con exactitud puede ayudarte a llegar a tiempo adonde quieres ir. Fíjate en el ejemplo del horario de autobús a medida que leas los consejos siguientes.

A Fíjate en el **título** para saber el itinerario que cubre el horario.

B Identifica **rótulos** que indiquen **fechas** o **días de la semana** para ayudarte a entender cómo funciona el horario diario o semanal.

C Fíjate en los **rótulos de los lugares** para saber qué paradas se mencionan en el horario.

D Busca **expresiones de tiempo** para saber qué horas o minutos se mencionan en el horario.

E Presta atención a la **organización** de la información. Lee de izquierda a derecha la fila para ver cuándo el autobús llega a cada parada.

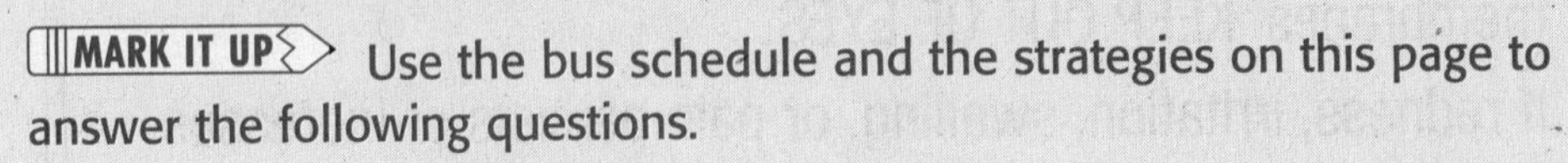

MARK IT UP Use the bus schedule and the strategies on this page to answer the following questions.

1. Circle the name of one stop on this route.

   Students should circle Quincy Station, S. Shore Plaza, Crawford Square, or Holb./Rand. Commuter Rail Station.

2. What time does the last bus leave Quincy Station for Holb./Rand. Commuter Rail Station on weekday mornings?

   10:55 AM

3. If you took the 7:25 AM bus from Crawford Square, when would you arrive at Quincy Station? *8:06 AM*

4. **ASSESSMENT PRACTICE** Circle the letter of the correct answer. If you have a 10:15 meeting at S. Shore Plaza on Tuesday, what's the latest bus you can take from Holb./Rand. Commuter Rail Station?

   A. 8:25 **B.** 8:55 **(C.)** 9:25 **D.** 10:05

A **Route 238 Quincy Center Station - Holbrook/Randolph Commuter Rail Station via Crawford Sq.**

WEEKDAY MORNINGS **B**

C Leave Quincy Station	Leave S. Shore Plaza	Leave Crawford Square	Arrive Holb./Rand. Commuter Rail Sta.	Leave Holb./Rand. Commuter Rail Sta.	Leave Crawford Square	Leave S. Shore Plaza	Arrive Quincy Station
D 5:25A	5:43A	5:58A	...	6:25A	6:29A	6:42A	7:08A
6:10	6:28	6:43	6:47A	6:50	6:54	7:07	7:35
6:25	6:43	6:58	7:03	7:20	7:25	7:38	8:06
6:45	7:03	7:19	7:24	7:50	7:55	8:08	8:36
7:05	7:25	7:41	7:46	8:25	8:30	8:43	9:11 **E**
7:30	7:50	8:06	8:11	8:55	9:00	9:13	9:41
7:55	8:15	8:31	8:36	9:25	9:30	9:46	10:14
8:15	8:35	8:51	8:56	10:05	10:10	10:26	10:54
9:10	9:30	9:46	9:51	11:00	11:05	11:21	11:49
10:05	10:25	10:41	10:46				
10:55	11:15	11:31	11:36				

Estrategias para prepararse para los exámenes

En esta sección pondrás en práctica estrategias que te ayudarán a tomar todo tipo de pruebas estandarizadas. Las estrategias se pueden emplear en preguntas basadas en lecturas cortas y largas, así como en preguntas sobre tablas, gráficas y etiquetas de diferentes productos. También practicarás con ejemplos de pruebas de revisión y corrección y pruebas escritas. Al emplear las estrategias con el material de práctica y al pensar en las respuestas podrás tener éxito en las pruebas que se te presenten.

Reading Terms found in Test Preparation Strategies

answer key clave de respuestas

antecedent nombre al que hace referencia un pronombre

compare and contrast comparar y contrastar

context clues pistas del contexto

excerpt extracto

focus enfoque en puntos específicos de la selección

graphic organizer organizador gráfico

italic letras cursivas o bastardillas que se ven inclinadas en la página

label rótulo

multiple choice pregunta de elección múltiple

open-ended pregunta de respuesta abierta

quotation cita, referencia

run-on sentence dos o más pensamientos adjuntos sin puntuación adecuada

setting ambiente

skim leer rápidamente

supporting detail detalle de apoyo

topic sentence oración temática

visual elemento visual

Test Preparation Strategies

APUNTES

You can prepare for tests in several ways. First, study and understand the content that will be on the test. Second, learn as many test-taking techniques as you can. These techniques will help you better understand the questions and how to answer them. Following are some general suggestions for preparing for and taking tests. Starting on page 180, you'll find more detailed suggestions and test-taking practice.

Successful Test Taking

Study Content Throughout the Year

1. **Master the content of your class.** The best way to study for tests is to read, understand, and review the content of your class. Read your daily assignments carefully. Study the notes that you have taken in class. Participate in class discussions. Work with classmates in small groups to help one another learn. You might trade writing assignments and comment on your classmates' work.

2. **Use your textbook for practice.** Your textbook includes many different types of questions. Some may ask you to talk about a story you just read. Others may ask you to figure out what's wrong with a sentence or how to make a paragraph sound better. Try answering these questions out loud and in writing. This type of practice can make taking a test much easier.

3. **Learn how to understand the information in charts, maps, and graphic organizers.** One type of test question may ask you to look at a graphic organizer, such as a spider map, and explain something about the information you see there. Another type of question may ask you to look at a map to find a particular place. You'll find charts, maps, and graphic organizers to study in your textbook. You'll also find charts, maps, and graphs in your science, mathematics, literature, and social studies textbooks. When you look at these, ask yourself, What information is being presented and why is it important?

4. **Practice taking tests.** Use copies of tests you have taken in the past or in other classes for practice. Every test has a time limit, so set a timer for 15 or 20 minutes and then begin your practice. Try to finish the test in the time you've given yourself.

☑ **Reading Check** In what practical way can your textbook help you prepare for a test?

Estrategias para prepararse para los exámenes

Puedes prepararte para los exámenes de varias maneras. Primero estudia y asegúrate de que entiendes el contenido que vendrá en el examen. Segundo aprende tantas técnicas como puedas para tomar los exámenes. Estas técnicas te ayudarán a entender mejor las preguntas y responderlas. A continuación tienes algunas sugerencias generales para preparar y tomar los exámenes. A partir de la página 180, encontrarás sugerencias más detalladas y práctica para tomar los exámenes.

Para tener éxito en los exámenes

Estudia el contenido a lo largo del año

1. **Domina el contenido de la materia.** La mejor manera de estudiar para los exámenes es leer, entender y revisar el contenido de la materia. Lee las tareas diarias con mucha atención. Estudia los apuntes que has tomado en clase. Participa en las discusiones de clase. Trabaja con los compañeros de clase en grupos pequeños para que se ayuden a aprender entre sí. Puedes intercambiar tus trabajos escritos con los de tus compañeros y comentarlos.

2. **Usa el libro de texto para practicar.** El libro de texto tiene muchos tipos diferentes de preguntas. Algunas pueden pedirte que hables del cuento que acabas de leer. Otras pueden pedirte que averigües por qué una oración es incorrecta o cómo hacer que un párrafo suene mejor. Intenta contestar estos tipos de preguntas en voz alta y por escrito. Este tipo de práctica puede hacer que tomar el examen sea mucho más fácil.

3. **Aprende cómo entender la información de los cuadros, mapas y organizadores gráficos.** Un tipo de pregunta del examen puede pedirte que te fijes en un organizador gráfico, como una red, y explicar algo de la información que tiene. Otro tipo de pregunta puede pedirte que te fijes en un mapa para buscar un lugar determinado. En el libro de texto vas a encontrar cuadros, mapas y organizadores gráficos para estudiar. También vas a encontrar cuadros, mapas y gráficas en los libros de texto de ciencias, matemáticas, literatura y estudios sociales. Cuando te fijes en ellos, pregúntate: ¿Qué información se presenta y por qué es importante?

4. **Practica con otros exámenes.** Usa copias de exámenes que hayas tomado antes o de otras clases para practicar. Todos los exámenes tienen un tiempo límite, por lo tanto pon un cronómetro durante 15 ó 20 minutos y luego empieza tu práctica. Intenta terminar el examen en el tiempo que te has propuesto.

APUNTES

☑ **Comprobación de la lectura**
¿De qué manera práctica puede ayudarte el libro de texto a prepararte para un examen?

Test Preparation Strategies

APUNTES

5. **Talk about test-taking experiences.** After you've taken a classroom test or quiz, talk about it with your teacher and classmates. Which types of questions were the hardest to understand? What made them difficult? Which questions seemed easiest, and why? When you share test-taking techniques with your classmates, everyone can become a successful test taker.

Use Strategies During the Test

1. **Read the directions carefully.** You can't be a successful test taker unless you know exactly what you are expected to do. Look for key words and phrases, such as *circle the best answer, write a paragraph,* or *choose the word that best completes each sentence.*

2. **Learn how to read test questions.** Test questions can sometimes be difficult to figure out. They may include unfamiliar language or be written in an unfamiliar way. Try rephrasing the question in a simpler way using words you understand. Always ask yourself, What type of information does this question want me to provide?

3. **Pay special attention when using a separate answer sheet.** If you accidentally skip a line on an answer sheet, all the rest of your answers may be wrong! Try one or more of the following techniques:
   - Use a ruler on the answer sheet to make sure you are placing your answers on the correct line.
   - After every five answers, check to make sure you're on the right line.
   - Each time you turn a page of the test booklet, check to make sure the number of the question is the same as the number of the answer line on the answer sheet.
   - If the answer sheet has circles, fill them in neatly. A stray pencil mark might cause the scoring machine to count the answer as incorrect.

☑ **Reading Check** What are at least two good ways to avoid skipping lines on an answer sheet?

4. **If you're not sure of the answer, make your best guess.** Unless you've been told that there is a penalty for guessing, choose the answer that you think is likeliest to be correct.

5. **Keep track of the time.** Answering all the questions on a test usually results in a better score. That's why finishing the test is important. Keep track of the time you have left. At the beginning of the test, figure out how many questions you will have to answer by the halfway point in order to finish in the time given.

Estrategias para prepararse para los exámenes

5. **Habla de tus experiencias al tomar los exámenes.** Después de tomar un examen o una prueba, coméntalos con tu profesor y tus compañeros. ¿Qué tipos de preguntas fueron las más difíciles de entender? ¿Qué hizo que fueran difíciles? ¿Qué preguntas parecían las más fáciles y por qué? Cuando se comparten las técnicas para tomar los exámenes con los compañeros, todos pueden llegar a tener éxito en los exámenes.

Usar estrategias durante el examen

1. **Lee las instrucciones con mucha atención.** No puedes tener éxito en los exámenes a menos que sepas exactamente lo que tienes que hacer. Busca palabras y frases clave, como *rodea con un círculo la mejor respuesta, escribe un párrafo* o *elige la frase que mejor complete la oración.*

2. **Aprende a leer las preguntas de los exámenes.** A veces es difícil averiguar el significado de las preguntas de los exámenes. Pueden tener expresiones poco familiares o estar escritas de forma extraña. Intenta hacer un resumen de la pregunta de una manera más simple usando palabras que entiendas. Pregúntate siempre, ¿Qué tipo de información se me pide en esta pregunta?

3. **Presta atención especial cuando se use una hoja separada para las respuestas.** Si accidentalmente te saltas una línea en una hoja de respuestas, ¡todas las preguntas siguientes pueden ser incorrectas! Intenta una o más de las técnicas siguientes.
   - Usa una regla en la hoja de respuestas para asegurarte de que pones las respuestas en la línea correcta.
   - Cada cinco respuestas, comprueba que estás en la línea correcta.
   - Cada vez que pases de página en el cuadernillo del examen, comprueba que el número de la respuesta es el mismo que el de la respuesta de la hoja.
   - Si la hoja de respuestas tiene círculos, llénalos con cuidado. Una raya de lápiz fuera de lugar puede hacer que la máquina dé un resultado equivocado.

4. **Si no sabes con certeza una respuesta, intenta adivinarla.** A menos que se te haya dicho que pierdes crédito por las respuestas incorrectas, elige la respuesta que pienses que tiene más probabilidad de ser la correcta.

5. **Ten en cuenta el tiempo.** Responder todas las preguntas de un examen normalmente hace que la calificación sea mejor. Por eso es importante terminar el examen. Ten en cuenta el tiempo que te queda. Al principio del examen, calcula cuántas preguntas deberás haber contestado para la mitad del tiempo para poder terminar en el tiempo dado.

APUNTES

☑ **Comprobación de la lectura**
Nombra por lo menos dos técnicas para evitar saltarte renglones en una hoja de respuestas.

APUNTES

☑ **Reading Check** What words in a multiple-choice question probably signal a wrong answer?

Test Preparation Strategies

Understand Types of Test Questions

Most tests include two types of questions: multiple choice and open-ended. Specific strategies will help you understand and correctly answer each type of question.

A **multiple-choice question** has two parts. The first part is the question itself, called the stem. The second part is a series of possible answers. Usually four possible answers are provided, and only one of them is correct. Your task is to choose the correct answer. Here are some strategies to help you do just that.

1. Read and think about each question carefully before looking at the possible answers.

2. Pay close attention to key words in the question. For example, look for the word *not*, as in "Which of the following is not a cause of the conflict in this story?"

3. Read and think about all of the possible answers before making your choice.

4. Reduce the number of choices by eliminating any answers you know are incorrect. Then, think about why some of the remaining choices might also be incorrect.
   - If two of the choices are pretty much the same, both are probably wrong.
   - Answers that contain any of the following words are usually incorrect: *always, never, none, all,* and *only.*

5. If you're still unsure about an answer, see if any of the following applies:
   - When one choice is longer and more detailed than the others, it is often the correct answer.
   - When a choice repeats a word that is in the question, it may be the correct answer.
   - When two choices are direct opposites, one of them is likely the correct answer.
   - When one choice includes one or more of the other choices, it is often the correct answer.
   - When a choice includes the word *some* or *often*, it may be the correct answer.
   - If one of the choices is *All of the above*, make sure that at least two of the other choices seem correct.
   - If one of the choices is *None of the above*, make sure that none of the other choices seems correct.

Estrategias para prepararse para los exámenes

Entender los tipos de preguntas del examen

La mayoría de los exámenes tienen dos tipos de preguntas: elección múltiple y respuesta abierta. Algunas estrategias específicas te ayudarán a entender y contestar correctamente cada tipo de pregunta.

Una **pregunta de elección múltiple** tiene dos partes. La primera parte es la pregunta en sí misma, llamada tronco. La segunda parte es una serie de respuestas posibles. Normalmente se dan cuatro respuestas posibles, y solamente una de ellas es correcta. Tu tarea es elegir la respuesta correcta. Aquí tienes algunas estrategias para ayudarte a hacer exactamente eso.

1. Lee con mucha atención y piensa en cada pregunta antes de mirar las respuestas posibles.

2. Fíjate muy bien en las palabras clave de la pregunta. Por ejemplo, busca la palabra *no,* como en "¿Cuál de los siguientes no es una causa del conflicto en este cuento?"

3. Lee y piensa en todas las respuestas posibles antes de decidir tu respuesta.

4. Reduce el número de elecciones eliminando todas las respuestas que sabes que son incorrectas. Luego, piensa por qué algunas de las restantes opciones pueden ser también incorrectas.

- Si dos de las opciones son muy parecidas, probablemente las dos sean incorrectas.
- Las respuestas que contienen alguna de las siguientes palabras son normalmente incorrectas: *always, never, none, all* y *only.*

5. Si todavía tienes dudas de la respuesta, ves si puedes aplicar alguno de los siguientes:

- Cuando una elección es más larga y más detallada que las otras, suele ser la respuesta correcta.
- Cuando una elección repite una palabra que se usa en la pregunta, puede ser la respuesta correcta.
- Cuando dos elecciones son directamente opuestas, es muy probable que una de ellas sea la respuesta correcta.
- Cuando una elección contiene una o más de las otras elecciones, a menudo es la respuesta correcta.
- Cuando una elección tiene la palabra *alguno* o *a menudo* puede ser la respuesta correcta.
- Si una de las elecciones es *Todas las anteriores,* ten la seguridad de que por lo menos dos de las otras elecciones parezcan correctas.
- Si una de las elecciones es *Ninguna de las anteriores,* ten la seguridad que ninguna de las otras elecciones parezca correcta.

APUNTES

☑ **Comprobación de la lectura**
En una pregunta de elección múltiple, ¿qué palabras podrían indicar una respuesta incorrecta?

APUNTES

☑ Reading Check What are at least three key strategies for answering an open-ended question?

Test Preparation Strategies

An **open-ended test item** can take many forms. It might ask you to write a word or phrase to complete a sentence. You might be asked to create a chart, draw a map, or fill in a graphic organizer. Sometimes, you will be asked to write one or more paragraphs in response to a writing prompt. Use the following strategies when reading and answering open-ended items.

1. If the item includes directions, read them carefully. Take note of any steps required.
2. Look for key words and phrases in the item as you plan how you will respond. Does the item ask you to identify a cause-and-effect relationship or to compare and contrast two or more things? Are you supposed to provide a sequence of events or make a generalization? Does the item ask you to write an essay in which you state your point of view and then try to persuade others that your view is correct?
3. If you're going to be writing a paragraph or more, plan your answer. Jot down notes and a brief outline of what you want to say before you begin writing.
4. Focus your answer. Don't include everything you can think of, but be sure to include everything the item asks for.
5. If you're creating a chart or drawing a map, make sure your work is as clear as possible.

Estrategias para prepararse para los exámenes

Una pregunta de respuesta abierta de un examen se puede presentar de muchas formas. Se te puede pedir que escribas una palabra o una frase para completar una oración. Se te puede pedir que elabores un cuadro, dibujes un mapa o completes un organizador gráfico. Algunas veces se te pedirá que escribas uno o más párrafos en respuesta a un comentario escrito. Usa las estrategias siguientes cuando leas y respondas a preguntas abiertas:

1. Si la pregunta tiene instrucciones, léelas con mucha atención. Fíjate en toda la información que requiere la pregunta.

2. Busca palabras y frases clave a medida que planeas cómo vas a responder. ¿Se te pide identificar una relación de causa y efecto o comparar y contrastar dos o más cosas? ¿Debes presentar una secuencia de sucesos o generalizar? ¿Se te pide escribir un ensayo en el cual establezcas un punto de vista y luego trates de persuadir a otros de que tu punto de vista es correcto?

3. Si vas a escribir un párrafo o más, planea tu respuesta. Escribe apuntes y haz un guión breve de lo que quieres decir antes de empezar a escribir.

4. Limita la respuesta a lo esencial. No incluyas todo lo que se te ocurra, pero asegúrate de contestar todo lo que se te pide.

5. Si estás elaborando un cuadro o dibujando un mapa, asegúrate de que tu trabajo sea lo más claro posible.

APUNTES

☑ **Comprobación de la lectura**
Nombra por lo menos tres estrategias clave para contestar una pregunta abierta.

APUNTES

Reading Test Model
LONG SELECTIONS

DIRECTIONS Following is an excerpt from an article entitled "The Empire of the Aztecs." Read the excerpt carefully. The notes in the side columns will help you prepare for the types of questions that are likely to follow a reading like this. You might want to preview the questions on pages 186–187 before you begin reading.

Examen modelo de lectura
SELECCIONES LARGAS

INSTRUCCIONES La lectura siguiente es un pasaje de un artículo titulado "The Empire of the Aztecs". Lee el pasaje con atención. Las anotaciones de los márgenes te ayudarán a prepararte para los tipos de preguntas que suelen hacerse después de una lectura como ésta. Tal vez quieras mirar primero las preguntas de las páginas 186 y 187 antes de empezar a leer.

from The Empire of the Aztecs

When the Spanish explorer Hernán Cortés marched into the Aztec capital of Tenochtitlán in 1519, he was amazed at what he found. Tenochtitlán, the site of present-day Mexico City, was built on two islands in the middle of Lake Texcoco. Tenochtitlán was connected to the mainland by causeways, or raised earthen roads. The city was much larger and more populous than any city in Spain. The people enjoyed a sophisticated lifestyle fueled by a prosperous economy. In fact, life in the Aztec empire five hundred years ago was remarkably similar to life in Mexico today.

READING STRATEGIES FOR ASSESSMENT

ESTRATEGIAS DE LECTURA PARA LA EVALUACIÓN

Find the author's main idea. Think about the focus of the article. What has the author set out to do?

Busca la idea principal del autor. Piensa en el tema central del artículo. ¿Cuál es la intención del autor?

Family Life The family was at the center of Aztec society. An Aztec family usually consisted of a husband and wife, their unmarried children, and some of the husband's relatives. Everyone had a role to play that contributed to the family's well-being. The husband supported the family by farming or working at a craft. His wife tended to the home. She cooked and wove cloth, which she used to make the family's clothing. Each family belonged to a larger social group called a *calpolli*. The *calpolli* was made up of closely related families who shared farmland. Its structure was similar to a small village.

Boys were taught by their fathers until around age 10. Then they attended schools established by their *calpolli*, where they received a general education and military training. Some children, especially the children of noble families, attended temple schools. There they received the religious training necessary to become priests or community leaders.

Housing The type of house an Aztec family occupied depended on where the family lived. At higher elevations, the climate required houses made of adobe, a mixture of sun-dried earth and straw. In the lowlands, where the climate was milder, houses were constructed with branches or reeds cemented together with clay. They were then topped with thatched roofs. Most homes consisted of several buildings: the main dwelling where

APUNTES

Draw conclusions How are Aztec families similar to families today? How are they different?

Saca conclusiones. ¿En qué se parecen las familias aztecas a las familias de hoy? ¿En qué se diferencian?

Notice topic sentences. A topic sentence reveals the purpose of a paragraph by telling you what the paragraph is about.

Fíjate en las oraciones temáticas. Una oración temática revela el propósito de un párrafo al decir de qué trata el párrafo.

APUNTES

the family lived and worked, a sweathouse for taking steam baths, and a storehouse.

Clothing In Aztec society, most people wore similar types of clothing. Men wore a piece of cloth that encircled their hips and a cape that was knotted over one shoulder. Women wore a wraparound skirt topped by a loose, sleeveless blouse.

As in many societies today, clothing was an indicator of social and economic status. The clothing most ordinary Aztecs wore was woven from the coarse fibers of the maguey plant. Nobles, however, enjoyed clothing made from soft cotton cloth. In addition, their clothing was often decorated with feathers and other ornaments to signal their status in society.

Diet The Aztecs dined on meat and vegetables, and some of their dishes remain popular to this day. Hunters brought home ducks, geese, rabbits, and deer. The farms of the *calpolli* provided corn, avocados, squashes, papayas, sweet potatoes, beans, and tomatoes.

A staple of the Aztec diet was the *tlaxcalli*, a thin pancake made from corn. We know it today by its Spanish name—*tortilla. Tlaxcallis* often were used to scoop up other foods. When the Aztecs wrapped *tlaxcallis* around bits of meat or vegetables, they called the result *tacos*.

Pay attention to foreign words and phrases. Foreign words and phrases will appear in italic type. Each word or phrase will be defined the first time it is used.

Presta atención a las palabras y frases en otro idioma. Las palabras y frases en otro idioma están en bastardilla. Las palabras o las frases se definen la primera vez que se usan.

The favorite beverage of the Aztecs was a drink made from chocolate. Because chocolate was made from expensive cacao beans, only wealthy nobles could enjoy it regularly.

Economy As in modern societies, the success of the Aztec empire was largely due to its economy. The Aztec economy was based on agriculture. In addition to fruits and vegetables, the Aztecs grew cotton and cacao beans and harvested latex to make rubber.

Aztec agricultural methods were similar to methods still in use today. In heavily forested areas, farmers used a technique called "slash-and-burn." They would cut down the trees and burn them, making a clearing in which crops could be planted. Where the landscape was hilly, farmers cut terraces into the hills. These terraces greatly increased the acreage of level land that could be farmed. In wetland areas, farmers created islands, called *chinampas*, by scooping and piling up the fertile mud of the wetland.

The bounty from the Aztec farmlands, along with the works of artists and craftspeople, found its way to marketplaces throughout the empire. The largest market anywhere in the Americas was in the city of Tlatelolco. Cortés himself estimated that this market attracted over 60,000 traders each day. The Aztecs traded because they had no money in the modern sense of that word. Instead,

APUNTES

Notice supporting details. What three types of farming methods did the Aztecs use? Where did they use each type?

Fíjate en los detalles de apoyo. ¿Qué tres tipos de métodos agrícolas usaban los aztecas? ¿Dónde usaban cada tipo?

APUNTES

they offered one type of good in exchange for another type—cacao beans for a richly decorated blouse, for example, or a jaguar pelt for brightly colored bird feathers.

Language The language the Aztec spoke, *Nahuatl*, belonged to a family of languages called Aztec-Tanoan. This language family included languages spoken by Native Americans, including the Comanche and the Shoshone.

The Aztecs had a written language, but it was based on pictures, not unlike the hieroglyphs of ancient Egypt. Each picture represented either an idea or the sound of a *Nahuatl* syllable. Because their written language was limited, the Aztecs used it mainly for government and religious purposes.

Think about the author's purpose. Is this article meant to inform, persuade, entertain, or describe?

Piensa en la intención del autor. ¿Se escribió este artículo para informar, persuadir, entretener o describir?

The Arts Artistic expression was important to the Aztecs. They created monumental sculptures to decorate their temples and other important buildings. Craft workers produced beautiful metalware, pottery, wood carvings, and weavings.

The Aztecs valued music and literature as well. Flutes, rattles, and drums provided a musical background for religious ceremonies. Poetry and historical accounts were handed down orally through the generations.

Religion The central focus of Aztec life was religion, and this is where Aztec society differed greatly from societies today. Hundreds of Aztec gods and goddesses presided over every aspect of human life: farming, the weather, war, fertility, the sun, the wind, and fire, to name just a few. In addition to a 365-day solar calendar, the Aztecs also had a 260-day religious calendar. This calendar helped Aztec priests decide the best time of the year to plant crops, go to war, or build new temples.

The Aztec gods demanded a great deal of attention from their followers. To appease their gods, the Aztecs held many religious ceremonies. The centerpiece of these ceremonies was human sacrifice. The Aztecs believed that the gods drew strength and bravery from the blood of sacrificial victims. Most of the victims were slaves or prisoners of war. In fact, the Aztecs sometimes went to war just to get prisoners for their religious ceremonies.

APUNTES

ANSWER STRATEGIES

ESTRATEGIAS PARA CONTESTAR LAS PREGUNTAS

Understand the meaning of *purpose*. An author's purpose is his or her reason for writing.

Entiende el significado de *la intención*. La intención del autor es la razón por la que escribe. El hecho de que una lectura sea entretenido no quiere decir necesariamente que entretener fuera la razón del autor para escribir.

Read foreign words and phrases carefully. This excerpt uses many foreign words and phrases.

Lee con mucha atención las palabras y frases en otro idioma. Este fragmento usa muchas palabras y frases en otro idioma. Asegúrate de que encuentras la que se menciona antes de elegir una respuesta.

Find main ideas. Remember that the main idea of a piece of writing describes what the author will talk about throughout the *entire* selection and not just one part of it.

Busca las ideas principales. Recuerda que la idea principal de una escritura describe lo que el autor expone a lo largo de *todo* el fragmento y no sólo en una parte.

Now answer questions 1–6. Base your answers on the excerpt from "The Empire of the Aztecs." Then check yourself by reading through the Answer Strategies in the side columns.

Ahora contesta las preguntas de 1 a 6. Basa tus respuestas en el pasaje de "The Empire of the Aztecs". Luego consulta las "Estrategias para responder las preguntas" de los márgenes para comprobar tus respuestas.

1. Which of the following best describes the author's purpose?

   A. to entertain

   B. to inform

   C. to describe

   D. to persuade

2. What is a *tlaxcalli*?

   A. a thin corn pancake

   B. a drink made from cacao

   C. a *tortilla* wrapped around meat or vegetables

   D. a social group

3. Which of the following best expresses the author's main idea?

   A. Hernán Cortés was amazed when he first saw the Aztec city of Tenochtitlán.

   B. The Aztecs enjoyed a sophisticated lifestyle.

   C. Life in the Aztec empire was similar in many ways to life today.

   D. The family was at the center of Aztec society.

4. Which of the following is NOT a conclusion you can draw about how Aztec and modern families are alike?
   A. Children went to school for their education.
   B. Parents provided for their families.
   C. Families are part of larger social groups.
   D. Relatives of the husband live with the husband's family.

Note key words. Pay attention to the key word or words in the question.

Fíjate en las palabras clave. Presta atención a la palabra o a las palabras clave de la pregunta. La palabra clave aquí es *not.*

5. Which method of farming involved clearing the forest?
   A. slash-and-burn
   B. crop rotation
   C. cutting terraces
   D. creating islands

Don't rely on memory. Each of the responses to this question is a type of farming. One of them, however, is never mentioned in the excerpt.

No te fíes de la memoria. Todas las respuestas de esta pregunta son métodos agrícolas. Uno de ellos, sin embargo, no se menciona en el fragmento. Antes de responder, vuelve a leer el fragmento y busca los métodos que sí se mencionan.

6. In what ways is the Aztec religion similar to and different from modern religions?

Plan your response. Read the question carefully. This question asks you to compare and contrast.

Planea la respuesta. Lee la pregunta con mucha atención. En esta pregunta se te pide comparar y contrastar. Busca semejanzas y diferencias y exprésalas en tus propias palabras.

Sample short response for question 6:

The Aztec religion shares many similarities with modern religions. The Aztecs recognized the existence of gods. They believed these gods would protect them if they respected and worshipped the gods. Also, the Aztecs held regular religious services and ceremonies. The most important difference between the Aztec religion and modern religions is human sacrifice. Today, people pray to their god or gods and make offerings, but no religions practice human sacrifice.

Study your response. Notice how the writer follows the same organization as the question–similarities first and then differences.

Revisa la respuesta. Fíjate cómo el escritor sigue la misma organización que la pregunta, primero las semejanzas y luego las diferencias.

Answers:
1. B, 2. A, 3. C, 4. D, 5. A

APUNTES

Reading Test Practice
LONG SELECTIONS

DIRECTIONS **Now it's time to practice what you've learned about reading test items and choosing the best answers. Read the following selection, "The Gauchos of the Pampa." Use the side columns to make notes about the important parts of this selection: the setting, important ideas, comparisons and contrasts, difficult vocabulary, interesting details, and so on.**

Práctica para un examen de lectura
SELECCIONES LARGAS

INSTRUCCIONES **Ahora vas a poner en práctica lo que has aprendido sobre cómo leer las preguntas de los exámenes de lectura y cómo elegir la mejor respuesta. Lee la siguiente selección, "The Gauchos of the Pampa". Usa el margen para tomar apuntes sobre las partes importantes de esta selección: escenario, ideas importantes, comparaciones y contrastes, vocabulario difícil, detalles interesantes, etcétera.**

The Gauchos of the Pampa

In the mythology of Argentina, no one sits taller in the saddle than the gauchos. Part expert horsemen and part outlaws, these free spirits of the Pampas played a brief but crucial role in the development of cattle ranching and agriculture in Argentina. Although the gaucho era lasted barely a century, it remains an essential part of Argentina's culture, celebrated in literature and song.

La Pampa Stretching across central Argentina from the Atlantic coast to the foothills of the Andes, *la Pampa*, the Pampa, is a nearly flat plain. It is bordered to the north by the Gran Chaco and to the south by

Patagonia. The Quechuas gave the Pampa its name. In their language it means "flat surface." Today, the region is commonly known as "the Pampas." It was onto this great plain that the Spanish introduced both cattle and horses. Soon, great herds of these animals were running wild throughout the eastern Pampas.

The Rise of the Gauchos Portuguese, Dutch, British, and French traders were eager to exploit the resources provided by the herds, namely hides and tallow, a waxy white fat used to make soap and candles. In turn, the horsemen of the Pampas were eager to help the traders because cattle and horse rustling was a profitable, if illegal, business. Thus were born the gauchos, who soon established their own culture on the plains of Argentina.

The gauchos lived simply, in mud huts with thatched roofs, sleeping on piles of hides. They formed families and had children, but their marriages were rarely officially recognized by the state or the church. Favorite pastimes of the gauchos included horseback riding and guitar playing.

Tools of the Gaucho Trade Everything about the gaucho lifestyle was geared to existence on the plains, including their clothing. Typically, a gaucho wore long, accordion-pleated trousers called *bombachas* that were tucked securely into high leather boots. A wide silver belt was cinched at the waist. A warm

APUNTES

APUNTES

woolen poncho and a brightly colored scarf completed the costume.

The gaucho's weapons were simple and effective: a lasso, a sharp knife, and, most importantly, a *boleadora*, or *bola*. The bola consisted of three long leather cords attached at one end. At the other end of each cord was a stone or iron ball. Galloping after a stampeding herd of horses or cattle, the gaucho would twirl the bola in the air and then release it, parallel to the ground, at the legs of a fleeing animal. The bola would wrap itself around the animal's legs and send it crashing to the ground.

The End of an Era Toward the end of the 18th century, many of the gauchos had become legitimate animal handlers. They were hired by businessmen who had acquired large herds of wild cattle and horses. Then, during the 19th century, large tracts of the Pampas were carved into vast ranches called *estancias* or estates. The wild animals of the Pampas were slowly replaced with purebred stock from Europe. Railroads were built across the Pampas to transport livestock and tractors replaced horses on the ranches. The gaucho lifestyle had come to an end, and the remaining gauchos were now *peones*, or farmhands.

Celebrating the Gaucho Although the gaucho lifestyle ended, the gaucho legend lives on. During the heyday of the gaucho, a rich literary tradition had begun chronicling their exploits. In 1872, José Hernández wrote his epic poem *El gaucho Martín Fierro (The Gaucho Martin Fierro)*. Fifteen years later, the celebrated gaucho minstrel Santos Vega was the subject of three poems by Rafael Obligado. As late as 1926, Argentinian writer Ricardo Güiraldes added to the body of gaucho literature with *Don Segundo Sombra: Shadows in the Pampas.*

Like the age of the American cowboy, the gaucho era was a colorful time in the history of the Pampas. Even today, the legend and spirit of the gaucho is kept alive through traveling gaucho shows, reminders of a time when the Pampas and the proud, independent people who lived there shaped the future of Argentina.

APUNTES

APUNTES

Now answer questions 1–7. Base your answers on the selection "The Gauchos of the Pampa."

Ahora contesta las preguntas de 1 a 7. Basa tus respuestas en la selección, "The Gauchos of the Pampa".

1. Which of the following best describes the main idea of this selection?

   A. The gauchos were free spirits.

   B. The gauchos played a crucial role in the development of cattle ranching and agriculture.

   C. The gaucho era lasted barely a century.

   D. The gauchos were expert horsemen and outlaws.

2. Patagonia lies in which direction from the Pampas?

   A. north

   B. west

   C. east

   D. south

3. Why did the gauchos agree to help the European traders?

   A. Cattle rustling was illegal.

   B. Cattle rustling was profitable.

   C. Cattle rustling was an outlaw's trade.

   D. Cattle rustling was not profitable.

4. Which of the following does NOT describe the gaucho lifestyle?

   A. The gauchos lived on large ranches.

   B. The gauchos lived in mud huts.

   C. The gauchos enjoyed playing the guitar.

   D. The gauchos slept on piles of hides.

5. Why was the bola an effective weapon?
   A. It had long leather cords attached at one end.
   B. It was easy to twirl and throw.
   C. It had three heavy stone or iron balls.
   D. It tripped the animal being hunted so the animal could no longer run.

6. Why does the author describe the gauchos as "proud, independent people"?
   A. because they were outlaws
   B. because they endured harsh conditions on the Pampas
   C. because they made a living successfully by their own rules
   D. because they agreed to work for others

7. Explain why the era of the gauchos came to an end.

APUNTES

THINKING IT THROUGH

The notes in the side columns will help you think through your answers. See the answer key at the bottom of the next page. How well did you do?

PIÉNSALO BIEN

Las anotaciones de los márgenes te ayudarán a pensar muy bien tus respuestas. Consulta la clave de respuestas de la parte inferior de la página siguiente. ¿Contestaste bien?

Each answer lists a detail from the opening paragraph. However, since the main idea tells about the focus of the entire selection, you can easily eliminate three of the four choices.

Cada respuesta incluye un detalle del párrafo inicial. Sin embargo, puedes eliminar tres de las cuatro respuestas fácilmente porque la idea principal se enfoca en la selección entera.

1. Which of the following best describes the main idea of this selection?

   A. The gauchos were free spirits.

   B. The gauchos played a crucial role in the development of cattle ranching and agriculture.

   C. The gaucho era lasted barely a century.

   D. The gauchos were expert horsemen and outlaws.

Skim the reading looking for the key word *Patagonia.*

Lee por encima para buscar la palabra clave *Patagonia.*

2. Patagonia lies in which direction from the Pampas?

   A. north

   B. west

   C. east

   D. south

Notice that answer choices A and C say the same thing. Answer choices B and D are opposites–a good clue that either B or D is the correct answer.

Fíjate que las opciones A y C dicen lo mismo. Las opciones B y D son opuestas, una buena indicación de que B o D es la respuesta correcta.

3. Why did the gauchos agree to help the European traders?

   A. Cattle rustling was illegal.

   B. Cattle rustling was profitable.

   C. Cattle rustling was an outlaw's trade.

   D. Cattle rustling was not profitable.

Read the question carefully. A word printed in capital letters is important to understanding the question correctly.

Lee la pregunta con mucha atención. Una palabra en mayúsculas es importante para entender la pregunta correctamente.

4. Which of the following does NOT describe the gaucho lifestyle?

   A. The gauchos lived on large ranches.

   B. The gauchos lived in mud huts.

   C. The gauchos enjoyed playing the guitar.

   D. The gauchos slept on piles of hides.

5 Why was the bola an effective weapon?

A. It had long leather cords attached at one end.

B. It was easy to twirl and throw.

C. It had three heavy stone or iron balls.

D. It tripped the animal being hunted so the animal could no longer run.

> Notice that the first three choices just describe properties of the bola. Only the last choice describes how the bola worked to bring down prey.
>
> Fíjate que las tres primeras opciones sólo describen propiedades de la bola. Sólo la última opción describe cómo funcionaba la bola para atrapar la presa.

6 Why does the author describe the gauchos as "proud, independent people"?

A. because they were outlaws

B. because they endured harsh conditions on the Pampas

C. because they made a living successfully by their own rules

D. because they agreed to work for others

> This question asks you to infer meaning. What do "proud" and "independent" mean? Which answer choice reflects the meaning of the two words?
>
> En esta pregunta se te pide hacer inferencias. ¿Qué significan "orgullosos" e "independientes"? ¿Qué opción refleja el significado de las dos palabras?

7 Explain why the era of the gauchos came to an end.

The gaucho era came to an end because Argentina was changing. First, the once wild herds were acquired by people who wanted to manage them and profit from them. The gauchos were hired by these people. Then, the Pampas was "carved into vast ranches." These ranches meant that the gauchos could no longer roam freely. Railroads were built to transport the cattle, making cattle drives unnecessary. Soon, the only way the gauchos could make a living was to work as farmhands.

> This is considered a strong response because it
> - directly addresses the question and stays focused on the topic.
> - uses supporting details from the selection, including a quotation, to make its point.
> - is written clearly, using correct spelling, grammar, and punctuation.
>
> Esta respuesta se considera buena porque
> - contesta directamente la pregunta y no se sale del tema.
> - usa detalles de apoyo del fragmento, incluyendo una cita, para explicar su planteamiento.
> - está escrita de manera clara, sin errores de ortografía, de puntuación ni de gramática.

Answers: 1. B, 2. D, 3. B, 4. A, 5. D, 6. C

APUNTES

Reading Test Model
SHORT SELECTIONS

DIRECTIONS "Warmth from the Andes" is a short informative article. The strategies you have just learned can also help you with this shorter selection. As you read the selection, respond to the notes in the side column.

When you've finished reading, answer the multiple-choice questions. Use the side-column notes to help you understand what each question is asking and why each answer is correct.

Examen modelo de lectura
SELECCIONES CORTAS

INSTRUCCIONES "Warmth from the Andes" es un breve artículo informativo. Las estrategias que acabas de aprender te pueden ayudar también con esta selección más corta. A medida que leas la selección, sigue las recomendaciones del margen.

Cuando hayas terminado de leer, responde las preguntas de elección múltiple. Usa las anotaciones del margen para ayudarte a entender lo que se pide en cada pregunta y por qué esa respuesta es la correcta.

READING STRATEGIES FOR ASSESSMENT

ESTRATEGIAS DE LECTURA PARA LA EVALUACIÓN

Find the main idea and supporting details. Circle the main idea of this article. Then underline the details that support the main idea.

Busca la idea principal y los detalles de apoyo. Traza un círculo alrededor de la idea principal de este artículo. Luego subraya los detalles que apoyan la idea principal.

Warmth from the Andes

Southeastern Peru and Western Bolivia make up a geographic region called the *Altiplano*, or High Plateau. This largely desolate mountainous area is home to one of the most economically important animals in South America—the alpaca.

The alpaca is related to the camel and looks somewhat like another well-known South American grazing animal, the llama. Alpacas live at elevations as high as 16,000 feet. At such altitudes, oxygen is scarce. Alpacas are able to survive because their blood contains an unusually high number of red blood corpuscles, the cells that carry oxygen throughout the body.

For several thousand years, the Native Americans of the region have raised alpacas both as pack animals for transporting goods and for their most important resource—wool. Alpaca wool ranges in color from black to tan to white. It is lightweight yet strong and resists moisture. Also, it is exceptionally warm. Alpaca wool is much finer than the wool from sheep. In fact, it is so luxurious that when the Inca civilization dominated the *Altiplano* region, garments made from Alpaca wool could be worn only by royalty.

Alpacas are usually sheared once each year by herders in Bolivia and Peru. Some of the wool is sold to manufacturers in the United States and Europe to be woven into cloth as soft and sought after as cashmere. The herders sell the rest to local weavers, who use it to produce beautiful shawls and other fine garments.

1 Which of the following best describes the main idea of the article?

A. Alpacas can survive at high altitudes.

B. The *Altiplano* is a high plateau.

C. The alpaca is related to the camel.

D. The Alpaca is one of the most economically important animals of South America.

READING STRATEGIES FOR ASSESSMENT

ESTRATEGIAS DE LECTURA PARA LA EVALUACIÓN

Use context clues. To discover what a "pack animal" is, study the words around it. Which phrase helps define it?

Usa pistas del contexto. Para averiguar qué es un "pack animal", fíjate en las palabras que vienen antes de y después de esta palabra. ¿Qué frase ayuda a definirla?

Notice important details. Underline the details that explain why alpaca wool is so desirable.

Fíjate en detalles importantes. Subraya los detalles que explican por qué la lana de la alpaca es tan codiciada.

ANSWER STRATEGIES

ESTRATEGIAS PARA CONTESTAR LAS PREGUNTAS

Identify the focus. Each answer choice offers information from the article, but only one choice explains what the entire article is about.

Identifica el tema central. Todas las opciones dan información del artículo, pero solamente una opción explica de qué trata todo el artículo.

Answers:
1. D

Pay attention to the context of unfamiliar words. Find the sentence in the article where *pack animals* is used. Notice that only one answer choice is a phrase found right next to *pack animals.*

Presta atención al contexto de las palabras desconocidas. Busca la oración del artículo donde se usa *pack animals.* Fíjate que sólo una de las opciones es la frase que se encuentra justamente después de *pack animals.*

2 Which of the following best describes what pack animals do?

A. transport goods

B. survive at high altitudes

C. provide wool for clothing

D. graze on the *Altiplano*

Evaluate details. Something "highly prized" has important qualities. Which answer choice talks about the qualities of alpaca wool?

Evalúa detalles. Algo "muy apreciado" tiene cualidades importantes. ¿Cuál de las opciones se refiere a las cualidades de la lana de la alpaca?

3 Why is alpaca wool highly prized?

A. It resembles the fur of camels.

B. It has been woven for thousands of years.

C. It is lightweight, warm, strong, and resists moisture.

D. It can be worn only by royalty.

DIRECTIONS Some test questions ask you to analyze a visual rather than a reading selection. Study this chart carefully and answer the questions that follow.

INSTRUCCIONES Usa la siguiente lectura para practicar tus destrezas. Lee los párrafos con atención. Luego responde las siguientes preguntas de elección múltiple.

ESTRATEGIAS DE LECTURA PARA LA EVALUACIÓN

Read the title. What does the title tell you the chart is about?

Lee el título. ¿Qué te indica el título acerca de lo que trata la tabla?

Read the labels. What do the labels on the chart tell you?

Lee los rótulos. ¿Qué te indican los rótulos de la izquierda de la tabla? ¿Y los rótulos de la parte superior de la tabla?

Largest Lakes of Central and South America

	Surface Area (sq. mi./sq. km.)	Depth (feet/meters)	Elevation (feet/meters)
Lake Maracaibo, Venezuela	5,200/13,468	197/60	sea level
Lake Titicaca, Bolivia and Peru	3,200/8,288	990/302	12,500/3,810
Lake Nicaragua, Nicaragua	3,150/8,159	230/70	102/31

Read the question carefully. Notice that the question asks for depth in feet, not meters.

Lee la pregunta con mucha atención. Fíjate que se te pide la profundidad en pies, no en metros.

4 What is the depth, in feet, of the deepest lake?

A. 990

B. 12,500

C. 302

D. 13,468

Answers:
2. A, 3. C, 4. A.

5. What is the surface area of Lake Titicaca in square kilometers?

   A. 3,200

   B. 302

   C. 8,288

   D. 3,810

6. At what altitude is Lake Maracaibo?

   A. 197 feet

   B. sea level

   C. 12,500 feet

   D. 31 sq. km.

Read the labels carefully. Be sure you understand which column represents square kilometers.

Lee los rótulos con mucha atención. Asegúrate de que entiendes qué columna representa millas cuadradas y cuál representa kilómetros cuadrados.

Follow rows and columns carefully. If necessary, use your finger to trace across a row or down a column.

Sigue las filas y las columnas con mucho cuidado. Si es necesario, usa el dedo para buscar a lo largo de una fila o columna para que no termines por accidente en un punto equivocado con una respuesta incorrecta.

Answers: 5. C, 6. B

APUNTES

Reading Test Practice
SHORT SELECTIONS

DIRECTIONS Use the following to practice your skills. Read the paragraphs carefully. Then answer the multiple-choice questions that follow.

Práctica para un examen de lectura
SELECCIONES CORTAS

INSTRUCCIONES Usa la siguiente lectura para practicar tus destrezas. Lee los párrafos con atención. Luego responde las siguientes preguntas de elección múltiple.

During the 1990's, Spanish opera singer Plácido Domingo teamed up with two other singers, Italy's Luciano Pavarotti and Spain's José Carreras, to form a wildly popular singing group known as The Three Tenors. They enjoyed worldwide success, touring and appearing on television. Domingo's musical career, however, got its start much earlier—mid-century, in fact.

Born in Madrid in 1941, Domingo and his parents moved to Mexico City in 1950 where he began studying singing at the National Conservatory of Music. Ten years later, Domingo made his opera debut in a production of *La Traviata* in Monterrey, Mexico. After a three-year stint with the Israeli National Opera, Domingo joined the New York City Opera in 1966. Two years later, he made his debut with the Metropolitan Opera of New York.

Over the next three decades, Domingo dazzled audiences with his technical skill and virtuoso acting. Thirty-six years after his debut in Monterrey, Domingo became the artistic director of the Washington (D.C.) Opera. Then, in 2000, he assumed the same post at the Los Angeles Opera.

1 What was the author's purpose in writing this selection?

A. to persuade readers that Plácido Domingo is a great opera singer

B. to explain who The Three Tenors were

C. to inform readers about the career of Plácido Domingo

D. to describe the roles Plácido Domingo has sung during his career

2 Which of the following is NOT a conclusion you can draw from the selection?

A. Domingo is the greatest opera singer of his generation.

B. Domingo has had a successful career as an opera singer.

C. Domingo, Pavarotti, and Carreras captivated audiences with their singing.

D. Domingo is widely respected in the opera world as a singer and an artist.

APUNTES

APUNTES

DIRECTIONS Use the graph below to answer the questions that follow.

INSTRUCCIONES Usa la gráfica que se da a continuación y contesta las preguntas que la siguen.

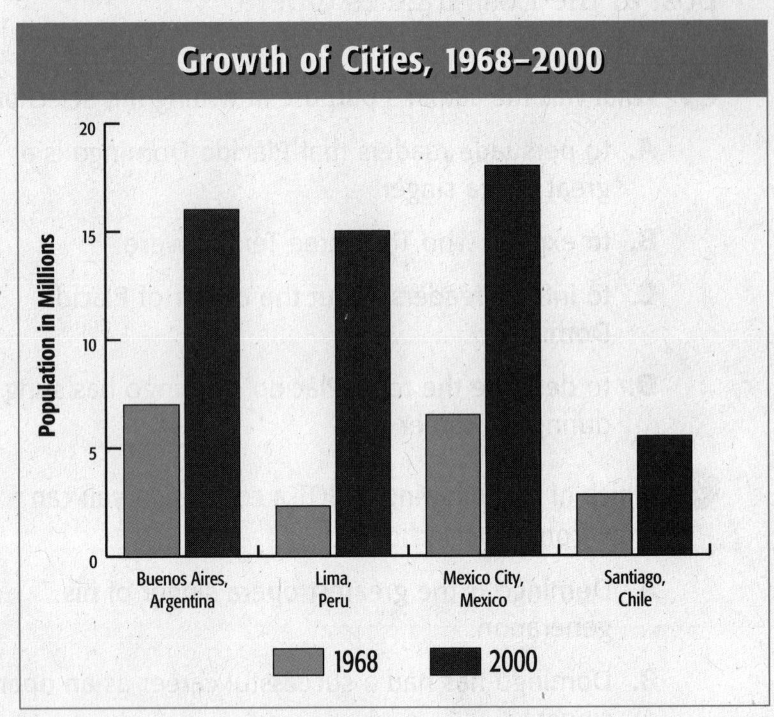

3 Which city had the SMALLEST population in 1968?

A. Lima

B. Buenos Aires

C. Santiago

D. Mexico City

4 Which city had the LARGEST population in 2000?

A. Lima

B. Buenos Aires

C. Santiago

D. Mexico City

5 Which city had the SMALLEST increase in population between 1968 and 2000?

A. Lima

B. Buenos Aires

C. Santiago

D. Mexico City

THINKING IT THROUGH

1 What was the author's purpose in writing this selection?

A. to persuade readers that Plácido Domingo is a great opera singer

B. to explain who The Three Tenors were

C. to inform readers about the career of Plácido Domingo

D. to describe the roles Plácido Domingo has sung during his career

First read all of the answer choices. Then think carefully about the kind of information the article does and does not contain. The author's purpose will become clear.

Primero lee todas las opciones para la respuesta. Luego piensa muy bien en el tipo de información que el artículo contiene o no contiene. La intención del autor se hará evidente.

2 Which of the following is NOT a conclusion you can draw from the selection?

A. Domingo is the greatest opera singer of his generation.

B. Domingo has had a successful career as an opera singer.

C. Domingo, Pavarotti, and Carreras captivated audiences with their singing.

D. Domingo is widely respected in the opera world as a singer and an artist.

Notice the word in capital letters in the question. Then ask yourself which of the answer choices is not supported by information in the selection.

Fíjate en la palabra en mayúsculas de la pregunta. Luego pregúntate cuál de las opciones no se basa en la información del fragmento.

3 Which city had the SMALLEST population in 1968?

A. Lima

B. Buenos Aires

C. Santiago

D. Mexico City

Look at the key to discover which color denotes 1968. Then look for that color in the graph.

Mira la clave para averiguar qué color indica 1968. Luego busca ese color en la gráfica.

4 Which city had the LARGEST population in 2000?

A. Lima

B. Buenos Aires

C. Santiago

D. Mexico City

The tallest bar on the graph will give you the correct answer.

La barra más alta de la gráfica será la respuesta correcta.

5 Which city had the SMALLEST increase in population between 1968 and 2000?

A. Lima

B. Buenos Aires

C. Santiago

D. Mexico City

This question asks you to compare 1968 with 2000. Look for the smallest difference in the two bars for each city to find the correct answer.

En esta pregunta se te pide comparar 1968 con 2000. Busca la diferencia más pequeña entre las dos barras para cada ciudad para responder correctamente.

Answers:
1. C, 2. A, 3. A, 4. D, 5. C

Functional Reading Test Model

DIRECTIONS Study the following nutrition label from a jar of tomatillo salsa. Then answer the questions that follow.

Examen modelo de lectura funcional

INSTRUCCIONES Lee muy bien la etiqueta de nutrición del frasco de salsa de tomatillo. Luego responde las siguientes preguntas.

ESTRATEGIAS DE LECTURA PARA LA EVALUACIÓN

Examine the structure of the label. Notice the type of information included in each of the four parts of the label.

Estudia la estructura de la etiqueta. Fíjate en el tipo de información que se incluye en cada una de las cuatro partes de la etiqueta.

Do the math. Remember that the "% Daily Value" and vitamin and mineral numbers on the label are for just a single serving.

Calcula. Recuerda que el "% Daily Value" y los números de las vitaminas y de los minerales de la etiqueta son sólo por una ración.

Nutrition Facts	
Serving Size 2 TBSP (30 g)	
Servings Per Container 15	
Amount Per Serving	
Calories 10	
Calories from Fat 0	
	% Daily Value*
Total Fat 0 g	0%
Saturated Fat 0 g	0%
Cholesterol 0 mg	0%
Sodium 230 mg	10%
Total Carbohydrate 2 g	
Dietary Fiber 0 g	0%
Sugars 1 g	
Protein 0 g	
Vitamin A 6% • Vitamin C 8%	
Calcium 4% • Iron 0%	
* Percent Daily Values are based on a 2,000 calorie diet.	

ESTRATEGIAS PARA CONTESTAR LAS PREGUNTAS

To find the correct answer, multiply the number of calories per serving by the number of servings in the bottle.

Para hallar la respuesta correcta, multiplica el número de calorías por ración por el número de raciones de la botella.

1. How many calories does this whole bottle of salsa contain?

   A. 10
   B. 150
   C. 15
   D. 30

Again, multiplication is the key to finding the correct answer.

De nuevo, la multiplicación es la clave para hallar la respuesta correcta.

2. If you ate two servings of salsa, how many mg. of sodium would you consume?

   A. 460
   B. 10
   C. 230
   D. 690

To answer this question, just look at that part of the label that tells how much fat each serving contains.

Para responder a esta pregunta, mira simplemente la parte de la etiqueta que dice cuánta grasa tiene cada ración.

3. Is salsa a smart food choice for people trying to limit their fat intake?

   A. No, because it has 230 mg. of sodium per serving.
   B. Yes, because the serving size is just 2 TBSP.
   C. No, because it has ten calories per serving.
   D. Yes, because each serving has 0 g. of fat.

Answers: 1. B, 2. A, 3. D

Functional Reading Test Practice

DIRECTIONS Study the following travel advertisement for a vacation package to Puerto Rico. Circle the information that you think is the most important. Then answer the multiple-choice questions that follow.

Práctica para un examen de lectura funcional

INSTRUCCIONES Lee muy bien el siguiente anuncio turístico para unas vacaciones a Puerto Rico. Traza un círculo alrededor de la información que te parezca más importante. Luego responde las siguientes preguntas de elección múltiple.

EXPERIENCE THE EXCITEMENT OF PUERTO RICO!

Snorkeling! Windsurfing! Sailing! Golf!
First-Class Entertainment!

4 days/3 nights at the
San Juan Adventure Resort

only $479 per person
airfare included *

Adventure Resort Package also includes continental breakfast, two beach passes, two spa treatments

* Price based on double occupancy. Airfare from New York City only. From Chicago add $175. From Los Angeles add $350. Single travelers add $200.

APUNTES

APUNTES

1. Which of the following is NOT included in the $479 price?
   A. beach passes
   B. windsurfing
   C. spa treatments
   D. continental breakfast

2. How much will this vacation package cost a single traveler from Los Angeles?
   A. $479
   B. $654
   C. $679
   D. $1,029

3. For which of the following is this vacation package the LEAST expensive per person?
   A. two sisters from New York
   B. a stockbroker from Los Angeles
   C. a single traveler from New York
   D. a college student from Chicago

THINKING IT THROUGH

The notes in the side column will help you think through your answers. Check the answer key at the bottom of the page. How well did you do?

PIÉNSALO BIEN

Las anotaciones de los márgenes te ayudarán a pensar muy bien tus respuestas. Consulta la clave de respuestas de la parte inferior de la página siguiente. ¿Contestaste bien?

1. Which of the following is NOT included in the $479 price?

 A. beach passes

 B. windsurfing

 C. spa treatments

 D. continental breakfast

> Although the ad mentions windsurfing prominently, it does not indicate that this activity is included in the price.
>
> Aunque el anuncio menciona el windsurfing de manera destacada, no indica que esta actividad esté incluida en el precio.

2. How much will this vacation package cost a single traveler from Los Angeles?

 A. $479

 B. $654

 C. $679

 D. $1,029

> To answer this question, read the small type at the bottom of the ad and add the extra charges to the advertised price.
>
> Para responder a esta pregunta, lee la letra pequeña de la parte inferior del anuncio y suma el precio extra al precio anunciado.

3. For which of the following travelers is this vacation package the LEAST expensive per person?

 A. two sisters from New York

 B. a stockbroker from Los Angeles

 C. a single traveler from New York

 D. a college student from Chicago

> Read each answer choice carefully. How many people are traveling? Where are they coming from? Then use the information in the ad to determine who will get the best deal.
>
> Lee con mucha atención cada una de las opciones. ¿Cuántas personas viajan? ¿De dónde vienen? Luego usa la información del anuncio para determinar quién conseguirá el mejor precio.

Answers:
1. B, 2. D, 3. A

Revising-and-Editing Test Model

DIRECTIONS Read the following paragraph carefully. Then answer the multiple-choice questions that follow. After answering the questions, read the material in the side columns to check your answer strategies.

Examen modelo para revisar y corregir

INSTRUCCIONES Lee con atención el párrafo siguiente. Luego responde las preguntas de elección múltiple que se dan a continuación. Después de responder las preguntas, consulta la información de los márgenes para comprobar tus estrategias para responder las preguntas.

[1]Madrid, the capital of Spain. [2]It is home to one of that nations cultural treasures—the Prado museum. [3]The building was constructed in the late eighteenth century as a museum of natural science. [4]Then they decided to change it to an art museum in 1819 and it has more than 9,000 works of art. [5]The museum is located on a street called the Paseo del Prado. [6]Their are many famous paintings they're, including works by El Greco, Velázquez, and Goya.

1 Which sentence in the paragraph is actually a fragment, or incomplete thought?

A. sentence 5

B. sentence 3

C. sentence 1

D. sentence 4

READING STRATEGIES FOR ASSESSMENT

ESTRATEGIAS DE LECTURA PARA LA EVALUACIÓN

Watch for common errors. Highlight or underline errors such as incorrect spelling or punctuation; fragments or run-on sentences; and missing or misplaced information.

Ten cuidado con errores comunes. Marca o subraya errores ortográficos o de puntuación; oraciones incompletas o seguidas; información que falta o está fuera de lugar.

ANSWER STRATEGIES

ESTRATEGIAS PARA CONTESTAR LAS PREGUNTAS

Incomplete Sentences. A sentence is a group of words with a subject and a verb that expresses a complete thought. If either the subject or the verb is missing, the group of words is an incomplete sentence.

Oraciones incompletas. Una oración es un grupo de palabras con un sujeto y un verbo que expresa una idea completa. Si falta el sujeto o el verbo, el grupo de palabras es una oración incompleta.

Answers:
1. C

2 In sentence 2, which of the following is the correct possessive form of *nation*?

A. nation's

B. nations's

C. nations'

D. nations

3 What is the best way to rewrite the first part of sentence 4?

A. Then he decided to change it to an art museum

B. Then the government decided to change it to an art museum

C. Then the government decided to change the natural science museum to an art museum

D. Then he decided to change the natural science museum to an art museum

4 Which sentence in the paragraph is a run-on sentence?

A. sentence 2

B. sentence 5

C. sentence 1

D. sentence 4

5 What is the best way to rewrite the first part of sentence 6?

A. They're many famous paintings their

B. There are many famous paintings they're

C. There are many famous paintings there

D. Their are many famous paintings there

6 Sentence 5 is out of place. Where should sentence 5 be?

A. after sentence 2

B. before sentence 2

C. after sentence 5

D. after sentence 3

Possessive Nouns. In sentence 2, the word *nation* is singular, so it takes the singular possessive form.

Posesivos. En la oración 2, la palabra *nation* es singular y necesita la forma singular del posesivo.

Pronoun References. Avoid unclear or inaccurate pronoun references.

Referencias pronominales. Evita referencias pronominales poco claras. En la oración 4 no se sabe a quién se refiere *they,* por lo tanto tiene que reemplazarse con el sustantivo *government. It* tampoco está claro y tiene que reemplazarse con *the natural science museum.*

Run-on Sentences. A run-on sentence is two or more complete thoughts joined without correct punctuation.

Oraciones seguidas. Una oración seguida ocurre cuando hay dos o más pensamientos completos juntos sin la puntuación correcta. Si la palabra *and* se usa en vez de un punto para unir dos pensamientos completos, indica una oración seguida.

Spelling Errors. Words that sound the same may be spelled differently and have different meanings.

Errores ortográficos. Palabras que se pronuncian de la misma manera pueden escribirse de manera diferente y tener significados distintos.

Logical Organization. The order of the sentences in a paragraph should be logical.

Organización lógica. El orden de las oraciones de un párrafo debe ser lógico. La oración que habla de la ubicación del Prado debe venir antes de la oración que se refiere a la construcción del museo.

Answers:
2. A, 3. C, 4. D, 5. C, 6. A

APUNTES

Revising-and-Editing Test Practice

DIRECTIONS **Read the following paragraph carefully. As you read, circle each error that you find and identify the error in the side column—for example, *misspelled word* or *incorrect punctuation*. When you have finished, circle the letter of the correct choice for each question that follows.**

Práctica para un examen para revisar y corregir

INSTRUCCIONES **Lee con atención el siguiente párrafo. A medida que lees, traza un círculo alrededor de todos los errores que encuentres e identifica cada error en el margen. Por ejemplo, *error ortográfico* o *puntuación incorrecta.* Cuando hayas terminado, traza un círculo alrededor de la letra de la respuesta correcta para cada una de las preguntas que se dan a continuación.**

[1]On December, 17, 1830, one of the most greatest leaders in South American history died. [2]He was born in Venezuela, which was ruled by Spain. [3]As a young man, Simón Bolívar tours Europe, and he vows to free Venezuela from Spanish rule. [4]After a series of setbacks. [5]Bolívar began winning his fight to oust the Spanish from South America. [6]By 1824, Spanish rule in South America was over and Bolívar is now known as *El Libertador* and the "George Washington of South America."

1. Which sentence in the paragraph is a fragment?

   A. sentence 4

   B. sentence 2

   C. sentence 6

   D. sentence 7

2. What is the correct way to write the date in sentence 1?

   A. Dec./17/1830

   B. December 17 1830

   C. December 17, 1830

   D. December, 17 1830

3. In sentence 1, which of the following is the correct form of the superlative adjective?

   A. greatest

   B. greater

   C. more great

   D. more greatest

4. Which of the following errors occurs in sentence 2?

   A. unclear pronoun reference

   B. incorrect capitalization

   C. incorrect punctuation

   D. incorrect verb tense

5. Which of the following is the correct way to rewrite the first part of sentence 3?

   A. As a young man, Simón Bolívar tours Europe, and he vowed

   B. As a young man, Simón Bolívar toured Europe, and he vows

   C. As a young man, Simón Bolívar is touring Europe, and he vows

   D. As a young man, Simón Bolívar toured Europe, and he vowed

APUNTES

APUNTES

6 Which of the following is the best way to punctuate the middle of sentence 6?

A. Spanish rule in South America was over: and Bolívar is now

B. Spanish rule in South America was over. Bolívar is now

C. Spanish rule in South America was over; and Bolívar is now

D. Spanish rule in South America was over—and Bolívar is now

THINKING IT THROUGH

Use the notes in the side columns to help you understand why some answers are correct and others are not. Check the answer key on the next page. How well did you do?

PIÉNSALO BIEN

Usa las anotaciones de los márgenes para ayudarte a entender por qué algunas respuestas son correctas y otras no. Consulta la clave de respuestas de la página siguiente. ¿Contestaste bien?

1. Which sentence in the paragraph is a fragment?

   A. sentence 4

   B. sentence 2

   C. sentence 6

   D. sentence 7

Remember that a sentence has a subject and a verb and expresses a complete thought. Which sentence is lacking either a subject or a verb?

Recuerda que una oración tiene un verbo y un sujeto y expresa una idea completa. ¿A qué oración le falta el sujeto o el verbo?

2. What is the correct way to write the date in sentence 1?

   A. Dec./17/1830

   B. December 17 1830

   C. December 17, 1830

   D. December, 17 1830

When writing a date, the name of the month should be spelled out, and the day and year should be separated by a comma.

Cuando se escribe una fecha, el nombre del mes se debe escribir con letra y el día y el año deben separarse con una coma.

3. In sentence 1, which of the following is the correct form of the superlative adjective?

   A. greatest

   B. greater

   C. more great

   D. more greatest

A superlative adjective is formed by adding *–est* to the adjective or placing the word *most* before the adjective. Never do both at the same time.

En inglés, un adjetivo superlativo se forma añadiendo la terminación *–est* al adjectivo o poniendo la palabra *most* antes del adjetivo. Nunca uses los dos a la vez.

First check that words are capitalized correctly, that the sentence is punctuated correctly, and that the verb has the same tense as other verbs in the paragraph. Then ask, "Who is *he*?"

Primero asegúrate de que las palabras que deben escribirse con mayúscula están escritas correctamente, que la puntuación de la oración es correcta y que el verbo tiene el mismo tiempo que los otros verbos del párrafo. Después pregúntate, "¿Quién es *he*?" A menos que puedas contestar con un nombre propio, la referencia del pronombre no está clara.

4. Which of the following errors occurs in sentence 2?

A. unclear pronoun reference

B. incorrect capitalization

C. incorrect punctuation

D. incorrect verb tense

Remember that all the verbs in a paragraph should agree—that is, have the same tense.

Recuerda que todos los verbos de un párrafo deben concordar, o sea deben tener el mismo tiempo. Por lo tanto los dos verbos de la oración 3 deben concordar.

5. Which of the following is the correct way to rewrite the first part of sentence 3?

A. As a young man, Simón Bolívar tours Europe, and he vowed

B. As a young man, Simón Bolívar toured Europe, and he vows

C. As a young man, Simón Bolívar is touring Europe, and he vows

D. As a young man, Simón Bolívar toured Europe, and he vowed

Remember that a run-on sentence is two or more sentences strung together with either no punctuation or incorrect punctuation. The solution is to create separate sentences.

Recuerda que una oración seguida es dos o más oraciones unidas sin puntuación o con puntuación incorrecta. La solución es escribir dos oraciones distintas.

6. Which of the following is the best way to punctuate the middle of sentence 6?

A. Spanish rule in South America was over: and Bolívar is now

B. Spanish rule in South America was over. Bolívar is now

C. Spanish rule in South America was over; and Bolívar is now

D. Spanish rule in South America was over—and Bolívar is now

Answers:
1. A, 2. C, 3. A, 4. A, 5. D, 6. B

Writing Test Model

DIRECTIONS **Many tests ask you to write an essay in response to a writing prompt. A writing prompt is a brief statement that describes a writing situation. Some writing prompts ask you to explain *what, why,* or *how.* Others ask you to convince someone of something.**

As you analyze the following writing prompts, read and respond to the notes in the side columns. Then look at the response to each prompt. The notes in the side columns will help you understand why each response is considered strong.

Examen modelo de escritura

INSTRUCCIONES **En muchos exámenes se te pide escribir un ensayo en respuesta a una sugerencia. Una sugerencia es una explicación breve que describe una situación sobre la que se te pide escribir. Algunas sugerencias te piden explicar *qué, por qué* o *cómo.* En otras se te pide convencer a alguien de algo.**

A medida que analizas las sugerencias siguientes, lee y sigue las recomendaciones de las anotaciones de los márgenes. Luego mira la respuesta para cada sugerencia. Las anotaciones de los márgenes te ayudarán a comprender por qué se considera buena cada respuesta.

Prompt A

Some child-rearing experts believe that young people should be kept busy after school and on the weekends with a variety of structured activities, such as music lessons, sports, dance classes, and so on. Others say that young people today have been "overscheduled" and need more time to themselves—to read, think about the future, and even just to daydream.

ANALYZING THE PROMPT

ANALIZAR LA SUGERENCIA PARA ESCRIBIR

Identify the focus. What issue will you be writing about? Circle the focus of your essay in the first sentence of the prompt.

Identifica el tema central. ¿De qué vas a escribir? Traza un círculo alrededor del tema central del ensayo en la primera oración de la sugerencia.

Understand what's expected of you. First, circle what the prompt asks you to do. Then identify your audience. What kinds of details will appeal to this audience?

Entiende lo que se te pide. Primero, traza un círculo alrededor de lo que se te pide hacer en la sugerencia. Luego identifica a quién va dirigido el ensayo. ¿Qué tipo de detalles atraerán a estos lectores?

Think about your experiences and the way your non-school time is structured. Do you think lots of structure, more personal time, or a combination of the two is most beneficial to young people? Remember to provide solid reasons and examples for the position you take.

ANSWER STRATEGIES

ESTRATEGIAS PARA CONTESTAR LAS PREGUNTAS

Capture the reader's interest. The writer begins by describing a typical busy day in his younger brother's life.

Capta el interés del lector. El autor empieza describiendo un día típico de la vida activa de su hermano menor.

State the position clearly. The last sentence of the first paragraph makes the writer's position clear to the reader.

Expresa la posición con claridad. La última oración del primer párrafo deja en claro la posición del autor. Ahora el autor puede pasar el resto del ensayo desarrollando el tema.

Address opposing views. The writer brings up an opposing view and admits that it might sometimes be true.

Trata puntos de vista opuestos. El autor menciona una perspectiva contrapuesta y admite que a veces puede ser así.

Use good examples to support the position. Here, the writer uses an example to make the point that not all busy kids stay out of trouble.

Usa buenos ejemplos para respaldar la posición. Aquí, el autor usa un ejemplo para establecer que no todos los niños activos no se meten en problemas.

Strong Response

Today was a typical day for my little brother Jeff. He got up at five o'clock to go to the local ice rink for hockey practice. Then he was off to school. At the end of the school day, Jeff had a piano lesson followed by a meeting of his Cub Scout troop. After a quick dinner, he did homework for two hours. He finally got to bed at ten o'clock. That's a lot to pack into a single day, especially since Jeff is just seven years old! I think that in addition to sports, music, and other activities, kids like Jeff need some time to themselves.

Many parents, mine included, think a busy kid is a safe kid. They believe that the less time a kid has on his hands, the less likely he'll wind up doing something he shouldn't be doing or being with people he shouldn't be with. That's probably true for many kids. After all, it's hard to get into trouble when you spend every day being carpooled from one activity to another.

But some busy kids do get into trouble anyway. Jeff's friend Mark got caught trying to shoplift a CD last weekend, and he's involved in just as many activities as Jeff is. So having a busy schedule is no guarantee that a kid won't get into trouble.

Plus, I think kids benefit from having free time to go to the movies, play video games, read, or even just be by themselves. Growing up isn't always easy, and kids need some time alone to figure things out, think about what's important to them, and decide what they really want to do.

Last Saturday afternoon, Jeff's soccer practice was canceled because of thunderstorms. We went to see a movie and later spent some time talking and listening to music in my room. It was the first time in months that we had time just to hang out together, and we really enjoyed it. Jeff said it was like having a day off. I think more kids like Jeff could use a day off too.

Use logical reasoning to further develop the position. The writer offers logical reasons why free time is important.

Usa el razonamiento lógico para desarrollar más la posición. El autor da razones lógicas de por qué el tiempo libre es importante.

Restate the position in the conclusion. Using another concrete example, the writer restates his position that kids need some time to themselves.

Repite la posición en la conclusión. Por medio de otro ejemplo concreto, el autor repite su posición de que los niños necesitan tiempo para ellos mismos.

ANALYZING THE PROMPT

ANALIZAR LA SUGERENCIA PARA ESCRIBIR

Look for the main idea. The first few sentences of the prompt present the subject you will write about. Try restating the subject in your own words.

Busca la idea principal. Las primeras oraciones de la sugerencia presentan el tema del que tienes que escribir. Intenta expresar el tema con tus propias palabras.

Understand what's expected of you. What does the prompt ask you to do? Explain something? Persuade someone?

Entiende lo que se te pide. ¿Qué se te pide que hagas? ¿Explicar algo? ¿Persuadir a alguien?

ANSWER STRATEGIES

ESTRATEGIAS PARA CONTESTAR LAS PREGUNTAS

Create an intriguing introduction. The writer arouses the reader's curiosity by leaving out one of the four seasons.

Crea intriga en la introducción. La autora aumenta la curiosidad del lector al no mencionar una de las cuatro estaciones.

Include the kind of information the prompt asks for. Notice how the writer follows the directions in the prompt by explaining what spring is like in her part of the country.

Incluye el tipo de información que se le pide en la sugerencia. Fíjate en cómo la autora sigue las instrucciones de la sugerencia al explicar cómo es la primavera en la parte del país donde vive.

Prompt B

Depending on where you live, each season of the year can be very different than it is in other parts of the country. Which season do you enjoy the most—summer, autumn, winter, or spring? What is that season like in your part of the country? What makes it special to you?

Strong Response

Here in the upper Midwest, the seasons seem as different from one another as night and day. Summer usually arrives suddenly. The temperatures soar, the humidity rises, and fierce thunderstorms add drama and sometimes destruction to the season. Autumn brings a crisp, cool, and colorful change as the leaves turn golden and the air turns chilly. Winter can be bitterly cold, and heavy snows often make the simple trip to school a real ordeal.

Then comes spring. Spring is a truly magical time of the year. I can sense spring long before it actually arrives. There's a certain scent in the air, and something is different about the way the sunlight looks. Soon the winter snows are reduced to muddy puddles.

The tree branches swell with buds, and the first green shoots of crocus and tulip leaves struggle up out of the ground. Most magical of all, the early morning hours just after dawn are filled with the cries of migrating birds heading back north.

Because my family lives in a small community surrounded by farmland, I get to experience a different kind of spring than many people do. The fields behind our house fill up with wildflowers that season the air with perfume and color. A trip to Jefferson's Pond offers a chance to watch ducks and geese resting on their long seasonal journeys. The apple and cherry trees at the McKlintock family orchards explode with blossoms until they look like giant balls of cotton candy.

Mostly, however, I love spring because it is a season of hope. The earth is coming back to life, filled with possibilities. I feel like I am, too.

Use sensory details. Details that appeal to the reader's sense of sight, sound, and smell bring the description to life.

Usa detalles sensoriales. Detalles que se dirigen a los sentidos de la vista, del sonido y del olor del lector hacen que la descripción sea viva.

Make comparisons. Comparing the blossoming trees to balls of cotton candy helps the reader experience the scene as the writer does.

Haz comparaciones. Comparar el florecimiento de los árboles con algodones de caramelo ayuda a que el lector sienta la escena igual que la autora.

Write a powerful conclusion. The writer ends the essay by comparing herself to her favorite season.

Escribe una conclusión poderosa. La autora termina el ensayo comparándose a sí misma con su estación preferida.

APUNTES

Writing Test Practice

DIRECTIONS **Read the following writing prompt. Using the strategies you've learned in this section, analyze the prompt, plan your response, and then write an essay explaining your position.**

Práctica para un examen de escritura

INSTRUCCIONES **Lee la siguiente sugerencia. Usando las estrategias que has aprendido en esta sección, analiza la sugerencia, planea la respuesta, y luego escribe un ensayo que explique tu posición.**

Prompt C

You have volunteered to participate in your community's semiannual blood drive. Your task is to write a letter to your community newspaper encouraging everyone in town to consider giving blood.

Think about all the ways your community benefits from having an adequate blood supply. Write a letter that explains what these benefits are. Include specific examples. End your letter by appealing to your fellow citizens' sense of civic pride and duty.

APUNTES

APUNTES

Scoring Rubrics

DIRECTIONS Use the following checklist to see whether you have written a strong persuasive essay. You will have succeeded if you can check nearly all of the items.

The Prompt

☐ My response meets all the requirements stated in the prompt.

☐ I have stated my position clearly and supported it with details.

☐ I have addressed the audience appropriately.

☐ My essay fits the type of writing suggested in the prompt (letter to the editor, article for the school paper, and so on).

Reasons

☐ The reasons I offer really support my position.

☐ My audience will find the reasons convincing.

☐ I have stated my reasons clearly.

☐ I have given at least three reasons.

☐ I have supported my reasons with sufficient facts, examples, quotations, and other details.

☐ I have presented and responded to opposing arguments.

☐ My reasoning is sound. I have avoided faulty logic.

Order and Arrangement

☐ I have included a strong introduction.

☐ I have included a strong conclusion.

☐ The reasons are arranged in a logical order.

Word Choice

☐ The language of my essay is appropriate for my audience.

☐ I have used precise, vivid words and persuasive language.

Fluency

☐ I have used sentences of varying lengths and structures.

☐ I have connected ideas with transitions and other devices.

☐ I have used correct spelling, punctuation, and grammar.

Normas de calificación

INSTRUCCIONES Usa la siguiente lista para ver si escribiste un ensayo persuasivo. Si la mayoría de las normas incluyen una marca, significa que lo has logrado.

APUNTES

Sugerencia

- ☐ Mi respuesta cumple con todos los requisitos indicados en la sugerencia.
- ☐ Mi opinión quedó claramente establecida con detalles que la apoyan.
- ☐ Me dirigí al público de manera apropiada.
- ☐ Mi ensayo cumple con el tipo de escritura sugerida (carta al editor, artículo para el periódico escolar, etc.).

Razones

- ☐ Las razones que presento apoyan mi opinión.
- ☐ Mis razones serán convincentes para el público.
- ☐ Presenté mis razones de manera clara.
- ☐ Expuse por lo menos tres razones.
- ☐ Apoyé mis razones con hechos, ejemplos, citas y otros detalles.
- ☐ Presenté mis razonamientos respondiendo a razonamientos opuestos.
- ☐ Mi razonamiento es sólido. Evité la falta de lógica.

Orden y organización

- ☐ Incluí una introducción atractiva.
- ☐ Incluí una conclusión interesante.
- ☐ Las razones están organizadas en un orden lógico.

Elección de vocabulario

- ☐ El lenguaje del ensayo es apropiado para mi público.
- ☐ Usé palabras precisas y vívidas, y un lenguaje persuasivo.

Fluidez

- ☐ Escribí oraciones de diferentes longitudes y estructuras.
- ☐ Uní ideas mediante elementos de transición y otros recursos.
- ☐ Utilicé ortografía, puntuación y gramática correctas.

Credits

Illustration

15–16 Nneke Bennett; **20–21** Ruben de Anda; **36–37, 41–42** Rick Powell; **56–57, 61–62** Enrique O. Sánchez; **141** Gary Hincks

Photography

3, 4, 5 Martha Granger/EDGE Productions; **9** Beryl Goldberg; **10** *top* Patricia A. Eynon, *bottom* Odyssey Productions; **11** Beryl Goldberg; **25** Martha Granger/EDGE Productions; **26** School Division/Houghton Mifflin Company; **31** John Boykin/PhotoEdit; **32** *top left* Martha Granger/EDGE Productions, *top center* Susan Kaye, *top right* J.P. Courau/DDB Stock Photo, *bottom left* Doug Bryant/DDB Stock Photo, *bottom center, bottom right* Martha Granger/EDGE Productions; **42** Robert Frerck/Woodfin Camp; **46** *top* Bob Daemmrich/Stock Boston, *inset* Robert Frerck/Odyssey Productions; **47** *left* Bob Daemmrich, *bottom right* Martha Granger/EDGE Productions; **51** *top* Raymond A. Mendez/Animals Animals, *bottom* Jaime Santiago/DDB Stock Photo; **52** *top* Thomas R. Fletcher/Stock Boston, *bottom* School Division/Houghton Mifflin Company; **97** "Cumpleaños de Lala y Tudi" ("Lala and Tudi's Birthday Party") (1989), Carmen Lomas Garza. Oil on canvas, 36" x 48". Collection of Paula Maciel Benecke & Norbert Benecke, Aptos, California. Photograph by Wolgang Dietze. © 1989 Carmen Lomas Garza; **135** Lee Foster/Bruce Coleman, Inc.; **141** *left* Galen Rowell/Corbis, *right* David Meunch/Corbis **147** Timothy Fadek/Corbis; **149** *quinceañera* Martha Granger/EDGE Productions; *Sweet 16 party* Ryan McVay/Getty Images; **151** Dennis MacDonald/PhotoEdit; **153** © 1978 George Ballis/Take Stock; **157** Jacques Jangoux/Getty Images

Apuntes

Apuntes

Apuntes

Apuntes